Rebels in the Name
of the Tsar

CLASSICS IN RUSSIAN AND SOVIET HISTORY

Series Editor: Ben A. Eklof
Indiana University

Advisory Editors:

Daniel Brower, University of California, Davis
John Bushnell, Northwestern University
Tom Gleason, Brown University
Carol S. Leonard, State University of New York, Plattsburgh
Brenda Meehan-Waters, University of Rochester
Richard Stites, Georgetown University
Allan Wildman, Ohio State University

Rebels in the Name of the Tsar

Daniel Field

Boston
UNWIN HYMAN
London   Sydney   Wellington

Unwin Hyman, Inc.
8 Winchester Place, Winchester, MA 01890, USA

Published by the Academic Division of Unwin Hyman Ltd,
15/17 Broadwick Street, London W1V 1FP, UK

Allen & Unwin Australia Pty Ltd,
8 Napier Street, North Sydney, NSW 2060, Australia

Allen & Unwin (New Zealand) Ltd, in association with the Port Nicholson
Press Ltd, 60 Cambridge Terrace, Wellington, New Zealand

Maps drawn by Dick Sanderson.

Page 30: Based on the maps of Kazan Province in the Brockhaus-
Efron *Entsiklopedicheskii slovar'*, vol. XIII, and in A.I. Iampol'skaia
and D.S. Gutman, eds., *Bezdnenskoe vosstanie 1861 goda*, Kazan,
1948.

Page 112: Based on AMS map #1404-233C, with additional information from *Istoriia mist i sil Ukrains'koi RSR: Cherkas'ka oblast'*,
Kiev, 1972.

Library of Congress Cataloging-in-Publication Data
Field, Daniel, 1938-
    Rebels in the name of the tsar / Daniel Field
        p.   cm. — (Classics in Russian and Soviet history ; 1)
    Reprint. Originally published: Boston : Houghton Mifflin, 1976.
    Includes bibliographical references and index.
    ISBN 0-04-445190-3 (pbk.)
        1. Soviet Union—History—Alexander II, 1855-1881.   2. Soviet
    Union—History—Alexander II, 1855-1881—Sources.   3. Peasant
    uprisings—Soviet Union—History—19th century.   4. Peasant
    uprisings—Soviet Union—Sources.   5. Monarchy—Soviet Union—
    History—19th century.   6. Monarchy—Soviet Union—Sources.
    I. Title.   II. Series.
    [DK221.F48 1989]
    947.08'1—dc19   88-20829
                                                                            CIP
British Library Cataloging-in-Publication Data

Field, Daniel
    Rebels in the name of tsar.
    1. Russia. Emperors. Allegiance of
    peasants, 1860-1880
    I. Title   II. Series
    323.6'5

    ISBN 0-04-445190-3

For Holly

Contents

Foreword

History, it is sometimes said, has lost its audience. The professional writing of history has become progressively denser, more turgid and obscure. The audience, historians reply, is less receptive, interested in the past, or willing to make an effort to understand "there" and "then." As a result, our culture remains trapped in the "here" and "now." Still, the fact that popular works of biography, military history, and grand synthesis continue to sell well speaks of a breakdown of communication rather than a loss of interest. Partly, I am sure, this stems from the new history's concern with introducing the methodologies and quantitative approaches of the social sciences, resulting sometimes in a tendency to use arcane language and to succumb to a numbing concern with numbers. Somewhere in the process, flesh-and-blood people and the drama of events are lost. This, despite the professed intention many of us share as social historians to make real the past lives of common people, so frequently excluded from textbooks.

All too often the first works confronted by students of history are simply too dense, too difficult, and too removed from the issues and dramas that initially drew most of us, in sheer fascination, into the world of the past. What is at the cutting edge of methodology may not be, upon reflection, the best place to begin a discourse upon the life of those who preceded us, whether great or small.

Such comments as these overlook, of course, the handful of wonderful works of social history that recreate the daily life, the strivings, and the pains of common people in ways—and with an empirical grounding—virtually unknown in earlier histories. But the direction of social history, away from the "epiphenomena" of great national events, and in search of the deeper structural forces and subterranean currents, the continuities that define the passage of history, carries the danger of entirely overlooking the real significance of such events, if only as national myths.

This series retrieves a number of works in Russian and Soviet history that have gone out of print and are no longer available for classroom use or for the general public. Some of these works retain their status as examples of unsuperseded primary research and sophisticated historical investigation. In fact, the volume at hand, *Rebels in the Name of the Tsar,* was perhaps a decade ahead of its time in its awareness of the complexities, and possibilities, of studying the elusive popular mentality.

Other works in this series may use categories and operate on assumptions that historians can no longer fully accept, but are unmatched as "you-are-there" history of a certain type. Many vivid first-hand accounts of events have disappeared from reading lists simply because historians no longer approach their subject in the same way, but it may well be a salutory exercise to bring back into circulation, for reconsideration, what we view as outmoded approaches. Still others bring back into print documents that have recently come under renewed scrutiny. Finally, additional works in this series will simply make available to the reader works that the editorial board feel deserve renewed circulation as lively, sophisticated, and engaging studies in Russian and Soviet life. We hope that this series will make a small step forward in restoring a dialogue between public and professional in the investigation of the past, which, as William Faulkner reportedly once said, "is not only not dead . . . neither is it really past."

* * *

Dan Field's *Rebels in the Name of the Tsar* tackles one of the most important and thorny of issues in the history of Imperial Russia; namely, the relationship between *narod,* or folk, and the educated public, including officialdom.[1] The author urges us to see that behind such terms as "peasantry" are "subsumed millions of individual men and women" and to recognize that peasants were actors as well as victims, capable of constructing as well as manipulating social myths. Political manipulation is at the core of these incidents, as each side sought to utilize a social myth to its own advantage; in the process, a stereotypical image was reinforced of the *muzhik* as gullible, easily misled, and blindly trusting in a benevolent tsar. As Field notes in the preface, this work endeavors to "show nonspecialists how a historian works through a problem and arrives, somewhat diffidently, at conclusions. . . ." It includes an interpretative essay and a study in documents of two famous incidents of peasant uprisings, "rebellions in the name of the Tsar" at Bezdna in 1861 and in the Ukraine (the Chigirin conspiracy of 1876-1877). By translations of documents interspersed with commentary, Field demonstrates the kind of detective work needed to work through the testimony of eyewitnesses and participants, and leaves bare for the reader the multiple discrepancies in these sources. He shows just how complicated working with primary sources can be. Reviewer Geoffrey Hosking noted:

> Field is not trying to state a thesis: he is trying to awaken our doubts about one that exists already. This negative characteristic of his enterprise gives the book a particular value to students, for it shows them how the historian endeavors to disentangle from the available documents the closest approximations to the ever-lost truth about what actually happened. Immediate impressions, notes and letters are brought up to be compared with later recollections. The author gives us a strong sense of how much we still do not know even when we have diligently sifted all these fragments. This might be a shock for undergraduates who like to make confident assertions in exam papers. But it would be a salutary shock. The book inculcates proper scepticism about historians' attitudes to subjects culturally very distant from them, while at the same time rehabilitating peasants by showing that they are not necessarily any more naive or superstitious than we are.[2]

Field's case studies predated by a few years the influential investigations of the peasantry of southeast Asia by James Scott, who developed the notion of "the weapons of the weak," by which oppressed cultures, avoiding direct confrontation with superior force, manage to subvert, evade and work their will. Although Field investigates peasants in crisis, his real interest is in breaking down conventional definitions of what is political and nonpolitical, and showing that the traditional dichotomies of peasant insurrection (romanticized by the left, minutely studied by Soviet historians) and passive, daily subordination, are falsely posed. As Scott points out:

> Formal, organized political activity, even if clandestine and revolutionary, is typically the preserve of the middle class and the intelligentsia; to look for peasant politics in this realm is to look largely in vain. It is also—not incidentally—the first step toward concluding that the peasantry is a political nullity unless organized and led by outsiders. . . . Most forms of [peasant resistance] stop well short of outright collective defiance. Here I have in mind the ordinary weapons of relatively powerless groups: foot dragging, dissimulation, desertion, false compliance, pilfering, feigned ignorance, slander . . . sabotage, and so on.[3]

To be sure, Field's case studies are precisely of those extreme, and rare, "flashes in the pan" (in this context, the phrase is Marc Bloch's), far less common than the "constant, grinding conflict over work, food, autonomy, ritual" that defines the relationship between peasantry and dominant cultures across the globe. What he shows, however, is that the boundary between the extraordinary and the commonplace is not a firm one; in the Bezdna and Chigirin crises, the peasants resort to the types of subterfuge and indirect assertion familiar from everyday contacts with their "betters." Even more revealing, these "betters" ultimately must accept peasant explanations of their actions in order to avoid punitive actions on a scale that would have brought, inevitably, further violence. Both sides, in their mutual self-interest, must reduce a large-scale event to more manageable dimensions.

One contemporary observer of the Russian social classes, Anton Chekhov, understood this relationship well. In a marvelous short story, "The Malefactor," he depicts a local peasant who is caught stealing nuts to fasten down rail ties that he was using as sinkers for his fishing rod. When dragged before a local official to explain his actions, the peasant initially demonstrates how useful such nuts are as sinkers, and proudly explains how he and his companions attached them to their lines. Sensing disapproval, he then adds that he was not alone in availing himself of state property, and that they, the peasantry, never took all the nuts, that they acted carefully and were "thoughtful" people. But then, when the local investigator explains that the theft of these nuts had caused a train derailment a year previously, the peasant understands the seriousness of the matter at hand, and begins to expostulate that "we are a benighted people" (*liudi temnye*). When the investigator tells him he is going to prison, he asks, "What for? I don't have time, I need to collect three rubles from Yegor for the suet I sold him." The investigator tells him to be quiet, but he adds, "I've done nothing, I didn't steal, I didn't fight. But maybe you think I haven't paid my arrears. . . ." In the space of a few minutes, the peasant tries out several different masks in front of his better, first boasting of his skills, next assuring him of his social consciousness, and then pleading that ignorance was endemic to his class. Finally, confronted with imprisonment, he feigns incomprehension.[4] In this case, the social myth of the "dark" peasantry does him little good, for as the story ends he is being led off to jail. But the manipulation of communication, and particularly the feigned naïveté, bears much in common with the actions described by Field below.

Rebels in the Name of the Tsar takes a commonplace assertion about the way peasants approached politics ("the myth of the tsar") and asks us to apply it to a concrete situation. We find that the comfortable generalizations we use to explain the way such peasants behave turn out, upon investigation, to be wanting.

Ben Eklof
Indiana University

Notes

1. For a discussion of recent work on this topic, see Ben Eklof, "Ways of Seeing: Recent Anglo-American Studies of the Russian Peasant (1861-1914)," *Jahrbucher fur Geschichte Osteuropas,* Vol. 36, No. 1 (1988), pp. 57-79.
2. *Times Literary Supplement,* October 22, 1976, p. 1335.
3. James C. Scott, *Weapons of the Weak: Everyday Forms of Peasant Resistance* (New Haven, 1985) pp. xv-xvi.
4. Anton Chekhov, "Zloumyshlennyk," *Sobranie sochinenii* (12 volumes: Moscow, 1961): Vol. 3, pp. 180-184.

Preface

One of the major problems of the history of late imperial Russia is the devotion of the common people to the person of the tsar. Soviet historians call this phenomenon "naive monarchism" and maintain that the Russian peasantry was under the sway of "monarchist illusions." Naive monarchism contributed to the survival of the tsarist regime, and its erosion or disappearance made the revolutions of 1905 and 1917 possible. Most historians assume that the modernization of Russia was fatal to naive monarchism, but no one has explained how it endured so long and then dissipated so quickly.

This book does not provide a comprehensive explanation of the evolution of naive monarchism. It does bring the problem down to earth by dealing with its concrete manifestations. There are several fascinating studies of the image of the tsar in Russian thought and literature. Discussions of naive monarchism, however, have always been very general; faith in the tsar is represented as an attribute of an abstraction—either "the peasantry" or "the common people." On this plane, it is hard to understand the shape and significance of a belief which is, from our point of view, outlandish and irrational. The two case studies that make up Chapters 2 and 3 in this book are intended to provide that kind of understanding.

There is a further reason for the format of these case studies. They are intended to show nonspecialists how a historian works through a problem and arrives, sometimes diffidently, at conclusions. They consist, in large part, of primary sources, which are prefaced and interspersed with commentary, relevant information, and questions. The reader is confronted with the raw material of the historian's craft, rather than with the distillate of erudition; thus the reader can participate in the scrutiny and reasoning that underlie conclusions about cases such as these and on which valid conclusions about general problems ultimately must rest. These cases were chosen because they were well known and generated a compact and diverse body of documents which could be laid before the reader without any specialized knowledge of the subject. However, specialists will find that the step-by-step exploration of these documents suggests some new conclusions about these familiar cases as well as about the broad problem of naive monarchism.

I have translated the primary sources (listed in italics in the table of contents) in their entirety, with two carefully noted exceptions; none of them has been translated before. Where I have injected a comment or a bit of information, my words are in italics and set off in brackets. These full-length sources are set in a different typeface to make them visually distinct from the main text. In addition, shorter excerpts from other sources appear in the midst of the main text. All these translations are faithful to the original Russian. All words italicized in translation were emphasized in the original. However, since many of these documents were hastily or carelessly written, punctuation and division into paragraphs have sometimes been modified in the interests of intelligibility. Also, slight variations in personal and place names have been silently corrected; the spelling of transliterated place names in the maps and text generally follows P.P. Semenov-Tian-Shanskii, *Geografichesko-statisticheskii slovar' Rossiiskoi Imperii,* 5 vols., St. Petersburg, 1863–1883, but many of the smaller villages mentioned in this book are not registered there. A glossary of English and Russian terms follows this preface.

I would like to express my gratitude to various persons and institutions who helped me. I am grateful to the librarians at the Butler Library of Columbia University and at the Houghton, Widener, and Russian Research Center libraries at Harvard. Charles Gredler deserves special thanks for securing two books on microfilm from the Soviet Union, and a general tribute for the excellence of the Slavic Division of the Harvard College Library, which he heads. James Bradley also procured an important microfilm for me.

Chapter 3 of this book was written in 1972, when I enjoyed the joint largesse of two splendid institutions: a Senior Fellowship at the Russian Institute of Columbia University and a Research Fellowship at the Russian Research Center of Harvard University. These grants were supplemented by a grant-in-aid from the American Council of Learned Societies. I am grateful both for this sub-

vention of my work and for the encouragement and moral support
which the directors and members of both institutions have lavished
upon me over the years.

In addition, I would like to thank Abbott Gleason, Robert C.
Williams, Eugene Vinogradoff, Patrice Higonnet, and Miriam Berlin,
who read parts of this book in manuscript, and the members of the
Slavic Seminar of Columbia, before whom I read a paper based
upon my work for this book. I am grateful for the help and encouragement I had from Robert I. Rotberg, Massachusetts Institute
of Technology, the general editor of a series in which this book
was to appear. A number of students read earlier versions of this
book, and I would like to single out Harold Henry, Cynthia Blake,
and Ann Mokrauer for their useful suggestions. All of these students
and colleagues favored me with helpful comments and criticism;
they should not be called to account for the shortcomings of this
book, from which they tried in vain to save me. I want to pay
tribute to Gwendolyn Andrews and Susan Dimitris for turning
my palimpsests into elegant typescript. I also had valuable help
and counsel from Orest Subtelny, Richard Henry Field, and John
Taylor Williams. The staff at Houghton Mifflin proved generous
in accommodating the peculiarities of this book and discerning in
making suggestions for its improvement. Finally, special thanks
are due to my wife and sons for their patience and sympathy during
my preoccupation with this project.

Daniel Field
Barnard, Vermont
June 14, 1975

Glossary

In the text that follows, some Russian terms have been systematically translated; these terms appear below listed under their English equivalents. Terms that have been uniformly transliterated are listed here in their Russian forms, with English translations.

aktoviki (also *akhtovye, aktovye*) — Chigirin peasants who accepted the acts of lustration

arbiter of the peace — *mirovoi posrednik,* a local official responsible for implementing the emancipation legislation

ataman — a cossack chief

barshchina — a peasant's labor service for a *pomeshchik*

batiushka — an affectionate term for "father"

boyar — one of the tsar's most senior officials in the sixteenth and seventeenth centuries

canton — *volost'*

constable — *uriadnik, gorodovoi*

desiatina (pl. *desiatiny*) — 2.7 acres

district — *uezd,* an administrative subdivision of a province

druzhina (pl. *druzhiny*) — fellowship

druzhinnik (pl. *druzhinniki*) — member of a *druzhina*

dushevik (pl. *dusheviki*) — peasant in the Chigirin area who favored reallocation of land on a per capita basis, as opposed to hereditary household tenure

hundreder	*sotskii, sotnik,* a village policeman
lustration	*liustratsiia,* an official review and modification of boundaries and dues
marshal (of the nobility)	*predvoditel' (dvorianstva),* the elected head of the nobility of a district or province, who also exercised public functions
mir	peasant commune (literally, "world")
muzhik (pl. *muzhiki*)	peasant, a pejorative in the usage of nonpeasants
narod	common people
narodosovetie	Shchapov's archaic term for representative government
nobles, nobility	*dvoriane, dvorianstvo,* often rendered in English as "gentry"
obrok	a peasant's cash dues to a *pomeshchik*
pomeshchik (pl. *pomeshchiki*)	owner of an estate; all *pomeshchiki* were noblemen, but not all nobles were *pomeshchiki*
regulatory charter	*ustavnaia gramota*
reviziia	census, for taxation
sheriff	*(uezdnyi) ispravnik*
tractholders	*uchastkovye, paishchiki* (Ukrainian), peasants with full allotments of land
ukaz (pl. *ukazy*)	decree
verst	*versta* (3,500 feet)
voevody (pl.)	seventeenth-century military governors
volia	freedom
warden	*stanovoi pristav*
zemskii sobor	Assembly of the Land, a deliberative institution in Muscovite Russia

1

The Myth of the Tsar

The Russian common people believed that the tsar was their benefactor and intercessor; he was a *batiushka,* or "affectionate father."
In the terminology of Soviet historians, the people were, until the
revolution of 1905, in the grip of "naive monarchism" or "monarchist illusions." Peasants blamed their misfortunes on fate, on
avaricious and powerful neighbors, or on their own sinful natures,
and believed that the tsar would take their side if only he knew of
their plight. Iurii Samarin, the nineteenth-century Slavophile and
reformer, described the peasants' faith in these terms.

> The nobility has separated the common people from the tsar.
> Standing as an obstacle between them, it conceals the com-
> mon people from the tsar and does not permit the people's
> complaints and hopes to reach him. It hides from the peo-
> ple the bright image of the tsar, so that the tsar's word does
> not get to simple people, or does so in distorted form. But
> the common people love the tsar and yearn for him and the
> tsar, for his part, looks fondly upon the common people,
> whom he has long intended to deliver from their woes. And
> some day, reaching over the head of the nobles, the tsar and
> the people will respond to one another.[1]

Almost fifty years later, Lenin wrote of the

> millions and tens of millions of Russian workers and peasants

1

who until now have been able naively and blindly to believe in
the tsar-*batiushka*, to seek relief from their unbearably hard
circumstances from the tsar-*batiushka* "Himself," and to
blame coercion, arbitrariness, plunder and all other outrages
only on the officials who deceive the tsar. Long generations
of the oppressed, savage life of the *muzhik*, lived out in ne-
glected backwaters, have reinforced this faith. . . . [Peasants]
could not rise in rebellion, they were only able to petition
and to pray.

Bloody Sunday, the day in 1905 when the tsar's soldiers had shot
down a crowd of workers peacefully petitioning the tsar, had been,
according to Lenin, "the agony of the inveterate peasant faith in the
tsar-*batiushka*." Now, "the masses of workers and peasants who had
still retained remnants of their faith in the tsar . . . can and will
rise in rebellion. The 'tsar-*batiushka*' by his bloody retribution on
the unarmed workers has himself driven them to the barricades."[2]

No one has seriously questioned that the Russian common people did idealize the tsar. Historians and contemporary observers,
both Russian and foreign, have attested to this faith. Recently,
historians in Russia have begun to dispute about the significance of
naive monarchism, but they all conceive the phenomenon in terms
much like Samarin's or Lenin's and agree that it was virtually universal.

The tendency of humble Russians to idealize the tsar gave com-
fort to nineteenth-century conservatives and monarchists, who liked
to point out that the masses had never risen in arms against a tsar
they recognized as legitimate. The great uprisings of the seventeenth
and eighteenth centuries had always been waged in behalf of the
"true tsar," against the supposed usurpers of his rightful authority.
Naive monarchism was correspondingly distressing to the populists,
the leading exponents of radicalism in Russia until the rise of Marxism in the 1890s. The populists sought to deliver the common people from poverty and injustice, and most of them tended not only to
identify with peasants, but to idealize them. Peasants were the in-
articulate bearers of pristine justice; they were natural socialists.
Some populists supposed they were natural revolutionaries, as well.
According to Bakunin, for example, radical intellectuals had nothing
to teach the people; their only role was to coordinate and to ignite
the people's insurrectionary potential. In this scheme, popular faith
in the tsar was a stumbling block. For Bakunin, the great obstacle

to be overcome was the peasants' "patriarchalism," of which the most important aspect was devotion and submission to the tsar.[3] Bakunin's more subtle comrade and contemporary, Alexander Herzen, was less optimistic about the promise of insurrection but no less aggrieved by the credulous monarchism of the common people. His anguish is clear in this apostrophe to the Russian peasants, written from exile in London.

> You hate the *pomeshchik* ["landowner"] and hate the government clerk, you fear them—and you are absolutely right. But you still believe in the tsar and the bishop. Don't believe them! The tsar is like the rest, and they are his men. . . . Oh, if only my words could reach you, toiler and sufferer of the Russian land![4]

The final sentence, in which Herzen seems to admit the impossibility of disabusing the people, points to one of the great themes of nineteenth-century Russian radicalism. At least some of the Decembrists, the constitutionalist army officers who rose in rebellion in 1825, tried to teach the common soldiers that an autocrat was a tyrant and hence a false tsar who must, as a matter of Christian duty, be overthrown. Their attempt was renewed, in a less disingenuous way, in the radical proclamations of the early 1860s and in some propaganda ventures a decade later. By the mid-1870s, populists were conceding, tacitly or explicitly, that a frontal assault on the people's faith in the tsar was a waste of time. This conclusion was decisive for the subsequent history of Russian populism, and played a role in the spread of Marxism, as well. Marxism claimed industrial workers as its special constituency; they were only a tiny segment of the whole body of "toilers," for whom the populists claimed to speak, but they were less benighted and superstitious than peasants and therefore more promising revolutionary material.

Radicals are not, of course, our only witnesses to the phenomenon of naive monarchism, but they are particularly telling witnesses because they struggled against it. More important, because of their concern for popular suffering, they bring us to the main problem of naive monarchism. Russian peasants were, by and large, destitute and oppressed; their oppressors were the tsar's agents or others acting under the tsar's patent. Yet whatever their level of misery and discontent, peasants appear to have believed that the tsar was their patron and benefactor. What we have to deal with, then, is something very different from the loyalty or chauvinism of the comfortable, the fortunate, or the suborned.

Despite their special dismay, radicals described popular monarchism in much the same terms as other observers did. Naive faith in the tsar was an attribute of the common people, the *narod*. For the eighteenth and nineteenth centuries, the *narod* meant "the peasantry" along with a few small categories akin to peasants. The term serves primarily to make a cultural distinction. The *narod* is counterposed to *obshchestvo*, or "educated society." Members of educated society—squires, officials, intellectuals, and professional men—differed from the *narod* in that they had broken out of the matrix of traditional culture. They lived amidst the *narod*, drew revenues from it and ruled over it, but they were no longer encrusted in what Bagehot called the "cake of custom." In their manner of life and of thinking, in their institutions and deportment, they resembled their counterparts in western Europe. They enjoyed a near monopoly of wealth and power in Russia, but they were not simply "the ruling class," for educated society included many of the powerless and poor who were nonetheless cosmopolitan in culture and alien to the ways of the village.

Obshchestvo and *narod* did not form a graduated hierarchy, for a social void separated them. Between the extremes were only those few elements of the population that were traditionalist in their way of life but at a remove from the *narod:* the merchant estate, the parish clergy, and some petty squires. These groups were politically and intellectually passive and, while they might be literate, literacy was simply an attribute of caste and profession. They did not mediate between *obshchestvo* and *narod* or report upon them for our benefit. What we can learn about the *narod*, then, is what individual members of educated society tell us. Our defining concepts and most of our raw material consist of perceptions and imputations made across a cultural gulf. This gulf was just about as wide for radicals, who ardently wanted to bridge it, as for government officials, for whom the gulf was a major justification for the power they exercised. In plain terms, literates produced the sources historians now use, and "literates" and *obshchestvo* were virtually the same.

The *narod*, then, was traditionalist. It worked the land, worshipped God, dressed, cooked, married, and buried according to the prescriptions of rigid and venerable custom. Custom was not always venerable, but it was always represented as such by the *narod* and perceived as such by educated society.[5] Neither expediency nor convenience provided the kind of justification for conduct that tradition did.

Among these traditions was faith in the tsar as the benefactor of the *narod*. As reported to us by educated Russians, this faith was very simple. It was simple in that it was naive and crude, but also in the manner in which it is reported. As a rule, the naive monarchism of the *narod* is adduced without elaboration or detail, like an axiom that everyone knows. In the writings of educated Russians and latter-day historians, it figures as a premise to prove some other point: Russia's might, the prospects for revolution, or whatever. It has nothing in common with the sophisticated monarchism of officials and intellectuals who, even when they were in accord with the *narod*, worked out their own justifications for belief and conduct.

If we turn to the recent investigations of Russian folklorists, the myth of the benevolent tsar turns out to be more complex. It reveals two distinct layers, corresponding to the past and the future. The historical correlative of the idealized tsar was the "just tsar" of the past. In popular tradition, Ivan the Terrible or Peter the Great played this role. The just tsar might be harsh, even impulsively cruel, but he is sympathetic to the *narod* in its sufferings. His acts of benevolence are limited in scale to the individual or at most the village. Often his favor is expressed in some symbolic act, such as standing godfather to the child of a poor peasant. And he visits his wrath on the oppressor by humiliating or executing arrogant nobles and officials. The tsars of the past, then, were "just" by virtue of particular acts of benevolence and vengeance which link them with the *narod*. Even according to the tradition that Ivan the Terrible was a servant boy who became tsar by divine intervention, he executed his former master rather than taking some general act in behalf of peasants or bondsmen. For while justice was one attribute of the legitimate monarch, so, too, was respect for the social order. Furthermore, these traditions were constrained by historical memory. Ivan and Peter did visit their wrath on the mighty, but they could not be represented simply as champions of the *narod*, for they were memorable first of all for the privations they inflicted on the *narod*. While sympathy for the *narod* was an attribute of legitimacy, it had to be represented as a personal quality of past tsars, which manifested itself only in particular instances.[6]

Projected into the future, the image of the ideal tsar was not so

constrained by bitter experience. The just tsar to come, the legendary deliverer, could show his love for the *narod* on a broad and
generous scale, through acts of policy as well as charity and vengeance. The popular myth of the tsar finds full expression in this
legend.

The legend of the tsar-deliverer circulated in various times and in
various versions. Underlying these versions, as K.V. Chistov has
shown, is a common scenario, which runs as follows: the deliverer
intends to free his faithful *narod* from serfdom, from oppressive
officials and heavy taxes. Wicked courtiers and officials forestall this
by overthrowing the deliverer and killing him. The deliverer miracu-
lously escapes (often thanks to a faithful servant from the *narod*)
and for some years he wanders from place to place as a pilgrim. In
his travels, he comes to know and share the sufferings of the *narod*.
From time to time he prefigures his triumphant return by declaring
his identity to those he meets. Eventually he returns to the capital,
is recognized as the true tsar, and is duly enthroned. Thereupon he
rewards the faithful followers who assisted in his restoration and
lavishes punishment on the wicked courtiers; in this he resembles the
historical traditions about the "just tsar." But the deliverer does indeed deliver the whole *narod* from bondage and oppression and
inaugurates a regime of liberty and tranquility.

The legend has its variants. Sometimes the deliverer is an infant
heir to the throne, and sometimes he is confined in prison. The
means by which he is recognized as the true tsar are various and
sometimes fanciful. Within the perimeter of these variants, the
legend is strikingly stable. It first emerged in the Time of Troubles
early in the seventeenth century and recurred again and again down
through the 1860s. It flourished in the aftermath of dynastic crisis
or confusion, for, while it was a clear expression of popular discontent, a kernel of fact was required to generate each new version. Its
span corresponds, by and large, to the rise and fall of serfdom
in Russia.

Serfdom as an institution can be traced to the sixteenth century,
when the Muscovite state began, as a matter of general policy, to
bind peasants to the lands of their masters. Serfdom was consoli-
dated in the Law Code of 1649; in the early eighteenth century,
Peter the Great made it more extensive and more systematic. The
proportion of the peasantry that was enserfed expanded steadily,
reaching its zenith early in the nineteenth century. A very large part

of the *narod*, to be sure, was not serfs. Parallel to the rise and expansion of serfdom, however, the state imposed burdens and restrictions on these nonserfs—townsmen, cossacks, and what would later be called "state peasants." By the eighteenth century, serfdom was only technically distinct from slavery. While the serf was likely to envy the peasant who was not enserfed, all elements of the *narod* were under the thumb of educated society, whether squires or administrators. The *narod,* both serf and nonserf, was eager for deliverance. What the legendary deliverer brought, quite simply, was freedom—freedom from the squire for the serf, freedom from overbearing administrators for the nonserf, and freedom from the tax collector and recruiting officer for all. The deliverer would confirm the peasants in possession of the lands they cultivated and which "belonged" to them (although they were legally the property of the *pomeshchik* or the state) and then leave them alone. The longed-for freedom, or *volnost'*, was purely negative—freedom such as Russians imagined they had enjoyed in the good old days. The legend of the tsar-deliverer, therefore, takes its origins from the time when freedom was perceived as something the state had withheld and only the state could restore; it died out when the state did turn the *narod* into free citizens—although, as we shall see, the abolition of serfdom and later reforms were very far from the popular ideal of *volnost'*.

The persistence of the deliverer legend testifies to the strength of monarchist illusions, particularly since it was not one single evolving legend but a series of similar ones. The denouement, enthronement of the "true" tsar and deliverance from oppression, did not vary, but all the other elements were compounded of folkloric commonplaces and contemporary details. Each new version required disillusionment with the reigning tsar of the moment and the designation of some person in the ruling house (rarely an imaginary person) as the deliverer to come. Unlike legends about Frederick II Hohenstauffen who was to return to deliver the common folk of Germany, or myths about heroes of the past, the Russian deliverer legend had to be periodically recreated almost from scratch, each time under the influence, as Chistov puts it, of "desperation and shattered hopes."[7]

The legend of the tsar-deliverer was not a mere fireside entertainment for, intertwined with other aspects of popular monarchism, it influenced the behavior of peasants, cossacks, and other humble Russians. In 1855, for example, thousands of serfs left their homes

and headed for the Caucasus where, it was said, the tsar was sitting
on a mountain distributing freedom to all who came to his feet. It
took armed force to make them turn around. More striking, and
more ominous for the regime, was the exploitation of the deliverer
legend by impostors.

Royal impostors are distinct from pretenders. A pretender claims
the throne on the basis of rules of succession different from those
that the reigning monarch relies on. Catherine the Great was a pretender, and a successful one; she substituted for the system of succession prescribed by Russian law the system that prevails among
black widow spiders, who, after the consummation of marriage, kill
their husbands. An impostor, on the other hand, represents himself
as the person who, under the commonly accepted rules of succession, would be the legitimate monarch. While pretendership is compounded of force and legalistic persiflage, imposture relies first of all
on a miracle: the claimant is not dead, as everyone had supposed.
Pretenders and impostors both figure frequently in Russian politics
during the 250-year span of the deliverer legend. The most notable
impostor was Emel'ian Pugachev.[8]

In 1773 Pugachev announced that he was the Emperor Peter III.
Peter's deposition and death a decade earlier, along with a new version of the deliverer legend, had evoked a rash of impostors. Unlike
these others, Pugachev managed to launch an insurrection in behalf
of his claim to the throne. Whether measured in territorial extent, in
blood shed, or in its impact on the minds of men, the Pugachev
rebellion was one of the greatest in modern Europe. Pugachev
had what we now call charisma, and also the capacity to exploit the
local grievances of cossacks, Muslim tribesmen, and other groups in
the area of his early operations in the Volga and Ural basins. Yet the
greatest single ingredient in his success was his use of the legend of
the tsar-deliverer.

Pugachev began by offering himself as the legitimate tsar whom all
Russians were bound to obey. Experience soon taught him that
officers, landowners, and officials rejected him, for which they often
paid with their lives. Cossacks, factory workers, common soldiers,
and serfs and other peasants, on the other hand, accepted him eagerly
and fought in his legions. So Pugachev learned to direct his propaganda to the *narod,* and against the favored classes, and to frame it
in terms of the deliverer legend. For this grizzled, illiterate cossack
to claim to be an effete German princeling was implausible, but

Pugachev played out the imposture as best he could. The thrust of his appeal, however, was not dynastic imposture but demagoguery. To his followers he promised the broadest freedom and the richest bounty, mercy, justice, and vengeance against the oppressors and possessors. He emphasized, in conformity with the deliverer legend, his years of wandering and the suffering he had shared with the *narod.* In his proclamations, he sometimes imitated the language of the imperial chancelleries, but often he drew upon the rhythm and tone of legend. He could preface an *ukaz* with a correct rendering of Peter III's ceremonial titles: "We, Peter III, by the grace of God Emperor and Autocrat of All Russia . . ." and so on. Sometimes he substituted a different set of titles with a different appeal.

I, the legitimate great sovereign, am come openly before the host and all the people, having revealed myself from a secret place, to pardon the people and all living creatures for their sins; I am the bountiful champion, the sweet-tongued, merciful, soft-hearted Russian tsar, Emperor Peter Fedorovich, now free before the whole world, pure in zeal, and the autocrat of all peoples of all descriptions.[9]

Pugachev's ultimate defeat was due to the narrowly military shortcomings of his host, and not to a lack of followers. The ghost of Pugachev and the prospect of a new *Pugachevshchina* haunted the regime for a century or more. Pugachev's exploitation of the deliverer legend demonstrated the wide spread and social power of the myth of the tsar, but also showed the dangers the myth might hold for the reigning tsar.

Grounds for Belief

Folklore and history testify to the sway of the myth of the benevolent tsar, but it remains to explain why the *narod* believed the myth. It may be tempting to substitute a few conventional epithets for an explanation. Russian peasants were "backward," "superstitious," perhaps even (we are told) "mystical." These words pay incidental tribute to our own rationality and sophistication, but their primary function is to eliminate the necessity of working out the kind of explanation we would apply to ourselves. Yet the epithets have no explanatory value. The peasants were superstitious, but so are we; our faith in higher education and sexual gratification is not much better based in analysis and experience than faith in the tsar. And to demonstrate that peasants were superstitious does not explain why they held this particular superstition. As soon as we recognize that peasants were people somewhat like ourselves, naive monarchism requires explanation. In the pages that follow, therefore, we will look for the roots of the myth of the tsar and then consider some of the difficulties that still remain in the emerging explanation.

In a sense, we do not have to explain why Russian peasants idealized the tsar, but why they continued to do so to the verge of the twentieth century. In the medieval and early modern eras, in eastern and western Europe, veneration of monarchs was the rule. This veneration often approached idolatry. The analogy between the royal and human natures of the king and the divine and human natures of Christ tempted learned royalists into what now seems blasphemy. Magical powers, deriving from the essence of legitimate kingship, were attributed to the kings of England and France. These were not simply the superstitions of the illiterate, for they were shared and developed by sober lawyers and ingenious theologians.[10] The cult of the monarch can be as sophisticated as any other. In time, however, even monarchists came to perceive and to justify the monarch's role without much resort to mystery. In England as early as the seventeenth century, kingship was conceived in anthropological and pragmatic terms.[11] The eighteenth-century Enlightenment was friendly to kings, but the *philosophes* were not disposed to venerate them. This kind of attitude spread gradually among the common people, and its spread was accelerated by the toppling and restoration of monarchs in the revolutionary and Napoleonic wars. By the nineteenth century, a king was a suitable emblem of sovereignty, and kings were duly supplied for the newly independent states of southeastern Europe. In the age of railroads and telegraphs, however, there was not much magic left in monarchy—except, apparently, in Russia.

In its ideology and symbols, the Russian monarchy was similar to its counterparts in the West. Like his brother monarchs, the Russian tsar of modern times ruled "by the Grace of God," as he reminded his subjects in the preface to each *ukaz*. The trappings of sovereignty in Russia were familiar and intelligible to westerners. The common European ideal of monarchy was Christian and imperial in its origins. In Russia, however, both empire and church were those of the Byzantine East. Russian tsars were able to assume their imperial

legacy with comparative ease. In the West, the idea of the divine
right of kings derived primarily from struggles between kings and the
pope; the concept of absolute monarchy was challenged by privileged
groups and corporations. These conflicts had no counterpart in
Russia, except for an episode or two. There were no real attempts to
subordinate the tsar to the law or to institutions. The Russian
Church strove in principal for cooperation and "symphony" with
the monarchy, and in practice it was compliant. Etymologically and
in the minds of men, legitimate sovereignty and autocracy were one
and the same.

In Russia, then, the ideological foundations of monarchy were
ample. Being relatively secure in this respect, the Russian monarchy
did not have to resort to the tortuous and idolatrous devices that
were common in other Christian countries. For Russian theologians,
the analogy between the awful power of the tsar and the power of
God remained only an analogy, and they laid full and proper emphasis upon the sinful humanity of the tsar as a person.[12] Russian
tsars never claimed the magical healing touch of the kings of England
and France. Their problem, by and large, was not in eliciting deference but in making their writ run throughout their domain.

The Russian monarchy was so secure in its theoretical underpin-
nings that it could survive Peter the Great. Peter brought the monarch into the light of day by substituting practical activities for the
cloistered and ceremonial routine of seventeenth-century tsars. In
addition, he designated himself not tsar but "emperor," a title
deliberately chosen for its resonance in western Europe. This change
of title was part of a systematic transformation of names and ceremonies. Perhaps no state has ever changed its symbols so completely
except as a result of conquest or revolution. The very name of the
state and nation, as well as the titles of almost all civil and military
officials and institutions, were changed between 1699 and 1725.
Peter removed the throne from Moscow to St. Petersburg, a new
city with a Western name and orientation. He abolished the patri-
archate and appointed an administrative board to rule over the
Russian Church. All the emblems of sovereignty and authority were
recast on Western molds and retained these new forms until 1917.[13]
Yet popular monarchism passed unaltered through this transformation. The monarchy presented itself in a new and alien guise, but the
monarch was still revered as the benefactor of the *narod*. In a sense,
the monarchist tradition simply did not register Peter's transforma-

tion. In folklore and in other expressions of naive monarchism, dating from the eighteenth and nineteenth centuries, the monarch is not the emperor; he is still the tsar, and surrounded not by ministers and senators but by boyars and *voevody*; and he rules, as of old, over *Rus'*, not Peter's *Rossiiskaia imperiia.*

Some Russians did reject the new image of monarchy, but they did so on religious grounds, as a by-product of the Great Schism in the Russian Church. From the middle of the seventeenth century, popular hostility to the monarchy was always associated with religious dissent and, ultimately, with the belief that the reigning tsar was the Antichrist.[14] The Old Believers and the members of the various sects that derived from the Great Schism were political as well as religious dissidents, and on this ground they were harassed by state officials and, in the nineteenth century, cultivated by revolutionaries, who vainly hoped to capitalize on their alienation from the state.

Correspondingly, for the majority of Russians who stayed within the fold of orthodoxy, the rites of the Church reinforced popular monarchism. Prayers for the emperor and for the members of his family were a regular part of the liturgy. Obedience to the powers that be was one of the obligations of the orthodox, as of other Christians since Saint Paul's time, but orthodox Russians also pinned their hopes for justice and security in this world on the tsar. The orthodox *narod* was inclined to associate God and the tsar. For example, lands such as forests which could not, according to popular concepts of property, justly belong to any single person were called either "God's" or "the sovereign's." For God and the tsar shared many attributes—might, justice, and remoteness. The Old Believers, in their own way, made the same association; they could not simply reject the tsar on the grounds of policy, the repudiated tsar must be the Antichrist, the polar opposite of divine.

The affinity between religion and monarchism goes beyond theology and liturgy. Veneration of the monarch and veneration of God may derive from a common impulse. Feuerbach and others since his time have argued that God is made in the image of man, and that the attributes and injunctions of the gods are simply the brightest hopes and best wisdom of human beings. Kavtaradze explains the cult of the tsar in similar terms, emphasizing that the will of the idealized tsar corresponded perfectly to the values of the *narod*. "The peasants *externalized* their sense of justice and fastened

it to the person of the tsar, who 'orders' them to do what they
want. Herein . . . is the meaning of peasant monarchism."[15] So it was
that the peasants' most intense desire, the desire for land, stood fore-
most in the will of the idealized tsar. A radical propagandist in the
1870s found that the ideal of the tsar was closely linked with "the
peasants' ideal of the land. The peasants have projected their desires,
their concepts of justice onto the tsar, as if they were his desires and
his concepts."[16]

This process of projection was, in a sense, a way of advancing a
political program, of which the cardinal points were land reform and
equality before the law. The peasants did not conceive or represent
themselves to be making political demands, for they stood outside
politics. Until the very last days of imperial Russia, peasants were
unable to advance political demands in the modern sense, by making
an argument on the merits or by invoking the number of supporters
for a particular demand. They justified worldly decisions by invoking an authority veiled in mystery and standing outside themselves—
God, immemorial custom, or "the will of the tsar."

Furthermore, monarchist illusions may also have shared some of
the other functions of religion. The central myth of Christianity
looks to the future: the way of the Christian is hard, but the faithful
will receive a heavenly reward. The myth of the tsar held a similar
promise of reward, not in the next world but in this. It was a source
of hope for men and women with little occasion to hope, and consolation for the oppressed and destitute. In a poem written by a
nineteenth-century serf, an old peasant is assured:

> Although you are oppressed by fate
> God and the tsar are always with you![17]

Along with hope and consolation, the myth of the tsar—again, like
the Christian myth—encouraged the *narod* to bear misfortunes
passively. Because deliverance must come from a powerful and
benevolent authority, there was no reason to disrupt the present
order of things or attempt a direct challenge to the immediate oppressor. The obverse of the message of consolation was a counsel of
prudence, for if you challenge the oppressor, he is likely to strike
back with devastating force.

The interrelationship between religion and the cult of the tsar is
complex and significant, but it may impair our understanding by
magnifying the differences between nineteenth-century peasants and

ourselves, and so reinforcing the stereotype of the stupid *muzhik.* Nineteenth-century peasants were ignorant of many things that twentieth-century intellectuals know; they were superstitious, if all belief in things unseen is superstition. Hence it is important to appreciate that naive monarchism was not limited to the unlettered and unsophisticated and that it had some basis in experience and observation.

In its simplest and most common expression, popular monarchism took the form of the adage, "The tsar wants it, but the boyars resist." "It," of course, was justice, or tax relief, or a redistribution of land—whatever the *narod* most wanted. Educated Russians did not resort to this adage to explain political events, but they perceived politics in much the same terms. For example, they were prone to blame official wickedness and folly on an evil genius who exerted a baneful influence on the tsar: Arakcheev or Pobedonostsev, for example. And from the eighteenth century to early in the twentieth, many a reformer would insist that all he sought was "to get through to the tsar with the whole truth."[18] The tsar, in other words, is surrounded by self-seeking bureaucrats—the wicked boyars of the popular adage—and they conceal the truth from him to prevent their exposure and dismissal. If only the tsar *knew* what is happening in that courtroom, in my bureau, in our village, then surely he would set matters right, so that justice would prevail. And justice is all we want.

This attitude derived from the plenitude of the tsar's power. He was an autocrat, not accountable to any constituency and not limited by any judicial or legislative body. All legitimate authority derived from him. If the tsar was not temporarily misled by false counselors, if, knowing the whole truth, he deliberately rejected what a subject wanted, then the matter was closed. The subject had either to resign himself to the tsar's decision or else take a revolutionary stance. On a vital issue, however, resignation is very difficult; it is the wordly equivalent of the worst of sins, despair. And while it is easy in retrospect to say that people ought to have risen in arms to attain what they wanted, a conscious revolutionary position is, in a traditional society, as difficult to adopt and sustain as resignation and does not hold much more promise of immediate practical success. Russia's alienated intellectuals, with the revolutionary experience of Europe before them, took generations to develop a revolutionary attitude. And through the middle of the

nineteenth century even the most steadfast of them were tempted
by the prospect of using the tsar's authority before destroying it.
For an enormous concentration of power in the hands of one man is
fascinating and dazzling. It does not require superstition, ignorance,
or tradition to cast its spell. Even the "boyars" themselves, who presumably had a cynical understanding of the political machinery of
the empire, resorted to a variety of naive monarchism. They blamed
their own disappointments on conspiracies or on lack of access to
the tsar himself: the tsar wants it (my promotion, say, or the enact-
ment of my cherished plan), but the boyars resist. In Stalin's time,
one man, unsupported by custom or tradition, enjoyed a plenitude
of power like that of the tsars and, by virtue of this power, was the
object of the same kind of wishful thinking. A concentration camp
song tells of a prisoner, a loyal communist and innocent of any offense, who praised Stalin with his dying breath, calling on him to
"investigate everything here." And sophisticated politicians and intellectuals would respond to each new outrage with the lament, "If
only Stalin knew."

Naive monarchism, then, is not simply a function of the traditional allure of the monarch nor is it limited to peasants and others
who are, axiomatically, naive. Yet there are special reasons for the
sway of this attitude among peasants. "God is high," according to a
well-known proverb, "and the tsar is far away." The proverb ex-
presses the peasants' sense of their remoteness from the sources of
authority and their isolation within the village. Some historians hold
that peasants regarded everyone outside the village as alien and suspect, so that the village boundary was the frontier between "us" and
"them." According to Rakhmatulin, "An understanding of their
community of interests was alien to the peasantry as a whole, and in
their midst there was no footing for an understanding of themselves
as a distinct class of the exploited counterposed to the class of
feudal exploiters." Litvak puts it more simply, finding that serfs
might regard a nearby village of state peasants or even a more prosperous serf village belonging to their squire as "them," for they
understood "us" to apply only to their own village commune—plus
God and the tsar.[19] While "the peasantry" was not a peasant
concept, they did use other words—*narod*, "orthodox Christians"—
which suggest that they vaguely identified with other peasants in
distant villages. But these other peasants, in any event, were as
isolated and powerless as themselves. Eric Hobsbawm argues that

the peasants' ignorance and helplessness, their sense of their own inferiority to the other estates of the realm, largely determined their political behavior. Hence "the normal strategy of the traditional peasantry is passivity."[20] This norm was imperative in imperial Russia, where even nonpeasants were forbidden to engage in open politics, and any manifestation of peasant self-will was liable to repression as a riot or rebellion.[21] The inferiority of the peasants as a caste, and their confinement to the village, was not merely the product of cultural and economic forces but a matter of Russian policy and law.

An authority that could act for peasants, therefore, must not be dispersed, diffused, and "base," but just the opposite. It must be the antithesis of the village. So Marx explained the success of Napoleon III in terms of the uniformity, but lack of cohesion, of small-holding peasants, who

cannot represent themselves, they must be represented. Their representative must at the same time appear as their master, as an authority over them, as an unlimited governmental power that protects them against the other classes and sends them rain and sunshine from above.[22]

The idealized tsar, then, was everything that the village community was not.

The ideal of the tsar was also supported by experience. It was not simply a projection of wishful thinking. Indeed, some historians seeking to explain naive monarchism stress the government's occasional actions on behalf of the peasantry.[23] From a peasant's perspective, however, these actions were rare. Much legislation and executive action that was intended to benefit the peasantry had no impact at all in the village, or had a negative impact. The government issued laws to encourage nobles to free their serfs, but few nobles did so, while the requirement that villages establish a grain reserve against the threat of famine seemed like a new tax. Moreover, the regime was careful not to seem to intervene for peasants against officials and landowners. When serfs rose in protest against an oppressive landlord, government officials were sure to punish the serfs openly for their presumption; if these officials also put pressure on the landlord to moderate his demands, they did so covertly. For the myth of the tsar was potentially explosive, as Pugachev had shown; in the interests of order and stability, the regime would not encourage the idea that landlords and officials were the common enemies of the peasants and the tsar.

The day-to-day actions of these landlords and officials, however, did provide indirect support for the myth of the tsar. They were, as a rule, exacting, corrupt, indifferent to peasant needs, and very easily perceived as oppressors. The distant tsar, on the other hand, professed his benevolent concern for his faithful *narod* in *ukazy* and proclamations. Expressions of this concern might be carefully framed and blandly worded, but there was a striking contrast between this rhetoric and the peasants' experience at the hands of local authorities.[24] The tsar's "paternal compassion" might only be an ornamental phrase, but the squire and the constable did not usually bother to profess compassion, if only because they would not be believed. Similarly, there was a striking contrast between the tone and letter of the law, emanating from the tsar, and the enforcement of the law in the village; this contrast sustained the impression that the tsar was, at the very least, more benevolent than his officials. Hence the maxim, "The tsar is merciful but the *psar* ['clerk'] has no mercy."

We can, then, find grounds for belief in the myth of the tsar in folklore and religion, in the social structure and the nature of the tsar's authority, and in experience. Taken together, these grounds are adequate to explain the myth's vigorous survival in the nineteenth century, provided we invoke "superstition" or some other magic word to get us past the remaining problems. If we must explain the behavior of peasants as we explain the behavior of other human beings, these problems are numerous and vexing.

Problems of the Myth

The most obvious problem of the myth is that the tsar was not the benefactor of the *narod*—not in the sixteenth century, and not in the nineteenth. The tsars delivered millions of peasants and their families into serfdom and upheld and enhanced the serfholders' authority with all the resources of the state. The merciless *psar* was the agent of the tsar. The tax collector and the recruiting officer came into the village at the tsar's behest. If we search the record from the establishment of the Romanov dynasty to the abolition of serfdom for some act of royal favor for the *narod*, the best example would have to be Paul I's ruling that serfs should not work more than three days a week for their *pomeshchik.* This ruling was not in fact a law at all but a casual remark buried in a law on the observation of the sabbath. Officials came to believe that this remark had the force of law. They did not enforce it. But, one could say, "The tsar wants it but the boyars resist."[25]

The myth of the tsar was false. Falsity need not prevent a belief from taking a deep, enduring hold in men's minds. For example, many Russian peasants also maintained that the world is flat and that thunder is caused by the rumbling wheels of Elijah's chariot. These beliefs are false, but village experience does not directly confute them, while tradition or common sense may support them. Indeed, it is hard to displace superstitions of this kind, as idealistic young Russians discovered when they tried. (How many of us could provide a correct explanation of thunder convincing enough to persuade a skeptic?) For the world seems flat; whatever causes thunder is out of sight in the heavens, and neither is a matter of immediate practical concern. The benevolence of the tsar was a matter of great practical concern, it ought to have been manifest in the village, and it was not. The deliverer never came.

The peasants were superstitious, but how could they maintain a belief which daily experience confuted? The myth of the tsar was so contrary to observation and experience that, at the first attempt to elaborate upon it, it disintegrated. One of the most remarkable expressions of naive monarchism is a long narrative poem, composed by an anonymous serf and sent to the royal family. It was called *News About Russia* and was meant to bring home to the tsar the truth about the plight of the *narod.* Again and again the poet wishes that the tsar will be enlightened, whether by information from below or intervention from on high, so that he will intercede at last for his faithful subjects. One expression of this hope is a long speech by the father of the peasant narrator, who says:

> It has been time long since to lead
> All the slaves out of the prison of serfdom
> And break the chain their common enemies impose,
> And enlighten their minds a little.
> God will help the tsar to do this.

The son replies, understandably enough:

> Could not we find among the *narod* such a man
> That we three could go off to the tsar
> And advise him to give liberty to all?

The father hastily advises him, "Forget forever my words."

> You, my son, would go to the tsar?
> You would give his majesty advice
> To give freedom to all?
> And answer his questions
> In your colorless words?
> He would listen—then order silence
> And ask you nothing more about anything.
> Or he might decide to exile you
> Where even the raven does not lay his bones.
> Or turn you over for trial
> Into the authority of our unjust courts.
> . . . .
> The judges would cite laws
> Against your good intentions,
> And then, the scriveners, the pharisees,
> Perhaps will kill you on the public square.
> . . . .
> Leave it! Cast it out of your head
> And henceforth think of it no more.
> Think instead, tomorrow we will go
> To plow in an open field.[26]

The old man's advice was sound. Peasants who went as emissaries (*khodoki*—literally, "walkers") to bring the truth to the benevolent tsar were invariably punished. This was a fact of common knowledge, so obtrusive that it found its way into this poem, which is otherwise a sustained expression of faith in the tsar. It was a fine thing to muse upon the grace of the tsar-*batiushka*, but as soon as the musing suggested acting upon the myth, musing abruptly gave way to bitter caution. It was possible to recall the "just tsar" of the past or to prophesy the coming of the tsar-deliverer, but even ardent exponents of the myth of the tsar could not, without a gross affront to experience and common sense, provide the myth with a scenario in the present tense.

If we look at the details of the myth of the tsar, difficulties mount. The myth was, we have seen, congruent with religious belief and abetted by the Church, but the benevolence of the ideal tsar was not like the benevolence of God. God, we are told, will reward us in the next world for our sufferings in this, and these sufferings are retribution for our sins. He chasteneth those whom He loveth. The benevolent tsar, however, is supposed to reward us in this world, to our ease and material benefit. He does not chasten us, he chastens *them*—the boyars, courtiers, and squires. The myth of the tsar rests upon a cardinal distinction between the *narod* (the orthodox people, Christians) and the oppressor. It is both social and secular. Being much simpler than religious myths, it provides no basis for the continued sufferings of the *narod* and the flourishing of those who are alien to the *narod*.

Furthermore, benevolence was basic to the popular concept of the tsar; it was an attribute of legitimate majesty, but so was boundless autocratic power. How could the boyars prevent the tsar from bestowing his favor on the *narod*? They might manage to frustrate him for a time, just as the deliverer legend indicates. If their resistance is not an episode prior to triumph, however, but a permanent fact of life, then the tsar is not mighty; he is in fact no tsar at all. The success of Pugachev and various impostors derived from this tension between power and benevolence, which were, along with piety, the defining attributes of the legitimate tsar. In its basic formulation, then, the myth was unstable. And yet the *narod* held to it for more than three hundred years.

Eventually, the *narod* lost faith in the tsar. In this process lies a further difficulty in the myth, or rather in standard assumptions about the myth. Until 1905, all observers agreed that the peasants idealized the tsar. After 1905, it is clear that they did not. Between 1906 and 1917, monarchist political parties enjoyed some support from the urban middle and upper classes, but they had almost no peasant followers. Peasants put their hopes in liberal or radical politicians, or in themselves; the myth of the tsar was dead.

Some American historians assume that the myth of the tsar must have died in the last decades of the nineteenth century, while others find manifestations as late as 1916, when the myth was reportedly invoked to explain Rasputin's murder. They prefer, perhaps prudently, to bypass the issue and concentrate on administrative and cultural history. Soviet historians address the issue forthrightly and maintain, following Lenin, that it was the massacre of Bloody Sunday, on January 9, 1905, that disillusioned the *narod*. Yet how could one dramatic event in far-off St. Petersburg have so immediate an effect throughout Russia? Faith in the tsar had endured through privation and oppression, in spite of the imposition of serfdom and disillusionment about its abolition, in the face of the partial modernization of Russia and with very little confirmation in experience.

Then, we are assured, this faith disappeared in the twinkling of an eye. It is easier for us to believe in Elijah's chariot than to believe that a deeply and widely held belief could simply be thrown out with the newspapers of January 10.

We can meet this difficulty by assuming that popular faith in the tsar must have eroded in the decades prior to 1905, and that Bloody Sunday was simply the final blow. A pattern of gradual erosion would correspond to our understanding of the process of modernization and explain the *narod*'s indifference to monarchy after 1905. It is almost impossible, however, to find evidence in support of this pattern. Indeed, the sources indicate that the myth of the tsar still held sway among the peasantry in the first years of the twentieth century, despite the growing mood of revolt. In 1902, the eastern Ukraine was swept by agrarian outrages. A magistrate on the scene conceded that a few peasants might have fallen "under the influence of the agitation of subversive persons," but that

> the great mass of the peasants is still faithful to its sovereign. The very conduct of the peasants during the disorders is proof of this, for they were never directed against the supreme authority and its representatives. On the contrary, the peasants justified themselves by maintaining that "the tsar gave permission" to take grain and land from the *pomeshchiki*, that there was "an *ukaz* from the tsar" about this, and so on.[27]

If the myth of the tsar was in decay, this magistrate and many like him could not detect the process. Magistrates are often deceived. But we have much the same kind of testimony about the myth of the tsar for 1902 as for 1802 or 1702. Perhaps we can dismiss the evidence provided by magistrates, journalists, and politicians early in the twentieth century because we understand the impact of modernization. We ought, however, to be unsettled by the realization that our knowledge of naive monarchism in the nineteenth or seventeenth century rests upon much the same kind of evidence as this magistrate's report. At any rate, if the peasants' faith in the tsar was in decay by 1900, the process passed undetected.

Any attempt to trace the decline of naive monarchism entails further difficulties. We know that the myth of the tsar was dead after 1905 because the regime could not draw upon it. Officials had to compete for the *narod*'s allegiance with politicians, and the great advantages they enjoyed in this competition were their command

of armed force and their manipulation of the election laws, not
their service to the tsar. Yet the tsar's officials had never been able
to *use* naive monarchism. It may possibly have facilitated some
administrative processes, such as recruitment into the army, but it
did not create a reserve of allegiance on which the regime could
draw in time of need. The myth held the promise that the tsar would
deliver the *narod* from oppression, but it also laid the blame for this
oppression on the tsar's officials. Since these officials had to do the
tsar's work, the myth could be disruptive, if not subversive. A canny
statesman explained in 1879 that the regime's only useful support
came from conscious conservatives, who perceived and shared the
regime's concern for stability. In this category he included most
nobles, the Roman Catholic clergy of western Russia, and the Old
Believers, none of whom were under the sway of naive monarchism.
As for the common people, they

> are ready at the first summons to aid the government
> against its enemies, but this aid is disorderly and violent, ·
> always verging on the anarchic, and is therefore too danger-
> ous to rely on. At the same time, the masses are easily
> reached by malign rumors or promises of a grant to them of
> some new favors or material benefits. Under the influence
> of these rumors and promises, they are capable of refusing
> to submit to the proximate governmental authorities, and
> they seek out enemies where these authorities do not
> perceive any.[28]

Indeed, the maxim which epitomized popular monarchism, "The
tsar wants it, but the boyars resist," teaches love for the tsar but
hostility to his officials, and the second lesson was of greater practical significance. In the 1820s a community of peasants in Saratov
Province maintained that they were illegally enserfed. The case
passed from one agency to another, and the peasants sent a series
of emissaries to far-off St. Petersburg, all the while refusing to submit to their *pomeshchik*. Finally the Senate, the highest court of the
realm, rejected their claim, and the verdict was duly sent off to the
unsuccessful litigants. Still the peasants remained insubordinate, insisting that they must send yet another deputation to the capital to
establish whether the Senate's verdict was the tsar's true will. And in
the meantime, they would not render any dues to their supposed
master. The governor of the province came to the village himself
and, reinforced by the local bishop and four companies of soldiers,

was able to procure a measure of submission. Yet he could not get the peasants to renounce their claim. Since he was enforcing the unfavorable verdict, he was yet another boyar and not the vessel of the tsar's true will. If the tsar himself had made the journey, we may suppose that the peasants would have rejected him as an impostor; in 1831, Nicholas I tried to subdue a rebellious community by the sheer force of his august presence, and suffered an embarrassing failure.[29] Even if these peasants would have acknowledged the tsar and submitted at last, a monarchism which only the monarch himself could call to life was not much use to the regime.

Officials could not manipulate the myth of the tsar against what the *narod* conceived to be its interests, but the matter did not end there. The great insurrections of the seventeenth and eighteenth centuries, and Pugachev's first of all, showed that the myth could be manipulated against the regime. Indeed, Pokrovskii maintained that the myth of the tsar was "the peasantry's revolutionary ideology," for the triumph of the idealized tsar would mean "the utter destruction of the whole social structure, which lay on the Russian peasant like a heavy burden."[30] Since the myth appeared to be in full vigor in the nineteenth century, could not some new impostor raise the *narod* in rebellion in the name of the tsar? According to one discerning conservative, it would be all too easy. Iurii Samarin explained to a friend that, from the point of view of the *narod:*

> A manifesto, a uniform, an official, an *ukaz*, a governor, a priest with his cross, an Imperial Order—all this is falsehood, deception, and fraud. To all this the *narod* submits, just as it puts up with cold, blizzards, and drought, but it does not believe in any of it, it does not acknowledge it, it does not yield its convictions. To be sure, before the *narod* stands the image of a tsar who has been separated from it, but this is not the tsar who lives in St. Petersburg, appoints governors, issues Imperial Orders and directs the army but some other tsar, a half-mythic impostor, who tomorrow may pop out of the ground in the form of a drunken clerk or a demobilized soldier.[31]

Many observers would agree that the myth of the tsar lay ready to hand for a demagogic impostor and yet, after Pugachev, the impostor never did pop out of the ground.[32] The legend of the tsar-deliverer continued to circulate, but the flesh-and-blood impostors of the latter eighteenth and the nineteenth centuries were a pathetic lot. They were deranged, or desperate fugitives, or inspired by religious ecstasy rather than social justice. In any event, they did not launch any insurrections; they operated briefly in restricted areas and were easily captured and exposed.[33] The Pugachev rebellion taught the authorities how explosive the myth of the tsar could be, but the bloody suppression of the rebellion taught the *narod* a lesson in caution. They had yielded to Pugachev's blandishments because they desperately wanted to believe his claims, and they had suffered for it. It did not take much scrutiny to detect the drunken clerk or demobilized soldier under the robes of the impostor.

Furthermore, the myth of the benevolent tsar was not simply fuel for rebellion. It taught hostility to officials and faith in the tsar. Insofar as these two elements could be reconciled, the lesson was passivity and patience. The *narod* should wait until the tsar's true will could be realized. And, sustained by the myth, the *narod* did wait. Particular villages would seize upon plausible or implausible pretexts to improve their fortunes by invoking the tsar's favor. They would seek relief from the exactions of a flagrantly oppressive *pomeshchik* or grasping official; they would seek transfer from a bad *pomeshchik* to a better one, or a change in status. Often they were remarkably stubborn and imaginative in these struggles for partial advantage. Yet it is fair to say that the *narod* as a whole simply waited for the tsar to put an end to bondage. When the tsar did abolish serfdom, the peasants were desperately disappointed by the terms of the reform. Because the legislation was unjust, by their standards, it could not be the tsar's true and final will. It was a fraud, perhaps a test of their patience and faith in the tsar. The tsar would proclaim his true will "at the hour that has been foretold"; the *narod* must wait a little longer. A decade passed, and the hour did not strike. The peasants gradually submitted to the terms of the emancipation acts, but their expectations of the tsar's favor only became more extravagant. Rumors began to circulate that the tsar would soon ordain a "black repartition," a sharing out of all the lands in the empire among his faithful peasants. The rumor became so pervasive in the latter 1870s that the minister of internal affairs published a denial.[34] But of course, "The tsar wants it but the boyars resist."

The myth of the tsar, then, was disruptive and even, as Pokrovskii held, a "revolutionary ideology." Yet it also contributed to political stability. The peasantry, as Avrekh has argued, provided the tsarist regime with a broad social base, and did so largely under the influence of naive monarchism.[35] This was, to be sure, an inert base. The regime was doomed because, as soon as its social base quickened to life, pent-up antagonisms found expression in revolution.

On the level of generality we have maintained so far, naive monarchism is a puzzling phenomenon. It was a myth of this world that could withstand infinite worldly disappointment. It could inspire rebellion and inculcate passive submission. The attributes of the idealized tsar were contradictory in their essence. It is easy to conceive such a myth taking hold in a moment of crisis or ecstasy, but hard to believe that millions of people could have put faith in it for centuries.

Some of the difficulties lie in those convenient abstractions "*narod*" and "the peasantry." It is easy to use them glibly and forget that these terms subsume millions of individual men and women. It may be easier still now that "peasant studies" is becoming a distinct field of research. Philologists and anthropologists are aware how diverse "the *narod*" can be, and they can plot on a map how vowel sounds or tools change as one moves through Russia. If we could plot social myths in the same way, we might well find that they ebbed and flowed with the passage of time, and varied in their intensity from place to place. We can be reasonably sure that the myth of the tsar did not simply stand like a stone building until the moment of its demolition. Yet it is least of all possible to get a bearing on popular monarchism because we cannot be sure of its manifestations. Village A might be chronically insubordinate and village B long-suffering, and both be inspired by their faith in the distant tsar.

Granted that the myth underwent fluctuations, most of which were not recorded, it is still difficult to understand what the myth meant to its adherents. Did the myth of the benevolent tsar have the same standing as the saga of Ilia Muromets, the legendary hero of ancient Russia, or the legend of Elijah's chariot? Was it akin to the traditions that regulated the sowing of seed and the contracting of marriage? On this level of inquiry, the folklorists are not much help. They can record the forms and details of the myth, but they cannot assay its social reality.

To get a better understanding of naive monarchism, we must

descend from the level of "the *narod*" and "the peasantry" and deal
with particular peasants—men and women with names. This descent
narrows the inquiry a great deal, perhaps too much.

Once we seek
for peasants acting in response to the myth of the tsar, we find, as
Besançon observes:

> While the divine and paternal nature of the Sovereign does
> have its concrete manifestations, it is most often masked. It is
> a truth of the heart, which comes to the surface only in rare
> moments of effusion.[36]

We must, then, investigate moments of effusion. Peasants who
ardently believed in the benevolent tsar and waited patiently for
his favor are lost to us. They were not subjected to examination and
interrogation, and, indeed, we can infer their motives and behavior
only from their inaction and from the structure of the myth. Those
peasants who challenged the tsar's officials in the name of the
benevolent tsar, on the other hand, attracted attention, so that
we have dossiers, not inferences or generalizations. Working from
these dossiers, we can try to understand the attitudes and actions
that followed from faith in the benevolent tsar. These peasants were
not typical, but they ought to be knowable. So the need for manifestations of naive monarchism, for documents we can analyze,
leads us to the central paradox of the myth of the tsar—the monarchism of rebels.[37]

Notes

1. Quoted in M. N. Pokrovskii, "Krest'ianskaia reforma," *Istoriia
   Rossii v XIX veke*, izd. "Granat," n.p., n.d., vol. III, p.78.
2. V.I. Lenin, *Polnoe sobranie sochinenii*, vol. IX (1960), pp. 216-
   218.
3. M.A. Bakunin, "Gosudarstvennost' i anarkhiia. Pribavlenie A,"
   in I.S. Itenberg, ed., *Revoliutsionnoe narodnichestvo semidesiatykh godov XIX veka*, Moscow, 1964, vol. I, p. 49.
4. [A.I. Gertsen], "Iskopaemyi Episkop," *Kolokol*, no. 105
   (August 15, 1861), p. 878.
5. See M. Confino, *Systèmes agraire et progrès agricole . . .*, Paris–
   LaHaye, 1969, ch. 1, for instances when peasants gave the sanction of custom to agricultural practices of recent origin.
6. On the "just tsar," see V.K. Sokolova, *Russkie istoricheskie
   predaniia*, Moscow, 1970, ch. 3.
7. K.V. Chistov, *Russkie narodnye sotsial'no-utopicheskie*

legendy XVII-XIX vv., Moscow, 1967, especially pp. 30-32, 64, 232. On the image of Frederick Hohenstauffen in popular eschatology, see Norman Cohn, *The Pursuit of the Millennium,* Harper Torchbooks ed., New York, 1961, pp. 107-123.

8. For a brief and thoughtful discussion of the Pugachev rebellion, see Marc Raeff's essay in R. Forster and J.P. Greene, eds., *Preconditions of Revolution in Early Modern Europe,* Johns Hopkins Press, Baltimore, 1971, pp. 161-201.

9. Quoted by Chistov, *Russkie narodnye sotsial'no-utopicheskie legendy,* p. 160. Chistov himself, however, disputes the view of S.F. Eleonskii that "epic influences" can be found in the style of Pugachev's proclamations (p. 157n).

10. For example, Blackstone held that the king, as a legal entity, "is not only incapable of doing wrong, but even of thinking wrong"; quoted in Ernst H. Kantorowicz, *The King's Two Bodies: A Study in Medieval Political Theology,* Princeton University Press, Princeton, 1957, p. 4. Kantorowicz goes on to show the influence of Christological doctrine on sophisticated concepts of kingship. On magical powers as an attribute of legitimacy, see Marc Bloch, *Les Rois thaumaturges,* 2nd ed., Paris, 1961.

11. On this transition, see J.N. Figgis, *The Divine Right of Kings,* Harper Torchbooks ed., New York, 1965.

12. Michael Cherniavsky, *Tsar and People. Studies in Russian Myths,* Yale University Press, New Haven, 1961, especially ch. 2.

13. On this transformation, see Cherniavsky, *Tsar and People,* ch. 3, especially p. 91, where Cherniavsky remarks of the new image and title of the tsar: "There was not really a dynasty one could identify, no sanctity one could feel, no piety one could admire. The Sovereign Emperor was such an abstraction that a German woman could fill the position."

14. Michael Cherniavsky, "The Old Believers and the New Religion," *Slavic Review,* XXV, 1 (March 1966), pp. 1-39.

15. G.A. Kavtaradze, "K istorii krest'ianskogo samosoznaniia perioda reformy 1861 g.," *Vestnik Leningradskogo universiteta,* no. 14 (1969), p. 58.

16. M.N. Pokrovskii, *Tsarizm i revoliutsiia,* Moscow, 1918, p. 30.

17. T.G. Snytko, ed., *Vesti o Rossii. Povest' v stikhakh krepostnogo krest'ianina,* Iaroslavl', 1961, p. 47.

18. For an eighteenth-century example, see Alexander Radishchev, *A Journey from St. Petersburg to Moscow,* Harvard University Press, Cambridge, 1958, pp. 71-76. For a late one, see "Peredovaia stat'ia Petra Struve," *Osvobozhdenie,* no. 12 (Stuttgart, December 2, 1902), p. 187.

19. M.A. Rakhmatulin, "K voprosu ob urovne obshchestvennogo soznaniia krest'ianstva v Rossii," *Voprosy agrarnoi istorii tsentra i severo-zapada RSFSR. Materialy vsesoiuznoi diskusii,* Smolensk, 1972, p. 161; B.G. Litvak, "O nekotorykh chertakh psikhologii russkikh krepostnykh pervoi polovine XIX v., " in B.F. Porshnev, ed., *Istoriia i psikhologiia,* Moscow, 1971, pp. 208-209.

20. Eric Hobsbawm, "Peasants and Politics," *Journal of Peasant Studies,* I, 1 (October 1973), p. 13.

21. Iakushkin remarked in the 1860s, "how educated people try to give everything a special interpretation. A misunderstanding, a complaint—for them it is always a riot! They don't have another word in their vocabulary"; P.I. Iakushkin, "Bunty na Rusi," *Sochineniia,* St. Petersburg, 1884, p. 56.

22. Karl Marx and Frederick Engels, *Selected Works,* 2 vols., Moscow, 1962, I, p. 334.

23. Litvak, "O nekotorykh chertakh," p. 209. See also V.A. Fedorov, "K voprosu ob ideologii krepostnogo krest'ianstva," *Voprosy agrarnoi istorii tsentra i severo-zapada . . . ,* p. 147.

24. Rakhmatulin maintains that the idealized image of the tsar was directly influenced by the language of *ukazy,* which represented the tsar as superhuman and without sin; "K voprosu," pp. 165-166. This kind of propaganda was distinct from the propaganda of official nationality, which was largely directed at *obshchestvo;* see N.V. Riasanovsky, *Nicholas I and Official Nationality in Russia,* University of California Press, Berkeley, 1959.

25. S.B. Okun' and E.S. Paina, "Ukaz ot 5 aprelia 1797 i ego evoliutsiia," *Issledovaniia po otechestvennomu istochnikovedeniiu,* Leningrad, 1964, pp. 283-299.

26. Snytko, *Vesti o Rossii,* pp. 56-61. In practice, a *khodok* was sure to be punished but would not be executed.

27. *Krest'ianskie dvizheniia 1902 goda,* Moscow-Petrograd, 1923, p. 63.

28. P.A. Valuev, quoted in P.A. Zaionchkovskii, *Kriziz samoderzhaviia na rubezhe 1870-kh-1880-kh godov,* Moscow, 1964, pp. 99-100.

29. I.I. Ignatovich, *Krest'ianskoe dvizhenie v Rossii v pervoi chetverti XIX veka,* Moscow, 1963, pp. 411-421; N. Ia. Eidel'man, *Gertsen protiv samoderzhaviia,* Moscow, 1973, p. 201.

30. Pokrovskii, *Tsarizm i revoliutsiia,* p. 3.

31. Quoted in P.A. Zaionchkovskii, *Provedenie v zhizn' krest'-ianskoi reformy 1861 g.,* Moscow, 1958, pp. 80-81.

32. Litvak finds that in the nineteenth century, imposture was re-

placed by documentary fraud—false charters and decrees from the tsar; Litvak, "O nekotorykh chertakh," p. 210. See also Fedorov, "K voprosu," p. 148.

33. On latter-day imposture, see K.V. Sivkov, "Samozvanchestvo v Rossii v poslednei treti XVIII veka," *Istoricheskie zapiski*, no. 31 (1950), pp. 88-136, and V.G. Korolenko, "Sovremennaia samozvanshchina," *Polnoe sobranie sochinenii*, 9 vols., Petrograd, 1914, III, pp. 316-320.

34. Zaionchkovskii, *Kriziz samoderzhaviia*, p. 110.

35. A.Ia. Avrekh, "Russkii absoliutizm i ego rol' v utverzhdenii kapitalizma v Rossii," *Istoriia SSSR*, no. 2 (1968), p. 101.

36. Alain Besançon, *Le tsarevitch imolé. La symbolique de la loi dans la culture russe*, Paris, 1967, pp. 89-90. Kavtaradze makes much the same point in "K istorii," p. 56.

37. While this book was in press, Phillip Longworth published two innovative studies pertaining to the myth of the tsar. They are "Peasant Leadership and the Pugachev Revolt," *Journal of Peasant Studies*, II, 2 (1975) and "The Pretender Phenomenon in Eighteenth Century Russia," *Past and Present*, no. 66 (1975), pp. 61-83.

Spassk District, Kazan Province (1860s)

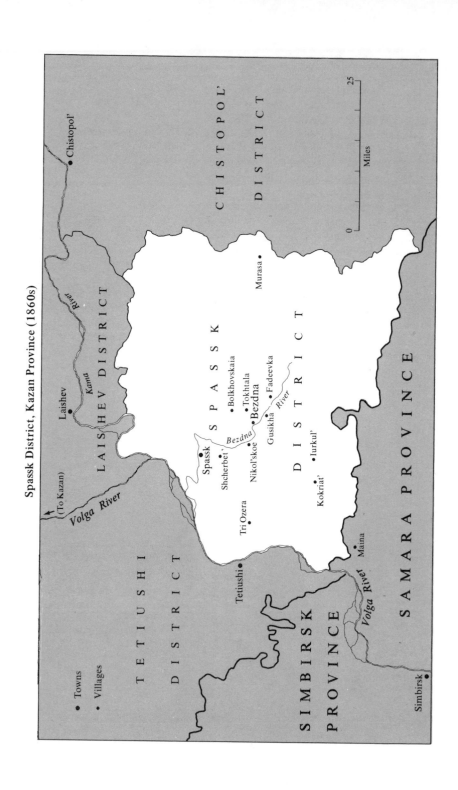

2

Bezdna

The emancipation legislation of February 19, 1861, was a compromise between serfdom and *volia,* or freedom. For the peasant, serfdom meant a network of obligations. He had to render labor service (*barshchina*) or pay dues (*obrok*) to his master; his master could choose between the two, demand both, or even take the serf into his household as a servant. The serf's obligations did not end there, for, unlike the American slave, he was liable to be drafted into the army and for taxes of various kinds. Yet in his relations to the state, as in all else, the serf was under his master's authority, for the master was responsible for the serfs' taxes and could choose which serfs would serve in the army. Every aspect of the serf's life was subject to the master's control: his vocation, his marriage, his children's fate, his place of residence, and the land he worked. In practice, the serf might make an arrangement with his master that satisfied them both, but under the law, the serf had multiple obligations and no will of his own.

    Volia, on the other hand, was the peasants' word for "freedom" in its broadest and most appealing sense: a life without obligations to others. A peasant in 1857 explained that when peasants are "completely free [*vol'nye*] they will not ask [us] for any taxes or recruits for the army, there will not be any bosses, and we will begin to rule over ourselves."[1] Under *volia,* then, life in the village would be wholly subject to the peasants' will; indeed, in Russian *volia* also means "will." *Volia* is what Pugachev promised emphatically, and it is closely akin to the *volnost'* which the legendary tsar-deliverer would bestow on the common people. Government officials and other nonpeasants complained that peasants could not understand freedom in any other sense, and that *volia* really meant complete anarchy and idleness—freedom even from the necessity of growing food. It would have been understandable if peasants had framed an ideal which was the perfect opposite of the obligations and dependence they knew, but their concept of *volia* was not as far-fetched as it was, whether in praise or blame, represented to be. Under *volia*, as the peasants understood it, custom, nature, and the will of the community would all prevail over the will of the individual peasant. These were all familiar forces, of which the peasant was a part and with which he could identify. *Volia* did preclude, however, any obligations to those outside the peasant community, apart from deference to a remote and benign tsar. In simplest terms, *volia* meant that the peasant community would be left alone. It is not so far from the ideal we express as "life, liberty, and the pursuit of happiness."

The statutes of February 19 abolished serfdom but did not put *volia* in its stead. The *pomeshchik's* arbitrary power over his serfs, which was the essence of serfdom, was terminated. He was obliged to provide most of the peasants on his estate with allotments of land, and the size of these allotments and the cash or labor that peasants must provide in return were regulated by the new statutes. These regulations were complex, and most of the detailed provisions that produced this complexity were clearly designed to benefit the *pomeshchik*. Far from being disencumbered of his squire, the ex-serf was put in a state of temporary obligation to him. By and large, he could end this obligation only by redeeming his statutory allotment at an exorbitant price. The peasants found themselves hedged about with a multitude of regulations and placed under the authority of a pyramid of new officials. Whatever advantages they might eventually find in the new arrangements, this was certainly not *volia*. Indeed, the framers of the statues took pains not to use the word *volia*, in any of its senses. One peasant reportedly complained that he had been told to expect freedom, but instead " 'cipation" was being imposed.[2] The squires, to be sure, were dismayed at the loss of their prerogatives, but this was small consolation to the disappointed peasants.

The promulgation and implementation of the emancipation legislation presented great difficulties to the regime. The lives of some 22 million men and women were to be run by the book, and the book was four hundred folio pages of legalisms, obscurities, and seeming contradictions. Most peasants were illiterate, and few of those who could read could make much sense of the statutes. Who, then, could interpret the legislation to them? In most villages, the peasants could choose among the squire, the steward, the priest, and the constable—that is, the beneficiaries and enforcers of serfdom. Even if the peasants had some trust in, say, the steward, could this trust withstand the peasants' disappointment at the impositions and limitations the steward elicited from the statues? As the head of the political police reminded the tsar, "A majority of the peasants hoped to receive complete freedom from obligations to the *pomeshchik* and a free allotment of land."[3] The problem was in the legislation itself, and not in the peasants' illiteracy or in the difficulty of understanding bureaucratic language and legalistic complexities.[4] And what, after all, did "understanding" mean? The legislation would be imposed by the authorities in any event. What had the peasants to gain by acquiring or feigning an understanding of it? For peasants, as Hobsbawm puts it, "The refusal to understand is a form of class struggle."[5]

The problems the emancipation legislation presented were no greater or less in Kazan Province than elsewhere. But in this province, these problems generated a situation in which a large number of peasants were shot by soldiers; this shooting in turn provoked a unique political demonstration in the city of Kazan. Much ink was spilled over the shooting and the demonstration, producing a considerable body of official reports, private letters, depositions, memoirs, and so on. By one of the perversities of historical inquiry, the historian benefits from the deaths of these peasants, since their deaths generated a rich array of source materials for his use.

Briefly, events ran as follows. Anton Petrov, a peasant living in Spassk District, Kazan Province, claimed to have discovered that the emancipation legislation did offer *volia*. The peasants of his neighborhood, disappointed with the terms of the legislation as interpreted for them by others, flocked to Petrov. Various officials tried and failed to disabuse the peasants and to persuade them to surrender Petrov. Peasants began to come from more distant villages to hear Petrov's interpretation, until a large crowd was gathered in Petrov's home village of Bezdna (which happens to mean "abyss").

On April 12, the tsar's adjutant general A.S. Apraksin came into Bezdna with a body of troops. Apraksin and other officials tried once again to persuade the peasants to submit, to disperse, and to surrender Petrov, warning them that they would be fired upon if they were stubborn. The peasants insisted that they and Petrov were loyal subjects of the tsar and that to submit to Apraksin would be to flout the true will of the tsar. The troops then fired repeatedly into the crowd, killing and wounding many peasants. The peasants stood firm under several volleys, but they finally scattered and Petrov surrendered. He was tried by court-martial and executed on April 18. In the meantime, a number of students at Kazan University and the Kazan Theological Academy held a requiem service in Kazan for the peasants killed at Bezdna. This service caused a scandal, largely because of a speech or eulogy delivered by Professor A.P. Shchapov. The events at Bezdna and the requiem service were both investigated throughout the summer by various central and local authorities. As a result of their investigations, a few peasants of Spassk District were beaten and given jail terms, some students were expelled from the Kazan Theological Academy, while Shchapov, who had been confined to jail through the summer of 1861, was fired from his post and forbidden to teach elsewhere.

Official investigators had to flesh out the skeleton of events with detail and then interpret and evaluate their findings. The immediate task of the historian is not so very different. It was necessary in 1861, for example, to establish whether Apraksin acted properly— whether the dimensions and character of Petrov's movement justified shedding blood to suppress it. A century later, it is natural to sympathize with the peasants and to brand Apraksin a murderer, but easy indignation is no help to the historical understanding. The historian must first of all establish whether Apraksin's action was anomalous—whether it was inconsistent with the policies, procedures, and standards of society and the regime at that time. And this question is really the same as the question before the government in the aftermath of the shooting.

Similarly it is necessary now, as it was then, to determine exactly what happened at Bezdna on April 12. Were the peasants adequately warned, and did they threaten Apraksin's troops in any way? Was there any way of dispersing them without bloodshed? As for Petrov, what were his motives? Did he believe his fanciful interpretation of the emancipation statutes was literally true? Did his followers? But along with the investigator's task of reconstructing events and fixing responsibility, the historian should bring a sympathetic understanding to bear. He must try to understand the mentality that made it possible for the peasants to stand firm under fire, and also the mentality that made it possible to fire upon them. Armed with this understanding, he can hope to master the paradox of offering resistance in the tsar's name to the tsar's own agents.

The Statutes of February 19, 1861, reached Kazan Province at the end of March and the beginning of April. The regime had announced its intention to reform serfdom more than three years before, and by the spring of 1861 the tension of expectancy was intense. This tension is described in the memoirs of N.A. Krylov, who at that time was a steward on an estate called Murasa in Spassk District. He recalled that in that spring the peasants believed that the tsar had granted them *volia* long ago, but that squires and officials had so far managed to hide it. The peasants maintained this openly and, according to Krylov, cheerfully, without animosity. Krylov insisted that the peasants were mild and friendly even in making terrible accusations against the squires and himself as their tool. He even managed to make light of an incident in which the peasants on his estate put him under siege and in fear of his life.[6]

The promulgation of the abolition of serfdom did not relieve this tension and hostility. The emancipation legislation arrived piecemeal—first the ceremonious and vague manifesto was delivered to be read in the churches, then various extracts from the legislation were published in the newspapers, and last of all the complete statutes, bound as a book, were sent to each estate. As the newspapers with extracts began to arrive in Murasa, Krylov was careful to leave them in the estate office so that the peasants could consult them.

> Word about *volia* in the newspapers spread through the estate [Krylov recalled], and many people came to hear *volia*. But the language of the legislation proved to be unintelligible to the peasants and even to the semiliterates who were reading it to them. I took a hand at reading it myself to a crowd of peasants sitting and standing in the office; I always found that the most clear and expressive reading was utterly incomprehensible to them. I tried to explain the articles of the legislation in my own words, and then everyone understood clearly, but

they did not believe the explanation. They would say, " You read well enough, but you interpret everything to benefit the squire." The cellarer and the clerk read to them, also with explanations, but they too were suspected of being hand in glove with the squire.

In their disappointment, the peasants maintained that anyone who got wages from a *pomeshchik* had sold out and could not be trusted to read and interpret the new legislation. When a venerable gardener picked through the newspapers to read aloud the articles that held out some tangible benefit to the peasants, they retorted that these benefits were trivial and that the gardener, too, was concealing the main thing, *volia.* "Soon," according to Krylov, "readers and listeners got so sick of one another that the newspapers lay untouched in the estate office."[7]

The immediate problem was the peasants' illiteracy and their estrangement from the few literates in the countryside. According to an aide to the governor of Kazan Province, they "had no one to turn to" for an explanation of their new rights and obligations.

> They did not dare to trouble the *pomeshchik* and also, of course, they did not trust him, suspecting that he could offer them lies of some kind to his own benefit. The educated segment of the household serfs could not understand anything in the Statutes either, and they themselves were cruelly disappointed. . . . The deacons and sextons had been terrified with threats that they would be unfrocked if they read the Statutes, while the priests, who were ready to lick the squires' feet for a glass of vodka, were trusted by the peasants no more than the squires themselves.[8]

Matters at Murasa did not improve when the complete and official text of the statutes was delivered to the peasant community. The peasants brought the statute book to a local cabinetmaker. He began to read the book aloud slowly and carefully from the first page, which happened to be a purely procedural directive from the tsar to the senate. The peasants, who had been expecting to hear about the allocation of plowland and forest, listened while this unintelligible document was slowly read through. The cabinetmaker claimed, "Every word is intelligible to me, but I can't make out where any of it applies. And I can't explain it to people." Giving up on him, the peasants appealed successively to the village priest, who refused; his deacon, who could make no sense of the laws; and a pious old peasant woman, who proved able to read only the archaic Slavonic of the Church. They then sent for a peasant in a nearby village, who turned out to have already tried and failed to construe the legislation for his neighbors. As one day followed another and *volia* had still not been found in the statute book, the peasants searched ever more widely and desperately for a satisfactory reading.[9]

The fundamental problem was not in the capacity of the readers and interpreters, but in the legislation itself. It contained various benefits and improvements for the peasants, but not the *volia* they expected. They were driven from reader to reader by their own false hopes. The authorities, anxious that the peasants not find any support for these hopes, made it plain that it was a serious crime to interpret the new legislation incorrectly; as enforced in the country-side, this ruling often meant that any interpretation was banned. Actions of this kind, however, only reinforced the peasants' belief that the real *volia* was somehow hidden in the statute book and could be elicited by a cunning reader. Disappointed by the interpretations of nonpeasants, they searched out literates from among their own kind. Anton Petrov was one such peasant "interpreter."

The government in St. Petersburg got its first word of trouble in Bezdna in this telegram from Kazan city.

Telegram from P.F. Kozlialinov, Governor of Kazan Province, to the Minister of Internal Affairs, April 13, 1861[10]

Complete insubordination to the authorities on the estate of Bezdna, in Spassk District. Anton Petrov, a schismatic who claims to be a prophet and an emissary from the tsar, has captivated everyone. Common people from almost all the estates of the district are assembling at Bezdna; there real *volia* is being proclaimed and food is prepared for the *narod*. All persuasion is fruitless, they are sure of complete liberty, that all the land is theirs, and that there is no authority but the tsar's, transmitted by Anton Petrov, since all the rest *[of the officials]* have been bought by the squires. Count Apraksin, the marshal *[of the nobility]*, the sheriff, and my adjutant are already in the Bezdna area with a company from Tetiushi. *Pomeshchiki* and officials are not being touched, but Bezdna is surrounded with peasants on horseback, who don't allow anyone in; yesterday there were already more than 2,000 people at Bezdna. The arrival of the rest of the troops is delayed while they assemble at the battalion headquarters, and also by the terribly muddy roads and the difficulty of crossing the Volga and the Kama *[rivers]*. I have moved up three companies from Tetiushi, four from Laishev, three from Chistopol', and the two that were assembled at Kazan, all under the command of division commander Skalon. I have taken all measures to suppress this; I know all the details, strong measures are necessary in order to finish this quickly and get the sowing done by the end of the month, otherwise the consequences could be major. I hope for success in curtailing the uprising and in the sowing. I will report in detail by mail the day after tomorrow. In two districts where there are *pomeshchiki,* it is absolutely peaceful, but in three districts there have been instances of insubordination, due to misunderstanding; they were ended by persuasion and explanation.

In this telegram, based on reports from Kozlialinov's subordinates in the field, are several themes that will crop up again in official explanations of the events at Bezdna. Observers emphasized that Petrov presented himself to his followers as a "prophet," and made much of the fantastic and ecstatic character of his appeal; the first few lines of this report indicate that Petrov operated as the chosen emissary of both God and the tsar. Petrov is variously reported to be a "schismatic," "a sectarian," and "an Old Believer." Officials did not distinguish among these terms nor did they investigate Petrov's links to a dissident and possibly subversive religious community.[11] These terms may, therefore, have been casual labels, appropriate for any peasant who, like Petrov, was pious, literate, and troublesome. And Petrov's eccentricity in matters of religion served to demonstrate the irrationality of his appeal, a matter on which all the official interpretations agreed.

Then there is the problem of mud. The troubles at Bezdna fell in the season known as *rasputitsa* or *bezdorozhitsa* (literally, "no-roadness"), the part of the spring when all country roads were a mass of mud, while high water made it difficult to cross the rivers. The mud made it difficult to bring large numbers of troops to Bezdna, and General Apraksin would invoke this consideration to justify shooting into the crowd. Yet Apraksin also maintained that still larger numbers of peasants came from long distances, and even other provinces, to hear Petrov; the mud was just as sticky and the rivers as treacherous for them.

When he sent off this telegram, Governor Kozlialinov, who was almost a day's ride from Bezdna, did not know that the troubles at Bezdna had already reached their bloody climax. The authorities in St. Petersburg learned of the denouement and the arrest of Petrov from another telegram sent the same day.

Telegram from Colonel Larionov
to V.A. Dolgorukov, Chief of Gendarmes
April 13, 1861[12]

Yesterday up to 60 peasants were killed at Pushkin's, the leader is taken but there is no repentance, there is a rebellion all around, they don't go to work.

The Pushkin referred to here is Count Musin-Pushkin, the owner of Bezdna. Larionov was the chief of the Third Section, or political police, in Kazan, and presumably he was anxious to get the news about the shooting at Bezdna to St. Petersburg before the regular civil officials could do so. At any rate, he sacrificed accuracy for speed; scarcely anything in this telegram is correct except the fact that Petrov had been captured. The question remains whether subsequent reports, longer and more carefully composed, could efface the alarm produced by this first report.

Even in this hasty communique, Larionov expressed concern about the beginning of the agricultural year, just as Kozlialinov had done. This may seem a curious preoccupation in the midst of this kind of crisis, but they feared, as many other officials did in the spring of 1861, that now that the servile foundation of Russian agriculture had been displaced, peasants would not sow and harvest the crops on which they and all Russians depended. More particularly, officials feared that while the peasants might provide for themselves, they would refuse to work on any terms for the *pomeshchiki*, so that the landed nobility would be ruined in short order. These fears would prove excessive, but they were rife in 1861, and the urgency of stamping out any work stoppage among the peasantry colored official attitudes towards the events at Bezdna.

The next day, the authorities in St. Petersburg received a report, more extended and more reliable, from the provincial governor.

Report (by Telegraph) of P.F. Kozlialinov to the Minister of Internal Affairs April 14, 1861[13]

Secret

The adjutant Polovtsov, who returned today at 8 o'clock in the morning from Count Apraksin's side at the scene of the events, reported orally that Bezdna has been taken and the crowd dispersed; Anton Petrov has been arrested and the loss of peasants is considerable, as many as 70 or more peasants were killed, which testifies to their terrible stubbornness, to the degree that they were aroused, and to their confidence that their cause was right. The reason I sent the 12 companies about which I reported yesterday was to avoid bloodshed. Apraksin, seeing that the mass of people at Bezdna was increasing every minute (yesterday there were up to 4,000) and bearing in mind that the marshal *[of the nobility]* was getting reports every minute that estates were in turmoil, decided not to wait for the other troops and moved into Bezdna with two companies. The peasant women had been sent out of the village. Although adjutant Polovtsov, the priest, the marshal, and Apraksin himself appealed repeatedly for Petrov's surrender, the people kept replying the same thing: "We will not surrender him, we are united for the tsar, you will be shooting at the Sovereign Alexander Nikolaevich himself." The soldiers, drawn up in ranks, made five or six volleys; they shot the first few without aiming, so that at a distance of 300 paces *[only]* three or four men fell, but then they became outraged by the peasants' stubbornness, and hit with every shot of the fourth volley. The poor people stood motionless like a wall and continued to shout, "We will not yield, it is the tsar's blood that is flowing, you are shooting at the tsar." After the last volley they wavered and fled, and then Anton Petrov appeared, holding the *[Emancipation]* Statute on his forehead, and was arrested. All measures for giving aid to the wounded were undertaken and the bodies were cleared away. The District Marshal Molostvov, who went alone into the crowd three times, and especially the sheriff conducted themselves in exemplary fashion. The soldiers are trustworthy.

Along with this I shall report briefly by telegram to the Sovereign Emperor. Anton Petrov will be tried by court-martial at Spassk. It is necessary to carry out the sentence immediately in Bezdna itself, because, it is said, he told the people he would be brought to trial, but the Sovereign would open the treasury to him for three minutes and give him a cross *[i.e., a medal]* and then he would return and do what he had promised for the peasants. I ask permission *[for his court-martial]*.

I have just received *[word]* from Apraksin that the mob is dispersed but the mood in the neighboring villages is heated. Another company has arrived and the rest are drawing near.

It must have been awkward for Kozlialinov to have Apraksin operating in his province outside the regular hierarchy as the tsar's own agent. One of the governor's later reports (see pages 64–66) indicates that relations between them were strained. But apart from mentioning his own desire to avoid bloodshed and expressing some sympathy for the peasants, Kozlialinov did not venture any criticism of Apraksin's resort to arms. Apparently his adjutant Polovtsov, who provided the substance for this report, did not offer any material for such criticism. It was Kozlialinov, not Apraksin, who first requested permission to try Anton Petrov by court-martial, which meant he could be executed; Russian law did not provide for capital punishment of civilian criminals. Once it became clear that the crisis was safely past, both Kozlialinov and Polovtsov would represent Apraksin as a swaggering bully, but in this report they acknowledged, at least implicitly, the necessity of shooting down the crowd.

Apraksin

It remained for Apraksin himself to explain the events at Bezdna and justify his actions. We know that he took pains over his report, which he sent to the tsar three days after the shooting.

Report from General Apraksin to the Tsar
April 15, 1861[14]

From the day when the *[emancipation]* manifesto was published until the time when the "Statute on Peasants Formerly in Servile Dependency" was received in Kazan Province, everything seemed calm. While the *pomeshchiki* complained somewhat that the peasants were carrying out their tasks very lazily, they did say that they had noticed this ever since the question of the abolition of serfdom was raised *[that is, since 1857, when the government publicly undertook to reform serfdom]*. As a rule, the illiteracy of the proprietary peasants *[i.e., serfs]* is so great that one can positively say that there are no people among them who can read and properly understand the sense of published articles *[of legislation]* and most of them can scarcely sound out written words. When they received the Statute, they turned for interpretation at first to the *pomeshchiki,* the household serfs, priests, and local officials, but when they saw that no one could extract from the Statute the *volia* they dream of—that is, *barshchina* is not abolished and the *pomeshchiki* are to retain control of the land—they began to distrust educated people and to seek readers among the literate peasants. These interpreters received money for this from the peasants. From motives of greed and some, one may suppose, because of hatred for the *pomeshchiki,* and seeing that under the present circumstances they could exploit the ignorance of the peasants, they began to make the most absurd interpretations of the new legislation.

One of the major interpreters, the peasant Anton Petrov of the village of Bezdna, in Spassk District, became a kind of prophet among the peasants, and even aroused fanaticism. He enthralled the peasants with his tales; as he told them, they corresponded to the dominant idea in their minds and to their concepts of *volia,* and he enhanced all his arguments by invoking Your Majesty and almighty God, who had given him the right to proclaim freedom to the peasants and deliverance from the *pomeshchiki.* To this notion he applied a point in the form for the regulatory charter, where it reads, "Released to *volia* after the 10th *reviziia*—so many."

["Released to volia," *or* otpushchennyi na voliu, *was the legal term for "manumitted." The article in the emancipation legislation to which Apraksin refers ran as follows:*

    33. In every regulatory charter should be indicated:
        (1) The name of the settlement, and of the province and district where it is located.
        (2) The rank or title and name of the proprietor.
        (3) The number of peasants in the settlement according to the last reviziia *[the census of 1857–1858] and also of*

those residing in the settlement but registered in the reviziia *on another of the* pomeshchik's *estates; the number of household serfs, with an indication how many of the latter have the right to receive an allotment; if among these peasants, some have been settled on another of the* pomeshchik's *estates or released to* volia *after the* reviziia, *then precisely how many; and how many, therefore, souls there are remaining in the settlement, according to the total of which the allotment of land should be carried out.*[15]

The purpose of article 33, as the last phrase indicates, was to relieve pomeshchiki *from the obligation to allot land to the serfs they had set free or moved elsewhere since 1858; it was perhaps the only instance where the compilers of the emancipation legislation could not avoid using the word* volia.*]*

He interpreted this to mean *[Apraksin's report continues]*, the tsar already gave you *volia* in 1858, but the *pomeshchiki* hid it, hence all the land belongs to you and all the grain gathered and sold for the past two years should be confiscated from the *pomeshchiki.* Another example of this kind of interpretation relates to the "Rules on the System for Implementing the Statutes on Peasants Formerly in Servile Dependency," where it says in point 2 that from the day of the promulgation of the Imperial Statutes Concerning Peasants Formerly in Servile Dependency are terminated . . . and then, without reading what follows, he explained this article to them thus: the word "terminated" means that everything is terminated, or pure *volia.* And by this expression they understand complete freedom from all dues and obligations and the right to all the land. There is an abundance of other examples besides these two and it is not possible to enumerate them all, but they all had the effect that the peasants simply did not obey[16] the authorities established by the government and those persons who might have an influence upon them.

Complaints from *pomeshchiki* about peasants refusing to do their work began to come in steadily from the marshals of the nobility to the governor, so that after conferring with him on the 8th of April I set out for Spassk District, where the marshal of the nobility had been complaining about significant disruptions. Upon arriving in Spassk on the 9th, I sent for the marshal and the sheriff, who were then at one of the biggest estates in Spassk District, the village of

Bezdna, belonging to the *pomeshchik* Active State Councilor
Mikhail Nikolaevich Musin-Pushkin; the estate consists of 831
souls *[male peasants]* and 10,639 *desiatiny* of land. In general
the peasants in this settlement are quite prosperous. *[Official rec-
cords indicate that Musin-Pushkin provided his serfs with land more
generously than any of the other major* pomeshchiki *in the district.*[17]*]*

At five o'clock in the morning on the 10th, the marshal of the
nobility came to me in Spassk and conveyed the following: an
interpreter had appeared in the village of Bezdna, a peasant from
the estate named Anton Petrov; he had elicited pure *volia* from the
Statute and begun to preach about it throughout the neighborhood.
Peasants were coming to him from all sides, even from rather distant settlements, and day and night they were guarding his house
and not letting anyone in, so that, in the absence of force, it was
impossible to seize this preacher or—as the peasants consider him—
prophet. It is reckoned that there are about 23,000 proprietary
peasants in Spassk District. No reserve troops are stationed in the
district, and there is only one company of invalid soldiers in the
town of Spassk. Besides, the Volga and Kama rivers separate this
district from the others in the province and impede rapid communication with it, especially in the muddy season. The marshal inform*[ed]* me that neither his own exhortations nor even those of
the priest served to disabuse the peasants of Bezdna; so soon as anyone began to reason with the peasants, the crowd set up a cry of
"volia, volia"—seeking in this way to eliminate the possibility of
securing the obedience even of those who might be brought to
their senses.

In light of this situation, I immediately wrote an order to the Commander of the Fourth Reserve Battalion of the Tarutino Infantry
Regiment, stationed in the town of Tetiushi, to send two companies
to the village of Nikol'skoe, which is seven versts from Bezdna;
meanwhile I set out for Bezdna with the marshal of the nobility, in
order to try the remedies of kindness and exhortation. *["The remedies of kindness," which several witnesses mention, was a stock expression, and perhaps an officially sponsored euphemism, for
nonviolent methods of inducing the peasants to accept the emancipation legislation.]*

When I arrived at the estate office, I sent the sheriff to tell the
crowd assembled in the village to come to the office, for an adjutant
of the Sovereign Emperor had arrived there, charged with clearing
up for them any misunderstandings that had arisen. To this they

replied, "We won't go, let him come here," and then arose as usual the general cry of *"volia, volia."* Then the district marshal of the nobility went to them and also tried to persuade them to come peaceably for discussions with the newly arrived adjutant of the Sovereign. He impressed upon them all the terrible consequences of their disobedience to the authorities and the means to which the government would have to resort to bring them to submission. When the peasants replied again that they would not come, the marshal of the nobility declared to them that the Sovereign's adjutant Count Apraksin would wait for them one-half hour more, and if they did not bethink themselves, he would take stern measures to bring their disobedience to an end. The reply to this was a repetition of the cry *"volia, volia."* After waiting for more than an hour without result, I went to the village of Nikol'skoe, resolved not to undertake anything against the peasants at Bezdna before the arrival of the troops I had ordered. Meanwhile, as I discovered from bulletins I received, an enormous number of peasants from surrounding villages had gathered in Bezdna and was continuing to do so; hence, in order to strengthen the two companies I was awaiting, I sent an order to the commander of the invalid unit at Spassk to bring all his men who were free of other obligations to Nikol'skoe on the evening of the 11th.

Having thus put together a force of 231 men by the evening of the 11th, I resolved to put it into action the next day, because I could not expect the two additional companies from Chistopol', dispatched by order of the governor of the province, to arrive for four or five days, and to leave matters as they were was dangerous, because the mob at Bezdna was growing with improbable speed. The peasants no longer recognized any authority; they appointed officials of their own from among the peasants, as selected by Anton Petrov, and boasted that they had driven the sheriff and the marshal of the nobility out of the village. Throughout the night of the 11th, crowds of peasants, on horseback and on foot, made their way to Bezdna, where this Anton Petrov was giving *volia* and land and appointing officials, saying that in a short time he would completely liberate 34 provinces. He was not displayed to the newly arriving crowds, on the grounds that he was busy with correspondence with Your Highness. On the morning of the 12th, in his crowd there were already people who had come even from Simbirsk and Samara Provinces, from state peasants, and from the Tatars.

In light of all this, at five o'clock in the morning I moved the force

I had assembled into Bezdna. With me were the district marshal of the nobility, the constable, and two of the governor's adjutants, Lieutenant Polovtsov and Captain Zlatnitskii. All during the march, the crowds of people continued to gather in Bezdna. As we entered, on the outskirts of the settlement we saw a little table with bread and salt and two old men, standing with their hats off; I asked them, "For whom was that bread and salt prepared?" to which they timidly replied, "For you, by order of the authorities" (meaning the authorities appointed by the rebels). It subsequently came to light that this reception was given to all who came to enroll as Anton Petrov's confederates. I ordered the table taken away and the old men to go home. Reaching the church, which stands in the middle of the village, I summoned the priest, in order yet again to try the remedies of kindness. Although he explained to me that he had exhorted the people several times without success and that stubbornness was so strongly instilled in them that there was scarcely any hope left of bringing them to their senses by words and persuasion, nonetheless I wanted to try these methods yet again and convince myself that they were useless, for I was counting in the present instance on the moral influence of the presence of troops, and so I asked him to come along with the detachment. *[Apraksin was not playing at irony when he mentioned "the moral influence of the presence of troops"; at least, his counterparts elsewhere shared this conception of moral influence and used the same phrase.*[18]*]*

Before us almost to the end of the street, by Anton Petrov's house and across the whole width of the street stood a solid mass, numbering up to 5,000 people. Coming to within a distance of 180 paces, I halted the unit and sent out the two governor's adjutants for the first exhortation; the crowd only tried to drown out their words with the cry of *"volia, volia."* The adjutants returned, after warning the peasants that if they did not surrender Anton Petrov and disperse to their homes, they would be fired on. Then I sent the priest, who exhorted them at length with a cross in his hand and said that if they would not submit, they should disperse, otherwise there would be shooting; they continued their cries even after this exhortation by the priest. Then I myself rode up to the crowd. I explained to them the commission with which I was charged and ordered them to surrender Anton Petrov or disperse, but nothing could have an effect on the terrible stubbornness and certitude of these people. They cried, "We don't need an emissary from the tsar, give us the tsar himself! Shoot—but if you do, you will not be shooting at us but at *[the tsar]* Aleksandr Nikolaevich." Then I made them be silent and said, "I am sorry for you, lads, but I must and shall shoot; those who feel they are innocent, get out of the way." But seeing that no one was going away and that the crowd was persisting in its stubbornness and in its shouting, I withdrew and ordered one rank to shoot a volley; after this there were more exhortations, but the crowd still kept up its shouting; then I was obliged to make several volleys. I was prompted to do this largely because the peasants, noticing a significant interval between the volleys, were beginning to come out of the yards in large numbers, shouting and taking up pikes; they were threatening to surround and crush my undermanned unit.

[This is as close as Apraksin came to charging that the peasants at Bezdna offered violence against his troops, and his language is strikingly ambiguous. The phrase about pikes (vykhodit' . . . s krikom za koliami) *may mean either "came out shouting in order to get pikes" or "came out shouting, 'Get pikes!'"* Kol'ia *can be murderous pikes or the pickets of an innocent fence, and the word here translated as "threatened" may either denote explicit verbal threats or convey Apraksin's judgment that the situation was dangerous. No other witnesses reported that the crowd took up weapons, and peasants later testified that new arrivals at Bezdna were made to throw away their walking sticks upon entering the village. Nor did other eyewitnesses report that the crowd uttered any threats. Apraksin was a graceless writer, but the ambiguity here may have been artful; it certainly served to justify his order to keep on firing.]*

Finally the crowd scattered and shouts were heard about the surrender of Anton Petrov; he had tried to slip out of the settlement by the back way, but was forestalled by two cossacks, who seized the horse that had been made ready for him. Then Anton Petrov came out of his house and faced the troops, bearing the Statute on the peasants above his head, and there he was seized along with his confederates, whom he pointed out to me, and sent under guard to the fortress in the town of Spassk. After the surrender of Petrov, an attempt was made to clear away the bodies and give aid to the wounded. It was established that there were 51 killed and 77 wounded.

This decisive action was taken by me in view of the paucity of troops and the minute-by-minute growth of the insurrection, which was assuming an enormous scale. It was necessary in order to restore tranquility not only in this village, but among the whole population of several districts of Kazan Province, which did not submit to any authority at all and had reached such a pitch of insolence, that when a *pomeshchik* (a staff-captain of the Life Guard of Your I.M.'s Hussar Regiment) entered his village of Shcherbet' one of the peasants assembled there seized him by the chest and told him, "Clear out, you've got no business here."[19] I had conversations with peasants in the villages of Nikol'skoe and Tri Ozera where I explained to them that I was sent by the tsar to clear up misunderstandings and restore order; the crowd drew back from me several steps and said that I was not a real adjutant of Your Majesty but someone dressed up in a uniform by the *pomeshchiki*.[20] In general, the situation, not only of the *pomeshchiki* but even of the senior officers of the rural police was intolerable, and without the resort to decisive action I undertook a general rebellion could have taken place in Kazan Province.

At present the tumult is somewhat suppressed, work is resuming, and the old authorities are restored, but subversive persons are still circulating rumors that the emancipation of the peasants of the village of Bezdna is now quite complete, and that the count sent by the sovereign, after patting the prophet Anton on the shoulder, dressed him in clothes of gold with a sword and sent him to the sovereign, whence he will soon return with perfect *volia*.

In my opinion, to restore complete tranquility in Kazan Province, it is still necessary to increase somewhat the number of troops stationed there and to carry out an exemplary execution of the main culprits, for whom a Military-Judicial Commission is now being empaneled.

Major General Count Apraksin

Apraksin's report was intended first of all to win the tsar's endorsement of the decision to fire on the peasants, and it succeeded. Alexander II noted in the margin, "I can only approve Count Apraksin's actions; sad though it is, there was nothing else to do." Apraksin received the Order of Saint Vladimir for his accomplishments at Bezdna and his version of events became the official one. A month after the shooting, the government issued its account of the events at Bezdna, and it corresponded to Apraksin's report; on the crowd and the rush for pikes, it followed Apraksin word for word. This account, which had the personal approval of the tsar, differed from what we would call a press release in that Russian journals and newspapers could not supplement it with their own information or call it into question.[21] These actions inhibited or silenced criticism of Apraksin and his report, even in confidential correspondence within the government. When, four months later, an official of the Ministry of Internal Affairs reported on his investigation of the Bezdna affair, his findings were implicitly very critical of Apraksin. On the vexed question of pikes, he would say only that, after three volleys, "It seemed to someone that the peasants were running to get pikes, and four more volleys rang out." The peasants killed were the "victims of their own ignorance and a fortuitous misunderstanding"—presumably Apraksin's misunderstanding. And yet the investigator "could not bring himself to pronounce an opinion" on the events at Bezdna "since in this matter the actions of Count Apraksin, who received a decoration, must be regarded as correct."[22]

Polovtsov

The award of a decoration to Apraksin was "sad news" for F.A. Polovtsov, the governor's military adjutant who had been at Apraksin's side at Bezdna. He wrote to his brother, "Granted that he lied up, down, and sideways in his report, surely more accurate information reaches the sovereign. And can he really think that this stupidest of men is capable of anything worthwhile?"[23]

Polovtsov underestimated the tsar. He gave Apraksin a decoration and publicly endorsed his justification of his actions. Anything resembling a repudiation of Apraksin would lend credence to the stories Anton Petrov had set in motion. Nor did the tsar recall Apraksin from Kazan Province; that would have given encouragement to Apraksin's critics at Kazan, and the tsar could be counted upon to support a general under attack from civilian officials and intellectuals. However, on April 16 the tsar sent Adjutant General I.G. Bibikov to Kazan as his personal representative, giving him explicit authority over Apraksin. Since Apraksin functioned in Kazan as the tsar's personal representative, he was, in effect, supplanted without being removed.[24]

Furthermore, the tsar did have sources of information other than

the report from Apraksin. There was the regular provincial administration, headed by the governor. And the Third Section, or political
police, functioned in Kazan Province as elsewhere, and reported
independently to the central government; we have seen that the
Third Section was first to report on the shooting at Bezdna. Along
with the observations of its own officials and agents, the Third
Section passed along the contents of private letters, which it intercepted and copied unbeknownst to writer and recipient. One of the
letters intercepted in this fashion was Polovtsov's indignant letter
to his brother, which was on the tsar's desk in a matter of days. The
upshot of these disrespectful (although private) remarks about
Apraksin and the tsar was Polovtsov's own summary removal from
Kazan and dismissal from the army.

Polovtsov fondly believed that his letter passed from his family,
who lived in St. Petersburg, to high government circles and thence
to the tsar himself because of the importance of his revelations and
the trenchancy of his criticism; it was an instance of the truth that
bureaucrats ordinarily prevented from reaching the tsar. However,
the provenance of the letter indicates that it was intercepted and
copied, along with other similar letters and another by Polovtsov, in
the normal operations of the Third Section. There is not much
doubt that the tsar was prompted to order Polovtsov's dismissal because of his unseemly letter.[25]

Polovtsov's dismissal may also have been a sop to the *pomeshchiki*
of Kazan Province. Their hostility to the provincial governor and his
supporters was intense even before the bloodshed at Bezdna; for
example, Polovtsov was blackballed by the nobles' club. In the aftermath of Bezdna, and perhaps encouraged by this vindication of their
warnings, sixty nobles formally complained to the central government that the governor was prejudiced against the nobility and too
indulgent to the lower orders.[26] The regime would never remove a
governor in direct response to public pressure, but Polovtsov's dismissal was sure to please the governor's enemies; it offered a practical
advantage to the *pomeshchiki,* since Polovtsov would otherwise have
been directly involved in the implementation of the peasant reform
on their estates.

One manifestation of the factional strife among the officials and
nobles of Kazan was a police informer's report that Polovtsov,
drinking in a tavern in Kazan, had said that Russia would never
flourish until the peasants waded up to their knees in *pomeshchik*
blood. The report was surely false. Polovtsov was no radical, and

protested his devotion to the tsar-liberator even after the tsar dismissed him; as we shall see, he believed that Russian peasants were virtually incapable of violence. The Third Section officials in Kazan, like the local nobles, were hostile to the governor, and therefore launched a slanderous canard against one of his vulnerable subordinates. Whether or not officials in St. Petersburg gave any credit to this denunciation, the very fact that responsible officials ventured to make it indicated, like the intemperate letter, that Polovtsov was the kind of man it was better to be rid of.[27]

At any rate, Polovtsov was dismissed, and he had reason to blame Apraksin and his admirers for his disgrace. The means of revenge were ready to hand. Not only was he a witness to the events of April 12, he had rifled Apraksin's wastebasket and taken copies of the drafts of his confidential reports to the tsar. Polovtsov sent these reports, along with his own extensive commentary, to Alexander Herzen's *Kolokol,* which was published in London, beyond the reach of Russia's censors. In writing for *Kolokol,* Polovtsov was somewhat constrained by the necessity of maintaining his own anonymity, since he could be punished for corresponding with the notorious "fugitive" Herzen. In his memoirs, published forty-five years later, he was free of this constraint and was able to add some further details. The *Kolokol* publication is more important, however; it casts doubt both on the honesty of Apraksin's reports and the rationale of his decision to fire upon the peasants.

According to Polovtsov, the peasants gathered at Bezdna for the most humdrum and innocent of reasons. They were confused by the terms of the emancipation legislation and full of naive hopes, but held no danger to anyone. He observed that the peasants in and around Bezdna did not take so much as a grain of rye or anything else belonging to the *pomeshchiki;* they could scarcely have been so restrained if Petrov had convinced them that "all the land belongs to you and all the grain gathered and sold for the past two years should be confiscated from the *pomeshchiki.*" He also observed that the peasants had not so much as insulted the owner of Bezdna; this was perfectly true, although not a telling point, since Musin-Pushkin was never in Bezdna during these events. And he offered the following anecdote about his own visit to Bezdna on April 11, the day before the shooting.

When the governor's adjutant came to Bezdna, all [the peasants] took their hats off to him; when his coachman dropped

his whip on the street, the crowd of peasants handed the whip
back to the coachman and bowed politely in farewell to the
adjutant. All these apparently insignificant facts are the best
possible proof that there was no malice among the peasants.

Polovtsov also initiated the long controversy about the number of
peasants killed at Bezdna. Apraksin, he maintained, initially intended
to report only five or six casualties, but a junior officer reminded
him that this was not the Caucasus, where body counts could be
adjusted to taste. Even so, Polovtsov charged, the figure of 51 dead
in Apraksin's report was a major falsification; by his reckoning, the
total was more than 100 and, in his memoirs, he charged that more
than 350 peasants were either killed on the spot or died afterwards
of wounds.

One of Polovtsov's most embarrassing revelations concerned
Apraksin's little speech of warning to the peasants. In Apraksin's
draft there are no less than four different versions of the speech he
claimed to have delivered. It would seem that he labored to find the
common touch, for his first version was so formal and bureaucratic
as to be scarcely intelligible to peasants. His second version was much
simpler and emphasized the peasants' loyalty to the tsar, but failed
to give them a clear warning. With his last two attempts, Apraksin
came closer to the version he sent to the tsar—brief, soldierly, com-
passionate, and clear.[28]

While it is clear that Apraksin labored after the event to concoct a
suitable speech, these labors mirrored his efforts beforehand.
Polovtsov related in his memoirs that Apraksin brooded on his way
into Bezdna about what tone to take with the peasants. He did have
a speech prepared, but his efforts were wasted, for when he confronted the crowd, he panicked and forgot his lines. Since he was too
frightened to get within earshot of the peasants, according to
Polovtsov, whatever he did say was lost upon them.

Of course, it would not matter what Apraksin said or meant to say
if the crowd shouted down all attempts to address it, but in fact,
Polovtsov insisted, it gave a respectful hearing to various officials.
When, on the twelfth, Apraksin could not find the courage to face
the crowd and sent out the adjutants in his stead, the peasants "all
stood with their hats off, in deep silence."

> I conveyed Apraksin's order to them [Polovtsov recalled in
> his memoirs] and they listened calmly, every one of my

words was clearly audible. When I finished, the crowd all together shouted in response, "We will not surrender Anton Petrov. We must die for him; for him and for the Emperor Aleksandr Nikolaevich we must let our blood flow." With all the force of my eloquence I tried to explain that they could not die for Aleksandr Nikolaevich, since Aleksandr Nikolaevich had sent us; that Anton Petrov was to blame for everything, and they must for their own safety surrender him at once. All my suasions had no effect . . . . Then the priest went out to the crowd . . . . When he returned, the whole crowd began to shout, "We want to see the tsar's emissary." Like it or not, Apraksin had to go out to the crowd.[29]

It was at this point that Apraksin tried to deliver his little speech of warning. Polovtsov produced two accounts of the general's reception by the crowd. In *Kolokol,* he reported that when Apraksin threatened to fire upon the crowd, "the peasants stood with arms folded, utterly unable to believe that the sovereign had sent a man to them with instructions like that. They became more convinced than ever that this was . . . some agent of the *pomeshchiki.*" In his memoirs, however, Polovtsov recalled that the crowd did shout Apraksin down. The peasants thought he was an impostor because he "cut a very unimpressive figure"; someone in the crowd identified him as the gardener on a nearby estate. Affronted as well as frightened, Apraksin took advantage of a lull in the shouting to curse and threaten the crowd. Then he scuttled back to his unit to make good on his threat.[30]

Polovtsov always insisted that it was Apraksin, not Anton Petrov, who attracted the crowd to Bezdna. "The *narod* assembled at Bezdna to hear an explanation of the Statute from the tsar's emissary—and Apraksin imagined that they wanted to kill him." The crowd was not swelling, as Apraksin charged; two days before the shooting, when Apraksin made his initial foray into the village, the crowd had been twice as big. Because Apraksin refused to appear before the crowd himself, and relayed threats through subordinates, the peasants became convinced that there was no emissary of the tsar in Bezdna. The peasants were beginning to disperse, when Apraksin returned on the twelfth with his soldiers.[31]

As for Anton Petrov, he was simply a well-meaning and exceptionally stupid young man, according to Polovtsov. He stumbled on the word *volia* in the statutes and innocently supposed that the tsar had proclaimed *volia* for the *narod* in 1858. Representatives of other villages came to him to have him find the magic passage in their copy of the statute book, but often the dimwitted and barely literate Petrov could not find it, and had to send the representatives away disappointed. He had not, Polovtsov insisted, pretended to be a prophet—that is, he did not claim any religious or supernatural authority. Nor did he claim any special relationship with the tsar. And indeed, the sentence in Apraksin's report about Petrov's pretending to correspond with the tsar was inserted as an afterthought.

If Petrov was no prophet, and Apraksin had attracted the *narod* to Bezdna, it remained for Polovtsov to explain the composition and behavior of the crowd. Apraksin represented the crowd as large and growing. Polovtsov, on the other hand, held that the crowd was "a few thousand" and dwindling. One of Apraksin's most telling points was the involvement of peasants from other provinces. Their presence at Bezdna suggested that a grand conspiracy might underlie the movement, and certainly indicated that it could spread very rapidly if not forcefully checked. Polovtsov held that this "absurd fable" was conjured out of one peasant from Samara Province, who happened to be visiting relatives in Bezdna. The peasants from Samara and Simbirsk are not mentioned in any other account, nor even in Apraksin's second report to the tsar (reproduced on pages 57–61), and we know that the peasants killed on the spot came from nearby villages, all of which indicates that Polovtsov was right on this point.[32]

Why, then, had the crowd stood firm under the fire of Apraksin's troops? In *Kolokol* Polovtsov explained:

> The peasants, seeing that they were being attacked in earnest, were terrified and began to run away; Apraksin ordered his men to overtake and attack them. As many as ten of the gravely wounded peasants were wounded in the back.[33]

This explanation was simple enough, but did not take into account the considerable intervals between the volleys, during which the peasants were exhorted yet again to surrender Petrov and disperse. In his memoirs, Polovtsov produced a more elaborate version. The peasants

> had stubbornly remained crowded around Anton Petrov's house without any definite purpose; they simply did not un-

derstand just what was happening. Furthermore, the configuration of the part of Bezdna village where the crowd stood made a rapid departure difficult. Anton Petrov's hut was not far from the end of the village, and the whole street between this hut and the end of the village was full of a crowd so dense that in the rear nothing that happened in the front could be known or heard; of course, the shots were audible, but the bullets did not reach the rear of the crowd. Furthermore, the street runs into a little river flowing through the end of the village, and the only passage is through a gate of the usual narrow width. Therefore, it would have taken a good deal of time for the crowd to go out through this one gate, but Apraksin let loose his volleys with very small intervals. Finally, those in the rear learned of the firing on the forward ranks and discovered that many had died, but the crowd was jammed up against the fence separating the village from the river. They broke down the fence and flung themselves headlong across the river, over the ice.[34]

The destruction of the awkward fence would also account (although Polovtsov did not say so) for the peasants' rush for "pikes."

As Polovtsov would have it, then, some innocent peasants blundered into Bezdna through a misapprehension. He did not deny that the authorities had to disperse these peasants, but by "patient and rational means." Among Apraksin's failings was his failure to find the right "tone," and Polovtsov was confident of his own ability to deal with crowds of peasants. He observed in *Kolokol:*

Incorrect interpretation of the Statutes produced disturbances not only in Bezdna, but in many other estates in Kazan and other provinces . . . but all these disturbances had a very peaceful outcome. For example, on L'vov's estate Iunusova, which is also in Kazan Province, thanks to the timidity of the steward and the village officials, such a tumult broke out that Apraksin doubtless would have shot up two hundred people or so, but fortunately, Apraksin was not yet in Kazan, and a visit from the governor's adjutant [Polovtsov himself, of course] was quite adequate to the occasion; the peasants tied up and surrendered the drunken defrocked deacon who had claimed to be an emissary from the tsar.[35]

Handling peasants, then, required a knack, and Polovtsov was sure that he had it. Indeed, underlying his dispute with Apraksin was a distinctive conception of the peasantry. In Apraksin's eyes, the peasants were credulous, superstitious savages; in Polovtsov's, they were trusting, childish innocents. His attitude toward Petrov and his followers was distinctly patronizing, and it was complemented by his conception of himself: he was the benign and rational authority figure the childish peasants needed. It was gratifying to play this role, as when he set free the peasants Apraksin had arrested a month earlier. He confessed, in the letter to his brother already quoted:

> I rejoice every day that I was appointed to this work [on the commission of inquiry]. There is a good deal of work, but it is a long time since I have been so pleased with myself as I am when I release the arrested peasants. Many of them were so terrified that they did not want to believe their good fortune.[36]

Polovtsov's and Apraksin's attitudes were distinct, but not utterly different. They agreed that (to quote Apraksin) "the credulity of the *narod* knows no bounds; the more absurd a rumor is, the more powerfully it affects the *muzhik*."[37] Furthermore, each cast himself in a paternal relationship to the *muzhik*. Apraksin was a stern and punishing father, Polovtsov was a loving and understanding father, but each set himself above and apart from the *narod*, and each acknowledged the necessity of keeping the *narod* in order and under control. Yet even this affinity opened the way to another line of disagreement, a question of logistics.

Apraksin's justification of his resort to firearms rested partly on the temper and tendency of the crowd and partly on the small size of force under his command and the impossibility of rapid reinforcement. Polovtsov agreed that the force was very small, "so that it would have been easy to overpower it without weapons, if the peasants had really been disposed to riot." Therefore Apraksin should have withdrawn to await reinforcements, and returned only when he had a body of troops large enough to overawe the peasants without shooting them. How soon could reinforcements arrive? On this point, Polovtsov's account is confusing. He noted parenthetically that Apraksin simply forgot about a company of soldiers quartered at Kokriat', some twelve miles away, but no other source indicates that there were any troops there. In his draft report, Apraksin remarked that on April 11 he went to meet an infantry company crossing the Volga to his staging point, but he omitted this from his final text. Polovtsov held that Apraksin crossed the sentence out in order to conceal the feasibility of bringing reinforcements across the

Volga, despite the high water and muddy roads. Yet Polovtsov did not challenge Apraksin's assertion, which appeared twice in the first draft of his report, that he could not expect significant reinforcements for three, four, or even five days.[38] More troops were, indeed, on the way. Three more companies arrived on April 13, which would have doubled the force at Apraksin's disposal but not significantly altered the imbalance between soldiers and peasants. The full complement of reinforcements did not arrive in the area until three days after the shooting.[39] This fact made it difficult for Polovtsov and others to push the narrow, logistical criticism of Apraksin very far. What was most seriously in dispute, then, was the character, mood, and size of the crowd at Bezdna. The essence of Polovtsov's position was that waiting several days would not jeopardize security and order, and that Apraksin systematically lied in order to give the impression that the Volga Basin would have gone out of control if he had not opened fire.

Apraksin may have felt that this position was weak, for he sent a second report to the tsar, offering further arguments to justify the shooting. He did have the pretext of reporting on Anton Petrov's court-martial and execution and conveying the evidence accumulated in the process. Indeed, in the first draft of this second report, Apraksin noted that much new evidence had been gathered "after the trial was over"—an observation which moved Polovtsov to new indignation: "And so it is clear: first they shot the man and then they began to assemble the reasons why they had shot him!"[40] For the dispute between Polovtsov and Apraksin extended to this second report, which Polovtsov also filched and published in *Kolokol.*

Apraksin's Second Report to the Tsar
April 19, 1861[41]

In communique no. 744, dated April 15, the Military Governor of Kazan informed me of Your Imperial Highness's order that the main culprit behind the rebellion in Spassk District should be tried according to martial law and that the sentence should be carried out at once. Consequently, on the 16th of April a field court-martial to try the peasant Anton Petrov was convened by me at the detachment's billet in the village of Bezdna; the court was required to conclude the case within 24 hours.

At the trial the peasant Anton Petrov was found guilty of provoking several thousand peasants to rebellion by a perverse interpretation of the Imperial Statute on the emancipation of peasants from serfdom; of circulating false rumors about freedom; of inducing peasants to gross insubordination to their masters and of resistance to the local authorities and armed forces, in consequence of which 51 people were killed and 77 wounded during the pacification of the peasants in the village of Bezdna. Hence the field court-martial, taking into account the seriousness of the rebellion caused by the defendant and its fatal consequences, on the basis of articles 93, 608, and 609 of book I of the Military Code of Criminal Justice, sentenced the peasant Anton Petrov to be executed by shooting.

[It is odd that Apraksin thought it necessary to cite the code to justify his actions, since he had the tsar's instructions to try and execute Petrov. At any rate, he was no lawyer. Article 93 simply holds that the punishment should correspond to the crime, while articles 608 and 609 have to do with cowardice under fire. The latter reads, "Whoever is insubordinate at the front in the face of the foe is punished by death."[42] *Apraksin may have supposed that, since Petrov was to be tried by a military court, he had been retroactively drafted into the army, and therefore his refusal to surrender constituted "insubordination at the front." The "foe," of course, was Petrov's followers.]*

The military court passed sentence on April 17, I confirmed it the same day, and it was carried out on the 19th *[in fact, on the eighteenth*[43]*]* in accord with the rules set forth in article 545 of book II of the Military Code of Criminal Justice and in the presence of an assembly of the residents of Bezdna and settlements throughout Spassk District. As a supplement to my first report, I consider it necessary to set forth the circumstances taken into consideration by the military court and by me when I confirmed the sentence of the peasant Anton Petrov.

When the Imperial Statute on peasants was received in the villages, the defendant Anton Petrov was invited to the village of Bolkhovskaia to read the Statute. By giving it a perverse interpretation and misrepresenting its meaning, he was able in the course of two days to bring the inhabitants of this village completely under his influence. Together with them, he arrived in the village of Bezdna and went before the village priest, demanding that he give an oath that they were absolutely free; when the priest emphatically refused to carry out his demand, he proposed to his confederates that they should attain liberty by their own efforts. *[Apraksin's phrase here,* sobstvennymi silami, *denotes "by their own efforts" but it carries connotations of violence because* sila *means "force."]* By this they meant absolute independence not only from the *pomeshchiki* but also from the local authorities. He persuaded the peasants that they should not go out to do *barshchina,* pay *obrok* or haul loads, that they should not even prevent the theft of the *pomeshchiks'* property, and should not render any aid in the event of a calamity, such as fire, flood, the bursting of a dam, etc.; he reinforced these suasions by invoking Your Imperial Majesty's name. By telling these tales Anton Petrov was able in a very brief period of time to win over all the peasants of Bezdna and the neighboring villages. In order to increase the number of his adherents still more, he dispatched his chosen emissaries to various remote villages and even to other districts of Kazan Province; to attract the common people he circulated various absurd rumors, for example: that the Grand Duke Konstantin Nikolaevich *[the tsar's brother]* was being kept in irons in the village of Bezdna and was asking the peasants to free him. With a view to increasing still more the peasants' hatred of the *pomeshchiki,* he charged them with the death of the late Emperor Nicholas and with failing to carry out the will of Your Imperial Highness. *[This charge, which so strongly evokes the legend of the tsar-deliverer, derives from the testimony of the villagers of Bezdna.]*

So it was that on the 12th of April he managed to assemble up to 10,000 peasants in the village of Bezdna and the immediate neighborhood. *[In Apraksin's first report, the figure was 5,000; a civilian commission of inquiry later estimated the crowd at a maximum of 4,000.*[44]*]* He had provoked as many as 90 villages of Spassk District to rebellion; the inhabitants of these villages were streaming in crowds to Bezdna, since it had been proclaimed to them that those who did not gather in Bezdna by the 15th would remain in eternal slavery. The tumult reached such a point that in several settlements the peasants assaulted their village officials and elected new ones, took the ledgers out of the estate office and demanded an account. According to the report of the commander of the Spassk Invalid Company, two shots were fired at the unit in the village of Shcherbet' on its way to the village of Nikol'skoe to link up with the two companies of the Fourth Reserve battalion of the Grand Duke of

Oldenburg's Tarutino Infantry Regiment; fortunately, however, these shots had no harmful results. *[A civilian investigator found that someone happened to be target-shooting when the Spassk Company passed through Shcherbet'.*[45]*]*

Taking into account the extremity of the situation and seeing that the slightest delay could have fatal consequences, I had to resort to the resolute measures about which I have faithfully reported to Your Imperial Majesty.

Among the major accusations against Anton Petrov, apart from stirring up an enormous mass of inhabitants and inclining them to flagrant insubordination to the authorities, there is also this: during the rifle fire he himself was out of danger, and not only did he not stop the resistance of the crowd, over which he had enormous moral influence, but he even incited it to be stubborn and not to surrender him until the last extremity, for he told them that after three volleys, the firing would cease and complete freedom would be proclaimed to the people. The result of the peasant Anton Petrov's stubbornness was a great loss of life. This information is derived partly from the defendant's own admissions and partly from reliable facts discovered by the court-martial and by me.

The execution of the sentence in the presence of the *narod* had an enormous moral influence. Not only did Petrov's fate fail to arouse any sympathy, but the *narod* acknowledged the full gravity of his crime and expressed this by repenting completely and shouting, "It's dead to rights, all our sufferings are his fault."

[The sheriff of Spassk District, like all officials in the area, found that the narod *was in an abjectly penitent mood. He reported that peasants were cursing Petrov and that many of those assembled to witness his execution said he deserved his fate. But he also reported, somewhat later, rumors that a halo was visible over Petrov's grave.*[46]*]*

At the present time, the area is quiet, but I submit that to bring about a final restoration of order, especially now, when work in the fields is beginning, it will be necessary for the duration of the summer to have one battalion stationed at the town of Spassk and another distributed in companies on the more substantial estates. I find it necessary not to leave these companies regularly in one place, but to move them about from one estate to another, so as not to overburden the inhabitants with feeding and quartering them.

A copy of the sentence of the court-martial, and of my confirmation of it, is attached.

Major General Count Apraksin

Polovtsov was especially outraged by Apraksin's account of the execution.

The people did not assemble for Anton Petrov's murder in an enormous mass. There were, to be sure, about a hundred people, but they were herded together by force. The cries of joy when he was killed were heard only by Apraksin, no one else heard them. The peasants regarded Anton Petrov as the best man in the neighborhood; they speak of him as mild to a fault; he always fled from fights and heated arguments, and so came to be generally loved—but this love did not reach the level of frenzy, as Apraksin liked to put it. All the wounded, when they received the unexpected news that Anton had been killed, wept for him and crossed themselves. The moral effect of this killing was indeed enormous, but not of the kind represented. Initially, peasants all over the province were convinced that they had been assaulted against the will of the tsar, as a result of bribery by the *pomeshchiki*. When they became convinced that it was indeed the tsar who had ordered the assault, then, since they did not conceive themselves to be guilty in any way, they began to think of their *batiushka-tsar* in a wholly different light. When they look at the telegraph by which Apraksin's dispatches were transmitted, the peasants say, *"So were those poles stuck there so that people could be shot?"* In general, if the government sends Apraksins to the provinces a little more often, our telegraphs will not last long—and there is perhaps something else that will not last long either!

Polovtsov was caustic about Apraksin's claim that the peasants repudiated Petrov and repented their involvement with him, for after the execution,

Apraksin set two cannon brought from Kazan in front of the porch of the estate office and with incredible pomposity passed judgment on the intimidated peasants. He made them kneel for hours at a time, reviling them all the while. Now his words flowed incomparably more easily [than on the twelfth]. It must be this occasion that gave him the pretext for writing in his report, "not only did Petrov's fate fail to arouse any sympathy, but the common people acknowledged the full gravity of his crime and expressed this by repenting completely." What could they do but make this acknowledgment when they had two cannon and a thousand rifles under their noses, and all of them at the disposal of a man who suddenly, for no reason at all, gives the order to open fire!

Apraksin's accusation that Petrov had incited the peasants to resist the troops elicited from Polovtsov an emphatic reaffirmation that Petrov was only a deluded simpleton.

If Apraksin had simply said that Anton had to be shot because of some consideration or another, that would have been better than thinking up lies and laying them to a defenseless peasant. In his ignorance, Anton misunderstood the Statutes; that is the whole of his guilt, and Apraksin simply thought up all the other counts during the twenty-four hours in order to justify himself. Where, for example, was there resistance to armed force? If to stand with empty hands and face loaded with rifles means resistance, then every wild duck is just as guilty when a hunter aims at it from behind a bush![47]

On almost every point of judgment and on many points of fact, we must choose between Apraksin and Polovtsov. It is obviously important to consider their motives in making these choices. Apraksin's interest is clear. He had to justify his actions to maintain his position in the tsar's service and his own self-esteem. Polovtsov's motives were more complex, although resentment at his own dismissal is a most obvious one. He was a subordinate of Governor Kozlialinov and may have shared his resentment toward the interloper Apraksin. In his memoirs, however, he ridiculed the governor as an ignoramus who made a killing playing cards during the Crimean War and bought his office with the proceeds. He recalled that Kozlialinov wept on hearing of the shooting at Bezdna, but also that the governor's grief soon gave way to relief that he himself was not directly involved.[48] In retrospect, at least, Polovtsov was not a loyalist in the governor's faction.

The primary consideration for Polovtsov may have been guilt and revulsion. In *Kolokol*, he presented himself as a disinterested observer, and the picture in his memoirs is much the same. Yet he was a responsible senior office, serving with Apraksin but not subordinate to him. Apraksin represented the decision to move into Bezdna on April 12 as his alone. Other evidence indicates, however, that all the officials involved concurred in this decision, taken the night before. Krylov, whose account we will examine shortly, reported that the four-man "council of war" that deliberated the night before was unanimous—Apraksin, the marshal Molostvov, the sheriff Shishkin, and Polovtsov.[49] The early reportage in Herzen's *Kolokol* also listed Polovtsov among Apraksin's counselors and, in addition, charged him with ordering sharpshooters to pick off the *krikuny*— "those who shouted loudest."[50] These reports made *Kolokol* a particularly appropriate vehicle for Polovtsov's attempt to lay all the responsibility on Apraksin. Furthermore, in the immediate aftermath, Polovtsov accepted the necessity of bloodshed, for Governor Kozlialinov's initial report to the central government (pages 40–41) took that position, and it was based solely on Polovtsov's eyewitness account of the events of the twelfth.[51] Against all this evidence, there is only Polovtsov's insistence in his memoirs that he prevailed upon Apraksin not to move into Bezdna on the twelfth but to wait for reinforcements, which (he maintained in his memoirs) would arrive the next day.[52]

It would not be surprising if the sight of the crowd assembled in Bezdna shook Polovtsov's image of the innocent peasants and his confidence in his capacity to deal with them. It would be no less surprising if, when the smoke had cleared, order was solidly restored, and he found himself questioning the pitiful survivors one by one, he repented of the resort to arms. His attacks on Apraksin expressed his revulsion at the bloodshed and guilt at his own responsibility. We cannot be sure of Polovtsov's mental processes, but we know that he underwent a change of heart.

A change of heart was commonplace once the apparent danger of peasant rebellion was over. Governor Kozlialinov underwent the same change. We have seen that in his initial report to the minister of internal affairs, he cited his own attempts to avert bloodshed but did not criticize Apraksin for shedding it. After nine days had passed, the governor sent the minister a more thoughtful and more critical analysis. Broadly speaking, he took a position between Polovtsov's and Apraksin's. He reiterated and amplified Polovtsov's tactical objections to the decision to shoot, but he by no means found the peasants to be as innocuous as Polovtsov had. Further, he attempted to explain both the shooting and the ensuing requiem in terms of social tensions in the province.

Excerpt from a Letter from
P.F. Kozlialinov to S.S. Lanskoi,
Minister of Internal Affairs, April 22, 1861[53]

Dear Sergei Stepanovich:

The sad events in Kazan Province impelled me to be completely frank with Your Excellency in setting forth various circumstances which, I am convinced, significantly influenced the whole course of this affair and its consequences.

Ever since the peasant question was raised, a majority of the nobles has been completely unsympathetic. The enthusiasm of all the other estates of the realm has put the nobles, who even formerly kept apart in a closed and exclusive circle of their own, in a more hostile relationship than ever to other groups—the men of learning, civil servants, and merchants. (I am speaking of civil servants on active service, for an enormous number of nobles in Kazan Province are nothing more than retired bureaucrats, who made their fortunes in office and bought estates; these are the most harmful and stubborn adherents of the old ways, through which they made their fortunes, and they have a powerful influence on the rest of the nobility because of their cleverness, experience, and what passes for knowledge of the law.)

The opinions of the nobles, reaching the peasants by way of the household servants, increased the peasants' antipathy and distrust for the *pomeshchiki;* the children of the *pomeshchiki* who were students stood out among their comrades for their prompt and strong renunciation of their parents' actions. Rumors circulated that even during the time of the Provincial Committee on the Peasant Question *[nobles elected to advise the government on the emancipation]*, the peasants knew by name those members who were considered hostile to the question that had been posed. ...

The nobles, nonetheless, expressed their lack of confidence in the merits of the legislation on the peasant question, and began to express it still more flagrantly when they detected that Major General in His Majesty's Suite Count Apraksin sympathized with them on this subject, for he spoke out incautiously in their presence. The nobles thought they saw in him the Sovereign Emperor's plenipotentiary, with special rights and powers, and he would not, or rather could not, disabuse them. Then, when news came from Bezdna about the methods of repression and the upshot of the peasants' stubbornness, some nobles foolishly and recklessly expressed their joy at home and even at the *[nobles']* club. Thus they provoked members of the other estates of the realm to sympathize with those killed at Bezdna and, moreover, excited anger against themselves and Apraksin. *[Even government officials sympathetic to Apraksin found fault with the nobles for toasting his victory in champagne and held that their behavior provoked the requiem service and other unwelcome expressions of sympathy for the peasants.*[54]*]* Both sides were aroused. The nobles found that it *[the repression at Bezdna]* was just, energetic and good—the others, that it was illegal, for they considered that adequate preliminary measures of suasion, to avoid bloodshed, were not taken; it was especially the university *[community]* and the students who were notable for their recriminations against the nobles and anger at Apraksin. The upshot of this was a requiem for the dead and the raising of money for the benefit of their families; professors and other private persons are taking part in the subscription.

I am trying to take all the measures at my disposal to prevent and forestall disorders, which would be all the more dangerous as they would sustain the upsurge of hostility between the estates; given the present tumultuous state of mind among the peasants, the students in their recklessness could cause great harm.

Concerning Apraksin's actions at Bezdna: As I have had the honor to inform Your Excellency, it was just because I foresaw this that I ordered twelve companies with two cannon dispatched to him, in order to prevent bloodshed, but the troops arrived on the 15th *[of April]* while he took action on the 12th; the truth is that even on the 13th he would have had five companies instead of two, and these people had one hundred rounds apiece, while the two companies ordered out by Apraksin had only ten apiece (as the commander of the battalion reported to me). It seems that it would have been better to wait until the troops could assemble, even though the crowd might grow larger still, than with two companies of a hundred men each to risk action against the crowd, which was still growing and by some accounts had reached 8,000 or more persons; a failure would not only have been fatal to the two companies, it would have had ghastly consequences for the area, for it would have aroused the peasants and imparted courage to them and provided them with 200 weapons; I consider acting with two companies still more of a risk because the companies at Bezdna, having been led onto the street and arrayed close together in four ranks in a company column, were subject to the danger of being encircled and crushed, with no opportunity of forming a square or retreating; the peasants could have had axes, pikes, and spears.

Since I am working from information submitted by persons who were there and was not an eyewitness myself, I do not venture to pass judgment, but, in any event, I believe that under these circumstances, a favorable outcome of this affair could not be expected. The worst result is that because of the number of victims, the case has aroused the anger of many people, especially because, apart from their unswerving stubbornness in false interpretation and their not surrendering Petrov, the peasants did not reach the point of fighting or causing anyone harm, and on the 12th they were absolutely unarmed.

Once again I have the honor respectfully to report to Your Excellency that the peasants in the districts are calm; insignificant misunderstandings, which are not to be avoided, are eliminated at once, and work is going forward. However, the public is alarmed by the tumult in the university and among the students, who are also alarmed.

The letter concludes with a paragraph of fragmentary evidence about the requiem service which students had held in Kazan for the peasants killed at Bezdna. This incident may have encouraged Kozlialinov to reconsider the Bezdna affair, for it focused public and official attention on the shooting, making it harder for Kozlialinov to take a passive or neutral attitude toward Apraksin's actions.

In appraising this letter and the interpretation it offers, it is important to remember that if Apraksin was right, Kozlialinov was at fault. Law and order in Kazan Province were his responsibility; if order could be restored only by shooting down a large number of peasants, then Kozlialinov would be blamed for letting the situation get out of hand.[55] To vindicate himself, he had to challenge Apraksin. Then, too, he was the target of mounting recriminations from the *pomeshchiki* of Kazan Province, who were on the point of formally complaining to St. Petersburg about the governor's prejudice against them. This attack so undermined Kozlialinov's authority that, two weeks hence, he made a pathetic request for a public endorsement of his activities from the tsar himself, in order to "strengthen his moral influence" over the province in his charge.[56] With the nobility, as with Apraksin, Kozlialinov's best defense was a good offense, and the sinister link he managed to find between these two threats to his position was felicitous. This does not mean that the link was simply invented to suit his purposes. Other witnesses (most of them close to Kozlialinov) reported that the nobles in Kazan city were elated at Apraksin's "victory" at Bezdna. N.N. Bulich, a professor at Kazan University, suggested that Apraksin set out for Bezdna under the "moral pressure" of his friends in the Nobles' Club of Kazan. K.N. Tatarinov, on the other hand, maintained that the nobles of Kazan were quick to spot Apraksin for the "fool and incompetent" he was, and embraced him only after he had taught the peasants a dramatic lesson in submission to the powers that be.[57]

At any rate, Kozlialinov's version of events corresponded as closely to his interests as Polovtsov's and Apraksin's did to theirs. Departmental loyalties and career considerations are an element, however disguised, in almost any document emanating from a government official.

Krylov

What we want is a comprehensive report by a disinterested observer with no superiors to fear and no official position to protect. We are lucky to have just such a report in the memoirs of the steward N.A. Krylov (already quoted on pages 35-36). Krylov wrote his recollections of the conflict at Bezdna thirty years afterwards; they make a striking contrast to the tendentious and self-serving accounts of government officials. For example, he made the most serious attempt to establish how many peasants were killed at Bezdna; this was so sensitive a matter that even in 1892 the tsarist censorship would not let him publish his findings. The government acknowledged that 55 peasants were killed (4 more than Apraksin's initial total) and 70 wounded. The Third Section, in its annual report for 1861, estimated that "up to 70" peasants were killed.[58] Krylov, however, questioned the cossack who piled up the bodies after the shooting, and his figure of 107 peasants killed on the spot was supported by the warden and the sheriff. The sheriff further estimated for Krylov's benefit that more than 200 peasants had fled Bezdna and died of their wounds elsewhere, while less than half of those who sought treatment from government doctors survived.[59]

Krylov was careful to distinguish between what he had heard and seen himself and what he learned at second hand. Furthermore, he was aware how memories fade after thirty years. He mentioned a "military conversation" with Apraksin and other officials on the eve of the shooting, but he refused to describe it because he could not remember it well and was "afraid of being inaccurate."[60] Along with his scrupulous and modest manner, Krylov had a good deal more of a gift for words than the officials involved. All these qualities contribute to the persuasive power of his account.

The most important part of Krylov's memoirs is his rendering of the mood of the peasants. He described his own visit to Bezdna the day before the shooting. The inhabitants were in a state of serene exaltation and calm confidence. Their spirit infected Krylov's coachman, Sidor, who looked at the crowds who had come to get *volia* from Petrov and wondered, "How is it that the lords resist the tsar's order? See how many are taking a stand for the tsar! Who will stand up for the lords? They're trying something silly, for if real *volia* has been revealed, then even they have to submit to the tsar!"

The polarity between the "lords" and the *narod* was almost palpable, and Krylov, as the hireling of a noblewoman, was clearly on the lords' side. Krylov, according to his memoirs, did not meet any hostility at Bezdna; his account recalls Polovtsov's story of the coachman's whip. Yet he realized that the peasants were trying to cow him by impressing him with the power on their side—not the power of force or numbers but the power of the Lord and the tsar. He reported a peasant woman's story of a deputation's visit to Petrov.

> "The petitioners come to him, they give him [their copy of the statute] book, but he sits there, the dear, with his elbows propped on the table and says nothing. 'Why don't you speak,' they say. He lifts his bright eyes like this and answers them, 'Wait, wait, the mass in heaven is not yet over.' That is how wise the Lord has made him: he knows when they're singing mass in heaven. And to think that we sinners took him for a puny little fellow, and didn't know that one of God's own saints lived here with us in Bezdna!"

Krylov was moved to inquire why, with God and the tsar on their side, they had to mount such a numerous guard around Petrov. Several peasants firmly explained that they were not there at Petrov's request but by the tsar's order, and not in vain.

"For the last three days the warden has been telling us to go back home; he wants to whip us and beat us, but just let him try! He's trying to please the lords; he jumps all around the guards, foaming at the mouth; he tries everything to get the *muzhiki* to leave Anton Petrovich [Petrov] alone, but you can't go against the tsar's order, can you? Then the tsar would say, 'You wouldn't stand firm for the *volia* I granted, so you must go on working for the lords.' No, my dear man, our backs have ached long enough. We were released to *volia* at the time of the *reviziia,* and for three years you tricked us into doing *barshchina,* and you kept our land."

Even this last remark, which was close to an accusation against Krylov, held no threat, for the peasants at Bezdna, as Krylov recalled them, were cheerful and peaceable. He reminded them that troops had been brought into the area, but they were undismayed.

"What of that? We've seen them in the towns; they stand guard around the forts, sing songs, and do their drill . . . . If they are brought here and posted in the villages, we will listen to their songs."

Krylov insisted that if the troops were brought into Bezdna, it would be to shoot, and blood would flow, but the peasants were undismayed. "We heard all that from the warden," they said. "But how could they shoot the *narod*? After all, we aren't rebels, are we?"[61]

"We aren't rebels, are we?" The phrase could serve as an epigraph for Krylov's memoirs. The peasants, as he portrayed them, were in the grip of superstitious fantasies and eager for *volia,* but they were devoted to the tsar and utterly passive. If only the authorities had been attuned to their mood, they would have realized that they were harmless, and the bloodshed at Bezdna could have been avoided. To be sure, Krylov did not condemn Apraksin directly. He did, however, describe his own efforts to help officials see the peasants in a proper light. Apraksin sent him to Kazan to take dispatches to the governor, and Krylov found that Kozlialinov and his staff completely misunderstood what was happening.

In Kazan, they remembered that once Pugachev had been in this area between the Kama and the Volga, and they imagined that Anton of Bezdna was emulating him. I said that the peasants had no organization at all, that this was simply a misunderstanding on the part of a credulous and illiterate crowd; that the peasants were coming and going with staffs and knapsacks, like pious pilgrims; that there is no need for cannon, because there is no reason to expect any action from the peasants. A few companies of soldiers would be useful, however, to prevent the peasants from dividing up the squires' grain.

Governor Kozlialinov, Krylov implied, was reassured by this analysis. As Krylov headed back with the governor's dispatch, he met the family of Molostvov, the marshal of the nobility, fleeing to Kazan, and he was fearful that their arrival would cause new alarm in the city and undo the effect of his assurances. Further along, however, he met Anton Petrov himself, under guard and in chains. While Krylov was on his errand to Kazan, Apraksin had brought events to their bloody denouement.[62]

Pathos pervades Krylov's account, from first to last. Inept and obtuse officials, out of touch with the *narod* and the countryside, had not known how to handle a "credulous and illiterate crowd," and many lives were lost as a result. The peasants' hostility to the "lords" was impersonal and nonviolent, and held no threat of vengeance. While Krylov's account differs in particulars from Polovtsov's, it supports Polovtsov's insistence that the peasants at Bezdna were innocent as babes, and innocent in both senses of the word: they were naive and they were guiltless.

We are fortunate to have Krylov's memoirs as a yardstick to hold up against the reports of the officials involved. We are more fortunate still to have a second account by Krylov, written the day after the shooting at Bezdna. Krylov did not imagine that this account, a long letter to his employer, would ever be published, still less that it would fall into official hands, as it did, and form part of the government's dossier on Bezdna. The literary polish of his memoirs is missing from this hastily written and somewhat elliptical letter. So, too, is the pathos.

Letter from N.A. Krylov to A.P. Ermolova
April 13, 1861[63]

I crossed the Volga *[into Samara Province]* early in the morning on April 9. At the chapel, I hired a troika to go all the way to Maina, and reached there by dinner time. At Maina, they had just received the *[Emancipation]* Statute. The peasants assured me that it came so late because Samara Province is younger *[i.e., newer]* than Kazan Province. The colonel who brought it apparently gave them a speech. As they understood the speech, on the 19th they will be brought a new, third *volia.* I was skeptical, but they assured me that they had heard it themselves and pointed out that in Simbirsk and Kazan Provinces, *volia* had been read out three times. And indeed, at our estate first the manifesto was read, then extracts from the Statute, and finally the Statute itself. So in Samara Province they have understandable reasons to wait for a third *volia.* I went on to spend the night in Volostinovka, at the house of the *pomeshchik* Gorlov.

By twilight I arrived at Kokriat' *[in Kazan Province].* Sidor *[the coachman]* was not at home. "Where is he?" "Gone to the estate office to sign up for *volia.* The menfolk have got hold of true *volia,* so they are all meeting now at the estate office," a woman told me. "There's an order to cut up the *pomeshchiki,* you know." I went to the estate office. There was noise and uproar, a mob all crowded together, with a kind of bestial excitement on their faces. *[In his memoirs, Krylov described the peasants at Kokriat' as "animated . . . joy and gaiety shone on all their faces."*[64]*]* The meeting was to decide how to divide the squire's rye, whether to thresh his store or divide among themselves at once, in sheaves. They had decided that the whole *mir [commune]* should thresh the squire's store. I listened—the talk was of slashing, hanging, chopping up the nobles with axes, setting axes on the ends of long pikes. In general it was on the order of the Pugachev rebellion. They had driven out the cellarer and the elder. Someone who could write was signing up the peasants by name for true *volia,* and the crowd was being sorted out. "Don't write him down," someone cried, "he is always hobnobbing with the lords, don't give him any land." By conversing with many people there I learned what was behind all this.

In the village of Bezdna a certain Old Believer named Anton Petrov has discovered true *volia* in the Statute; many looked at it before him, but no one could understand it. But in the Statute, where the form for the Regulatory Charter is printed, it reads:

Household serfs	00
Peasants *[serfs]*	00
Land	00

And so on. These zeroes were no problem for Anton; he explained that this is real *volia,* and it is sealed with the cross of Saint Anne.

And the cross of Saint Anne? Turn back the page and just opposite "household serfs 00" there is "10%." This, he says, is the cross of Saint Anne, by which true *volia* has been secretly sealed.

Anton sits in his hut at Bezdna looking at these naughts and smoothly reading out, "Land for the *pomeshchik:* the hills and the hollows, the ravines and the roads, the sandbanks and the reedbeds, and not one twig of the forest. If he takes a step over the boundary of his land, drive him back with a kind word, and if he doesn't obey—cut off his head and you will get a reward from the tsar." The *narod* liked this kind of *volia,* and crowds came in from all sides to hear real *volia.* They brought the Statutes with them and he marked in them where real freedom is to be found. Anton preached like this for five days in a row. Then he put abroad rumors that he had received a charter from the tsar, read the Bible until he attained the power of prophecy, and, mixing the one and the other together, preached: "You will only attain true *volia* when you protect the man who finds it for you. Real *volia* will not be given until much Christian blood has flowed. The tsar has ordered you to guard that man closely and firmly, day and night, on horseback and on foot. Protect him from any attack and don't let either the lords or the priests or the officials through to him. To make sure of not surrendering him, do not go away from his hut. If they set one end of the village on fire, don't go away from the hut, if they set the other end on fire, don't go away from the hut. Old men and young will come to you, keep them away from me and do not surrender me. They will deceive you and say they come from the tsar, but don't believe them. To tempt you there will come old men and middle-aged, bald men and hairy, and all kinds of officials, but do not surrender me. And when the hour is come, a mere youth of seventeen years will come here from the tsar, with a gold medal on his right shoulder and a silver medal on his left. Believe him, and turn me over to him. They are going to frighten you with troops, but don't be afraid; no one dares to kill the orthodox people without the tsar's order. And if the nobles distribute bribes and you are shot at, then get your axes and chop up those who disobey the tsar."

I transcribe the speech of Anton of Bezdna word for word, as I heard it at Kokriat'.

[In Krylov's memoirs, the account of Petrov's teaching is much briefer. There, too, the peasants are urged to guard Petrov day and

night and not to be frightened "whether by the firing of guns or by the blows of swords." The necessity of shedding of Christian blood, however, and the threats of vengeance against those who disobey the tsar are missing. In retrospect, the tsar's true emissary is shorn of his youth and his medals; instead, "on his head there will be a star, on his right shoulder a star, and on his left shoulder a star." [65] *In either version, the legend of the tsar-deliverer is clearly evoked, especially since Krylov renders Petrov's words in the cadence of an incantation. It is important to remember, therefore, as historians have tended not to do,* [66] *that Krylov never pretended to transcribe Petrov's teaching directly. At best, Krylov was able to report rumors, as they passed from one of Petrov's adherents to another, over the twelve miles that separated Kokriat' from Bezdna. He may tell us something about the peasants at Kokriat', but does not provide much leverage on Petrov.]*

At the meeting it was decided not to go out to *barshchina* the next day. I heard a few little jokes, such as: the manor houses should be torn apart, reduced to so much lumber, because Anton says that everyone has been free since the tenth *reviziia;* the nobles have stolen *volia* until now and imposed labor unjustly, consequently, they must be punished.

I found Sidor at the meeting, and while he prepared the horses for me, I mused fondly about the Pugachev rebellion and was lost in admiration of our officialdom. Several peasants told me to my face that the constable and marshal had been driven out of Bezdna and said that the marshal will be put to the flames and that the tsar has given an order not to spare the nobles but to cut their heads off.

Sidor harnessed the horses and I went to Murasa *[the estate where Krylov served as steward]*. The sled scarcely moved over the dry ground, and a cold wind chilled my head. I became very worried for Molostvov. I began to cross-question Sidor; he honestly believes the nonsense. He is sorry for the *pomeshchiki* and frightened that his name will not be inscribed for real *volia* at Anton's. "Perhaps," he says, "they won't give me land now, because I have kept company with the lords." I reasoned with him as much as I could, without effect. I lay down to sleep in the sleigh, but could not *[and mused]*....
People have also rioted at Molostvov's, even all the household serfs; I heard this at Kokriat', and Sidor says the same. Molostvov is a wonderful man, he received me very kindly.... Perhaps now he is alone in this scrape, fearing for his family and the whole district....

Who knows, perhaps I can be useful, I have six shots in my revolver, that's force enough. . . .

Sidor is going through the forest, and I still can't sleep, the riot at Molostvov's is still on my mind. . . . Who knows, perhaps I will not be in the way and will manage to return the kindness with which he has received me. And if I am not needed, I will go away. A detour of fifty versts is not much. . . . But what if something delays me, and I am late in getting to Murasa! Well, I think, my employer will understand and forgive me, after all, I am not going for some silly diversion. "Sidor, turn back!" "Where?" "To Tri Ozera, my boy. I left a letter there." *[Tri Ozera, about fifteen miles from Bezdna, was the estate of Marshal Molostvov.]* Sidor reluctantly turned the horses around. We did not get very far and had to spend the night at Kokriat'.

On the morning of the 11th, while Sidor was getting ready and I was chatting with a peasant, the hundreder came into the courtyard. "Well, it seems no good will come of it to our people," he said. "It's one thing that they think they shouldn't work for the landlord, but now no one will transport couriers; after all, it's government business, even if you go on your own horse."

When I arrived at Molostvov's, I said, "Vadim Vladimirovich, I have come to ask what measures to take if the peasants refuse to work for the squire; in the villages around here they have stopped going out to *barshchina*. The riot is spreading and will reach Murasa. Shall I be firm or let it be?"

"Let it be."

"But then surely plundering will begin, and the manor house will go up in flames."

"What can be done? I expect it every day, we are powerless."

It was, I think, disconcerting to hear this from a marshal, all the more from a very intelligent one. It must be they are indeed powerless. I learned from Molostvov that everything I heard at Kokriat' is true. A riot is under way, and it's no prank. Although it was appropriate, I was too sorry for him to remind him of the "remedies of kindness" about which he had read to me so recently.

Count Apraksin had come to him that night and by morning a company of soldiers arrived. The peasants, seeing the company, went out to do *barshchina* without being ordered. It was well that I had come, for Molostvov really was all alone. They asked me to help them in their trouble by taking a dispatch to the governor general *[Kozlialinov]* in Kazan. I agreed with pleasure. They gave me luncheon, the company commander came in, and they held a little council of war. *[This is the "military conversation" Krylov could not clearly recall thirty years later.]* The company commander wanted to surround six thousand people with a hundred men. The general *[Apraksin]* wanted to wait for more troops. I asked the company commander whether he could give assurances that his company would act against peasants. "In times like these, one can only give assurances about oneself." This reply by the company commander still rings in my ears. These words filled my head without let-up for twenty-six hours. If you take a broad view of the matter, a company commander can only say these words when he has absolutely no confidence in his company. *[It is not clear whether the officer Krylov referred to as "the company commander" was Polovtsov. He was the governor's military adjutant, and each of the companies involved would have had its own officer in charge. On the other hand, the sources indicate that he took overall responsibility for these companies and that he was the only army officer, apart from Apraksin, to take part in the "military council" at Tri Ozera.]*

It's a bad business, I think; I put all my hopes on my revolver. I roll along into Kazan. By order of the authorities thirteen companies and two cannon have been sent to Spassk District. I don't know whether they know how to take charge, but with a force like this, it is possible to restore order very nicely and then, perhaps, the remedies of kindness may have an effect.

Now, however, it is time to lay hold of the remedies of kindness. *[In this letter, Krylov does not mention his conversation with the governor nor explain how he learned of the shooting at Bezdna; it is clear, at any rate, that the following account, however reliable it may be, is based on what Krylov learned upon his arrival at Bezdna on the evening of the twelfth.]* On the morning of April 12, the company moved into Bezdna. Count Apraksin was there with Molostvov, Shishkin, and several adjutants. They drew up opposite Anton's house, about 150 paces away. Anton's house, courtyard, roof, and all the street in front of the house for fifty paces or so were full of people. They began to exhort the people, asking them to disperse or surrender Anton; they spoke for a long time but got nothing from the crowd but shouts and rude jokes. The priest began to make a speech; first he beseeched them to disperse, and they reviled him. Then he took a different line and declared they would be shot for insubordination, and whoever didn't want that, let him stand aside. "If you are so stubborn in your ignorance, then does not some one of you at least want to die like a Christian? Perhaps someone wants to take communion and repent of his sins; let him come forward and take communion. Don't die like pagan Muslims!" And so on. The priest was reviled again. Once more they exhorted the crowd and tried to persuade it to disperse, they argued for a long time but got nothing but abuse.

"Captain, give the command!" A volley from several rifles resounded; three men fell in the middle of the crowd. "Cease fire!" Again the exhortation began, and there were more lengthy explanations, as before; nothing but abuse from the crowd.

"Give the command!" Again a volley, and five men killed. "Cease fire!" Still more exhortation, and still unsuccessful. They increased the number of rifles [engaged]; after the volley fifteen men or more fell, but it did not have discernible influence on the crowd. After each volley they tried to persuade the peasants to disperse or surrender the culprit Anton, but nothing was to be heard from the crowd but insolent words and threats. The whole company was ordered to fire, forty men fell from the volley, the crowd remained unsubmissive. Another volley by the company, and everything was in turmoil and in flight, and those who could not flee because of the press of people howled: "We surrender, we surrender!" The shooting stopped and the peasants fled as they might; many jumped across the river, crushing one another, while some fled through the backyards, over fences and sheds. Anton was led out of his hut, with a crowd of people from the courtyard following behind and with the Statute on his head. Apraksin cried out to the people to stop, so that Anton would come alone. As soon as Anton separated from the rest, cossacks came up and bound him.

Anton is about thirty-five, thin, small, pale as a sheet, and terribly frightened; he thought he would be shot at once. The crowd scattered, the dead were brought together and the wounded carried off to the hospital. There were about one hundred and fifty dead and wounded.

At once fifty men were set to digging a grave for the dead, patrols were sent out, and all was quiet. In an hour the wailing and lamentation began. Toward evening people came from the surrounding villages for their dead. Gravecloths and candles were brought for the outsiders. Late in the evening, when I left Bezdna, the whole village smelled like a grave. The soul turns cold at the sight of the number *[killed and wounded]*, but no one can be blamed. Two days of delay and there would have been total ruin. To those on the spot it was so much the easier to see that all could have been lost. You can judge of this from the fact that all those present remained satisfied with the happy outcome. *["All those present" would, of course, include Polovtsov.]* Only Molostvov was distraught. I am sorry for him, noble soul, but even he admits the necessity of what was done. One has to be especially grateful to him. How many times he went into the crowd at the risk of his life and attempted persuasion!

If in Simbirsk they are not mad for the remedies of kindness, then there will not be hundreds of corpses there.

I spent the night at Gusikha, three versts from Bezdna. There they regard Anton as a saint and the dead as martyrs. Although the rioting has quieted down, the lunacy has not been knocked out of their heads. They say, "Thank God, now that *volia* has been washed with Christian blood, it will be much easier to get." *[In his memoirs, Krylov was more specific. He quoted one old man of Gusikha as saying, "A matter is always more certain when human blood flows. Without blood, the tsar would not know what is happening here, but now, perhaps, he will intervene for us and, in his sorrow for the blood, will remember about* volia. *"67]*

I arrived at Murasa toward noon on the 13th. I found out that yesterday agents arrived from Bezdna to incite the people to riot. They stopped at the hundreder's house and the hundreder called a meeting; two emissaries for *volia* were appointed (Elikhov and Levanov, of course) and set off with others. They provided the agents with transportation and took them on to rouse more people. I want to write about this to Molostvov. Four of them left from Murasa and fifteen men from Erykla.

Our pilgrims did not reach Bezdna. On the way they learned of the outcome of the riot and turned back. According to their story, the count put his own clothes and decorations on Anton, set him in a cart and took him to the tsar. They say that black wagons *[smolianye kibitki]* are being prepared to take the nobles who shot the people to Siberia. And that somewhere the people were slaughtering the nobles when suddenly *[the Grand Duke]* Konstantin came up. "My children, softly there, what are you doing?"

"Carving up the nobles, Your Highness!"

"Well, thank you then, you are serving the tsar. Dogs should die like dogs!"

I can't relate all these fables. They are all silly, all utterly stupid and...all this is told and believed by free citizens, with whom we must make agreements by mutual consent.

[Krylov's final remark refers to the regulatory charters, by which the emancipation legislation would be applied. On each estate, the squire and his peasants were supposed to agree to the terms of the charter. In the short run, at least, Krylov's anxiety was vain. The peasants in his area were so terrified by the shooting at Bezdna, according to a government official, that they would consent to any terms. [68] *]*

The sense of tragedy that characterizes Krylov's memoirs is absent from this letter, which is suffused with bitterness and, above all, fear. Krylov's panic even penetrates the fabric of his prose. In the memoirs, the shooting at Bezdna is presented as the unnecessary product of mutual misunderstanding; in the letter, there is no doubt that Krylov endorsed the decision to shoot. In both their tone and their overall significance, the letter and the memoirs are worlds apart.

Krylov's memoirs are lucid and comprehensive, and have the advantage of incorporating his findings and observations subsequent to his letter. And Krylov's panic may have distorted his perception of the events and tendencies recorded in the letter, while he wrote the memoirs calmly, when his panic had long since passed. The letter, on the other hand, was written fresh upon events. The choice between the two versions is not self-evident, but it is easier if we resort to the humdrum device of plotting the journey described in the letter and the same journey in the memoirs. The two routes turn out to be quite different. In particular, it is clear from the letter that Krylov did not get to Bezdna until after the shooting was over. The account of his visit on the eve of the shooting, then, was an invention, and the touching snatches of conversation he transcribed— including, "We aren't rebels, are we?"—are wholly imaginary. This finding casts suspicion on other aspects of Krylov's memoirs, such as the assurances he claimed to have given the governor and, indeed, the tone of the whole. In the memoirs, sentimental and ideological notions prevailing at the time of writing were projected upon a painful experience thirty years past; this was a process of coloring, distorting, and effacing—not necessarily a deliberate process nor even a conscious one, but very thorough.[69]

It is necessary, then, to discount the memoirs in favor of the grimmer version of the letter, and to be grateful for the possibility of verifying the memoirs in this way. For historians frequently must and do rely on memoirs more fanciful and less reliable than Krylov's (or Polovtsov's, for that matter). And Krylov's memoirs cannot simply be discarded, for they have something to tell about circumstances before and after the period of panic covered by the letter.

On one important point, Krylov's letter and his memoirs are in accord: both emphasize the "prophetic" and irrational character of Petrov's appeal, the extent to which he relied on Christian and monarchist myths. Indeed, among the commentators on Bezdna, Polovtsov was almost alone in maintaining that Petrov did not pretend to be a prophet or an emissary of the tsar, and this contention was part of his charge that Apraksin had inflated a village squabble into a frenzied insurrection. The irrational elements of the Bezdna affair have always had a special fascination. Yet these elements also had a distinct practical significance for the regime. If the peasants at Bezdna were in a state of frenzied exhaltation, they could not have been dispersed by threats and exhortation, or by any means other than those Apraksin used. And if we are to understand what "naive monarchism" meant to its peasant adherents in this instance, we must establish the dimensions and force of Petrov's appeal.

This most important task is a difficult one. Official documents or, indeed, any writing emanating from the educated classes, have the limitation that their authors were not part of Petrov's audience; he was not appealing to bureaucrats, army officers, and stewards, and the most we can get from them is what Krylov provides: a report of the impact of Petrov's teaching after it had passed through many hands. But the men and women in Petrov's audience do not speak to us directly. They are uncommunicative or, if pressed, they are likely to dissimulate. The only documentary sources we have emanating, even indirectly, from peasants are the transcripts of depositions taken by the court-martial and the commission of inquiry. A man implicated in the crime of insurrection—and Petrov's fate showed that this was a capital crime—is the least disinterested of observers. Furthermore, even under more relaxed circumstances, Petrov and his followers were not as articulate and lucid as Polovtsov, Krylov, or even Apraksin. For these reasons, perhaps, historians have not paid much attention to their testimony.

Petrov

Testimony of Anton Petrov[70]

At the beginning of April, when the Statutes on the Emancipation of the peasants from serfdom arrived at Bezdna, the elders invited me to the village of Bolkhovskaia to read the statute. When I read it, not knowing how to read well, I misinterpreted the first article of the regulatory charter, where it says: "Of these, given *volia* after the *reviziia*—00." I took these signs to be an expression for *volia* and therefore started to tell all the peasants that *volia* had come. In two days, I returned to Bezdna with almost all the peasants of Bolkhovskaia; among them I recall Ivan Nikolaev, Vasilii Fedorov, and Roman Kondrateev. There I went before the priest with these peasants, asking him to give an oath that we had found *volia* in the Statute, but the priest did not agree to this. After this we went home, and I said to the peasants, "Let's eke out *volia* together."
[A good deal hangs on the pungent word vykhlopatyvat', *here translated as "eke out"; the* Oxford Russian-English Dictionary *offers "to obtain (after much trouble)"; a better, if clumsier, equivalent might be "to elicit after prolonged pleading and fussing."]*
From that time on, I began to proclaim to all comers that the peasants are free. I told them not to listen to the *pomeshchiki* or to those in authority, I ordered the peasants not to go out to do *barshchina*, not to pay *obrok*, not to haul loads, and even not to interfere when peasants see that others are taking grain from the squire's barn; and if the waters destroy the mill, they should not fix it themselves *[but]* they should not take anything from the *pomeshchiki*. I explained that all land belongs to the peasants, and the *pomeshchik* is left with only one-third of it. *[If all the land belongs to the peasants, how can the* pomeshchik *keep one-third? Here Petrov was obviously inspired by the provision in the emancipation legislation that, however much land the* pomeshchik *was otherwise required to allot to his ex-serfs, he was entitled to keep one-third of the estate for himself.]*
All this I though up out of my own head, in order to attract more peasants to my side, for I supposed that the more peasants there

were, the sooner I would receive liberty. Many peasants came to me, and I proclaimed liberty to them. When the marshal of the nobility, the sheriff, and the warden came to our settlement, I, in my foolishness, ordered the peasants not to listen to them and not to go to them, for I feared they would lead the peasants astray. In order to attract more peasants to my side, I proposed that the *mir* elect new elders and send them, along with other peasants, to various villages to gather peasants *[who would]* listen to *[the proclamation of]* liberty.

When the military detachment came to our village, I was in my hut and saw that at first two officers *[Polovtsov and Zlatnitskii]* approached on horseback; then the priest approached, and they all exhorted the peasants to disperse, but the peasants replied, "We do not want to, we will die for the tsar." When the first and second volleys were fired from the rifles, I prayed and said nothing; after the third volley, I told the peasants, "Don't give in, boys, it's not yet time. They won't fire any more, they'll begin to read *volia.*" I said these words to defend *volia.* After the fourth volley, I wanted to go out, but while my relatives were blessing me, there were several more volleys. When I had said farewell to my family, I took the Statute and a blessed copper image and, carrying the Statute above my head, I went out to the troops. I did this because I supposed that they would not shoot at me with the tsar's *ukaz* on my head. I did not mean to flee and no one prepared horses for me, there was only an escape route, for which I had arranged for safety's sake, so that I would not be burned out or captured.

I did not give myself out to be a prophet or soothsayer and I did not say to anyone that I had a letter from the Sovereign Emperor. Indeed, on the very day before April 12 a Tatar named Savelii from the village of Tokhtala came to my house and said that he was just about to seek out *volia,* with the help of the merchant Iunusov. Whereupon he besought ten silver rubles for the trip to Iunusov's and to have a petition written. For this I got three rubles from my father and seven rubles from whom I don't remember and turned them over to the Tatar Savelii along with a piece of white paper on which I had signed my name; I asked Savelii and my fellow villager Gavrila Tarasov, who was going with him, to have a petition to the tsar written at Kazan, thanking him for the peasants' liberty. Whether the petition was sent off I don't know; I had no special purpose in writing the petition, I only hoped to receive liberty as Savelii assured me that I would. *[Two rather jumbled footnotes attached to Petrov's deposition indicate that Tarasov and other witnesses confirmed this part of his testimony.* [71]*]*

During the assembly at Bezdna, the peasants collected one silver kopeck from each soul and brought the money to me; why this was done, I don't know, I suppose it was for clerical work. Almost all the peasants of Bezdna and other settlements participated in the uprising I caused. I did not have any close collaborators. The *[new]* hundreders were appointed not by me but by the *mir*, so I can't remember all of their names; I know only Nikolai Ivanov, Egor Leont'ev, and Petr Pimenov. *["Hundreders" were petty village officials. Some of them were reluctant to surrender their offices to Petrov's followers and, they later testified, were beaten up. What disturbed the regime most was not assault on peasants by peasants but the insubordination of replacing officials who served at the pleasure of the* pomeshchik.*]* They were chosen to gather the people together and to keep them from dispersing. I did not direct the people to plunder, murder, be insolent to the authorities, and such like, but on the contrary, said that they should not offend anyone. I did not have any purpose in gathering the crowd except the desire to be free of serfdom. All of this testimony of mine is honest and I can add nothing more to justify myself; I do not acknowledge that I am guilty of the death of my comrades killed by the detachment, and I am ready to suffer for them.

Petrov's deposition was scarcely a spontaneous utterance. We may suppose that this is not his language but a clerk's, and that the subjects raised were determined by the questions put, for these subjects correspond closely to the sentence that was passed upon him and so, given the haste with which the court-martial worked, to the counts in the indictment.[72] Polovtsov saw Petrov immediately after he surrendered and recalled his abject terror.

Still and all, Petrov's courage does show through. While he refers once to his "foolishness," he showed more pride than peasants generally did under interrogation. His matter-of-fact tone is striking. There is scarcely a hint of the prophecy and mystery of which his teaching was supposed to be compounded, for he represented his words and actions in terms of mundane strategy—"I said these words to defend *volia*."

On the basis of this deposition, what seems irrational is not

Petrov's message but the strategy itself, which his message was meant to serve. There is a striking lack of correspondence between means and ends. How could a reasonable man hope to attain *volia* by interpreting statues to suit himself, ordering a work stoppage, and cutting off all communication with officials? Two lines of interpretation are possible. One of these would impute to Petrov and his followers a high degree of naive monarchism and lay special emphasis on the petition to the tsar, which the Tatar Savelii and Gavrila Tarasov were to transmit. Such a petition was a common, although illegal, resort of aggrieved peasants. This particular petition has not, apparently, survived, and Apraksin and other officials who emphasized the peasants' irrationality paid no attention to it, but there is ample evidence that an attempt was made to send it. Petrov's other tactics can be explained as devices to attract the benevolent tsar's attention to this petition and to the plight of his faithful subjects in Spassk District.

Another interpretation must focus on the intensity of Petrov's yearning for *volia* and acknowledge how meager were his chances of securing it for himself and his neighbors. This interpretation entails a realization that rationality is situational and an appreciation that the situation of Petrov and his followers was desperate. They had no weapons, no influence, and no rights that promised any benefit. All they could manipulate was their numbers, and the fear that these numbers might arouse in the territory where Pugachev had flourished ninety years before. This is what all of Petrov's tactics came down to: solidarity, work stoppage, and confronting officials and soldiers with an overwhelming mass of human bodies. These tactics did not secure *volia*, and the chance that they might have done so was remote. Before we dismiss them as irrational, however, we must either devise a more effective strategy that Petrov and his followers should have pursued, or else pronounce that the *volia* they sought was not worth seeking against such heavy odds.

We might get a perspective on the confrontation at Bezdna by thinking of it as a demonstration. In this country there were numerous political demonstrations not so long ago. These demonstrations were often accompanied by instances of silliness, or violence, or rhetorical enthusiasm, and government officials made much of these details. The participants in these demonstrations had at their disposal an arsenal of political devices which Petrov and his followers lacked: the right of assembly and petition, freedom of speech, and the ballot. But still they sought to attain their goals by putting massive numbers of human bodies on the streets and so impressing the authorities with their determination and conviction. These demonstrators did not have naive faith in the head of state. And while they failed, by and large, to achieve their goals, who will say that they were incorrigibly irrational?

Petrov did not hope that the court-martial would spare his life, and his testimony may have been colored by resignation. We have, however, the depositions of other peasants who could hope to save their lives with their testimony. The collective depositions of three nearby villages are particularly striking.

Village of Iurkul', Belonging to the Pomeshchik Aristov[73]

When there was a rumor circulating in the bazaars that on the 12th of April a ruling about *volia* would be read in the village of Bezdna, they refused to work for the squire and went there, because they fully believed the rumor about *volia* that was circulating. They were confirmed in their conviction that the rumor was true by the fact that the Statute on Peasants had been sent out *[to them]*, while it had never been sent out to their fathers and grandfathers, who had remained in serfdom. They had been ordered to read the Statute. They hired readers to do this and paid them money. Supposing that these *[statute]* books had not been sent to them to no purpose, they thought that their readers did not know how to find *volia* in the Statute, while in Bezdna the readers were better and so had found it. Not to go to Bezdna and not to check whether *volia* was there or not would be unnatural (as they put it), because in former times they had to pay money for freedom, and now it was being proclaimed without even any solicitation on their part. Those who went to Bezdna did not see Anton and do not know who it was that surrounded him. No one ordered them to go to Bezdna on the 15th of April, and they did not hear from anyone that he *[Petrov]* wanted people to assemble there on that day.

[The investigators asked about April 15 because they believed that Petrov had promised a denouement on that day and had hoped to attract the largest possible crowd for it. The source of this notion, which appears in Apraksin's second report, is unclear; peasant testimony does not support it.]

Since Thursday—i.e., since April 13—they have been performing all their work for their squire, as they are supposed to do.

Village of Kokriat', Belonging to the Pomeshchik Naumov

[This is the village where Krylov learned of Petrov's teaching; see pages 71–73. Two peasants from Kokriat' died at Bezdna.]

On the 12th of April, seeing that others were doing so, 25 men went to Bezdna. When they arrived there, the Bezdna peasants told them that they, being outsiders, must stand to the rear because they supposedly did not know how to respond to the authorities. However, anyone who arrived with a stick or cudgel in his hands was ordered to throw it away. When asked who was the first to shout, "Get pikes!" all the peasants replied in one voice, "It would be a sin even to say that anyone spoke of pikes; on the contrary, at that time they all stood (as they expressed it) as if at prayer, holding their hats in their hands." As to whether they were to assemble in Bezdna at some other time, no one spoke to them and there were no rumors about it. After the interrogation all the peasants went to their knees three times and, almost in tears, asked forgiveness; they said they fully realized their guilt, especially since up to that time they had never been at fault with their *pomeshchik* in any respect and would now make every effort to try to efface the deeds that had transpired.

Village of Bolkhovskaia, Belonging to the Pomeshchik Musin-Pushkin

[Six peasants from this village, which was part of the same estate as Bezdna, died under Apraksin's bullets.]

When they received the Statute on the 2nd of April, one of them, Matvei Mikhailov, who had learned to read a little from Anton in Bezdna, proposed that they should invite Anton to read the Statute. Therefore, Vasilii Semenov, Vasilii Fedorov, and Evdokim Nikolaev set out for Bezdna with Matvei and asked the steward Pavel Rodionov to allow Anton to come with them. The steward released Anton, and he was with them from Monday, April 3, until dinner on Tuesday. During this time he read them the Statute and said that the peasants should work only forty days a year for the *pomeshchik.* *[The emancipation legislation specified forty days of* barshchina *as dues for the statutory allotment.*[74]] He said nothing about *volia.* Then he came to them again Wednesday evening and said they should come as a whole *mir* to Bezdna, because he would reveal *volia* to them there, and he added that if he had been a resident of Bolkhovskaia, he would reveal *volia* to them in that village. Then they went, the whole *mir,* to Bezdna. Coming first to the house of the hundreder Andrei Matveev, they told him of Anton's words. Seeing them, people began to gather, and when there were enough, they went to the priest and asked him to swear that *volia* had been given to them. The priest refused to do this for them and asked Anton to read him where he had found *volia.* Anton refused and said to the people, "It's better to go to my house." After this, Anton began to read them the Statute and said that all work for the squire should be halted, the nightwatch should be abolished, the mills should be abandoned, and so on, but he forbade them to take anything of the *pomeshchik*'s. From that time the *narod* began to come to Anton from all the villages, but they themselves all went home that first day, and thereafter, until the day the soldiers drove them out, every day ten men, sometimes fifteen or more, went to Bezdna from their village. On the day of the shooting, they were all there; they did not go away because Anton assured them that the soldiers would only frighten them, that they would fire at them three times using blank cartridges, and the fourth time, with bullets, they would shoot to the rear. A bullet would kill anyone who stood to the rear, while it would not even graze those standing forward, and therefore they and all the peasants of Bezdna stood in front of everyone and ordered those who came from other villages to stand in back of themselves. *[Compare the deposition of the Kokriat' peasants.]* Anton said that after three volleys, there would be drumbeats, and he would then come out to the authorities; they would bind him and take him to the Sovereign, who would send them *[the peasants]* a gracious manifesto and give them *volia.* Anton did not designate a day when they should come to Bezdna, he only said to come when the soldiers did; furthermore, he gave an order to all of them that in the event of a discussion with the authorities they should speak quietly and they should join the crowd with nothing but their hats, not carrying any stick with them. During the exhortations *[on April 12]*, the crowd was noisy because, as they put it, *muzhiki* do not know how to speak quietly, especially when several thousand of them are gathered, as it was then in Bezdna. Finally, the peasants said that it was the sending of the Statute, and that only, that obliged them to believe Anton that they had been given *volia,* since up to that time no books of any kind had ever been sent to the commune.

Despite some discrepancies, these depositions are consistent one with another and also with other testimony elicited from individual peasants. Whether or not the witnesses were Musin-Pushkin's peasants, whether or not they had followed Petrov (among those interrogated were the village officials whom Petrov had replaced), whether they were interrogated by Apraksin's court-martial or by Polovtsov's commission of inquiry, they gave a similar picture of events and motives. And they all supported Petrov's version. They substantiated his claim that he insisted upon passivity and non-violence, and provided very little support for the view that Petrov represented himself as a prophet or emissary of the tsar. The Bolkhovskaia peasants did say that Petrov predicted he would be arrested and brought before the tsar, and the peasants of Bezdna charged that he forbade them to go to church, charging that the priest was a heretic who mixed poison in the communion wafers;[75] since this priest had attempted to frustrate Petrov's movement at the beginning, there were strong practical reasons for estranging him from the peasants. Otherwise, the peasants explain their adhesion to Petrov in wordly and rational terms. It was in their interest to explain their actions in terms of mystery and superstitious folly, since that would make them deluded victims, not willing and culpable rebels. Yet they do not represent Petrov as a "prophet," but simply as a leader—a lay attorney, so to speak.

At the same time, the peasants emphasized their ignorance and gullibility and tried to show that these qualities were the reasons why Petrov had been able to seduce them into insubordination. Petrov himself made only a halfhearted attempt to exculpate himself by pleading "foolishness," to maintain that he had honestly misread the statutes. His followers, however, did advance this kind of excuse and maintained that they, in all innocence, had been deceived by Petrov. As the miller Larion Timofeev put it,

> I suppose that if our squire . . . had been in Bezdna at that time and had explained to me and to one or two others what rights had been given to us, then there would not have been

any of those gatherings. . . . Apart from Anton, we are all equally guilty. How can anyone who was in the crowd say that another was more guilty than he was when he himself was in the wrong when he believed a stupid *muzhik*?[76]

It was in the peasants' interest to display their naiveté, to convince their interrogators that they had been innocently deluded. Here and there, even through the crabbed language of the depositions, we can almost detect what we would call a put-on. When the peasants of Bolkhovskaia ruefully observed that *"muzhiki* do not know how to speak quietly," we may, substituting "niggers" for *muzhiki*, hear Sambo speaking in a Middle Volga accent.

The peasants maintained that they were deluded and they convinced their interrogators. Indeed, no one from educated society expressed any doubt on the matter. For Apraksin, the sway of delusion proved that the peasants were beyond the reach of rational appeals. Even though Polovtsov's rendering of Anton Petrov is similar to Petrov's own account of himself, Polovtsov yielded to no one in emphasizing the naiveté and irrationality of Petrov's followers. Yet all these witnesses perceived the peasants across a social and cultural gulf, a gulf so wide that a semblance of delusion might look like the real thing.

Is there any reason to suppose that the peasants at Bezdna were not sincerely deluded? One source suggests that there may be. It was written four days before the shooting, when there was as yet no "Bezdna affair," but only a little trouble on Musin-Pushkin's estate. Official investigators paid no attention to it, but it is worth our scrutiny.

Report of R. V. Shishkin, Sheriff of Spassk District, to the Governor of Kazan Province April 8, 1861[77]

After making my report of April 7[78] on the subject of the insubordination of the peasants in the village of Bezdna, which is Mr. Musin-Pushkin's property, I set out that same day for the village of Bezdna and went into action as follows: at once I sent a cossack for[79] the selectman and the elder, but they didn't come. I sent for the police hundreder, to summon them, and all three came with the information that all the people were gathered around the house of their fellow villager Anton Petrov, a literate who had elicited for

them from the Statute that the peasants are completely free at
once and acquitted of any labor or obligations for the *pomeshchik*.
When I summoned the reader himself and everyone around him to
come to me at the estate office, no one came except the hundreder.
I went out to them, inviting the priest to go with me. Their reader
was looking out from the open window of his hut, with a houseful
of peasants behind him, while around the house there was a crowd
of people, including women and children, from the village of
Bolkhovskaia, which belongs to the same proprietor; all the people
[of that village] were there. In the presence of the priest, I began to
exhort the people, and they seemed to listen attentively; I ended by
saying that the people should disperse to their houses and meekly
await the outcome of their case, in accord with the rules appended
to the manifesto. To this they replied with a shout that they would
not listen to anything except what their reader had proclaimed, that
is, that they are absolutely free, unconditionally and at once. I
called out the reader and proposed that he read the Statute, while I
listened along with the people. He did not come out, and the people
passionately shouted, "Don't come out, we won't surrender you."
I demanded an explanation of the part of the Statute which had
convinced them so firmly that they could follow their own sweet
will; the reader replied that this was a secret, and the people said
the same. The reply was the same to my argument that the Statute
was granted just so that one and all could know it. So it went until
twilight on the seventh. Returning to my quarters, I ordered the
assembly to send to me the next day their venerable men together
with their reader and their Statute; they replied that not one man
would come or listen to any Statute whatsoever, except the one at
Anton Petrov's; they would not do so even though it was explained
to them that the Statute I have and they have and all peasants have is
one and the same.

Then I went to bed at the estate office, after taking measures to
prevent breaches of the peace in the village during the night, and
that night I sent for the marshal *[Molostvov]* , 28 versts away, informing him about all that had happened. The cossack returned
from him the next day at six o'clock in the morning and transmitted
the marshal's verbal order that if he did not arrive by two o'clock
of that day, it meant he would not come.

The next day *[April 8]* I was at the same place with a copy of the
Statute on Peasants and the priest, and after a short exhortation I

proposed to the assembly to collate my copy of the Statute with theirs. After some argument and my energetic insistence, I was successful: their reader began to read, very badly. I followed along in the Statute in my hands, correcting him every now and again. Then by persuasion I arranged to have the reading turned over to me while the reader, conversely, followed along. I read loudly and distinctly, without hurrying, and calling out the number of each page and paragraph. After each subsection, I would ask Anton Pavlov *[sic]*, "Is that right?" and he would answer, "Right." Taking turns with the priest, I read everything that he considered most necessary and also what the reader proposed, but nothing helped. During the reading of the rules on the system for implementing the Statute on Peasants Formerly in Servile Dependency, the reader turned to paragraph 33 and, reading subsection 3 as far as the comma, the following words: "those settled on another estate of the same *pomeshchik* or released to *volia* after the *reviziia*," he stopped and cried, "There, *volia* really is there." And then all voices, "*Volia, volia!* You've read enough." I tried hard, after this great howl of theirs, to read the subsection to the end, with a few repetitions, but nothing would help. My arguments and those of the priest were in vain. Then they began to come up for us to certify by our signatures that they were completely free, with all the land. Noise and shouting without any restraint ensued, and try though I might, I could do no more, so I hastened to report to Your Excellency about everything that happened, supplying a real and detailed description of events so as to characterize this affair more faithfully. Bezdna is surrounded by the estates of other *pomeshchiki*, and I noticed that at the assembly there were fairly many peasants from neighboring estates, who had responded to the argument of the peasants here that real *volia* had been sent only to them.

Having reported this to Your Excellency, I consider it my duty to add that it is past two o'clock in the afternoon, but the marshal has not come *[Marshal Molostvov arrived the next day.*[80]*]*, and the warden of the first ward is sick. Along with this, I am inviting the constable to come to the village of Bezdna, and have also ordered the warden of the second ward here.

The confrontation with Shishkin on April 8 was the first and last time when Anton Petrov was willing to defend his reading in a public dispute with an official. As article followed article, he had to concur in Shishkin's reading of the text, until finally his followers broke off the confrontation by shouting Shishkin down. The behavior of the crowd suggests that both Petrov and his followers were made to understand that Petrov's "reading" had no basis in the statute. The article about the *reviziia* may have acquired decisive significance for them because of this incident, for Petrov had been preaching *volia* for several days without making any special use of it. At any rate, after the encounter with Shishkin, the peasants would not listen to "exhortation" from officials and were careful not to allow themselves to be disabused. They had seen once how officials could cut the ground from under their leader's feet and deflate their own hopes.

The investigating authorities did not attach any significance to this confrontation between Petrov and Shishkin. They may not have known of it. It is not described in any of the collective depositions, and, apart from them, the investigators relied primarily on the testimony of reliable peasants—that is, the village officials whom Petrov had replaced. By April 8, they were lying low, and were not, apparently, present at this confrontation. Indeed, the only confirmation of Shishkin's account comes from Krylov, who reported that Petrov had been willing to go off to Spassk with the sheriff and his deputies but that the crowd of peasants would not permit his "arrest." [81]

The authorities may, however, have chosen to ignore the possible significance of the confrontation between Petrov and Shishkin. Within a few days of the shooting at Bezdna, it was clear that order was most emphatically restored; work in the fields was going smoothly and the peasants were effusive in their expressions of penitence. Polovtsov recalled that he had the task of conveying the tsar's ceremonious thanks to the villages in Spassk District that had not yielded to Petrov. The sheriff drew up a list of villages that had kept aloof.[82] When Polovtsov arrived in the first village, however, the assembled peasants fell to their knees, professing their submission and their regret that "in their silliness they had run off to Bezdna." In the other villages on the list, Polovtsov had to keep the peasants silent so they would not disrupt the ceremony with protestations of repentance and submission.[83] In this climate, it was tempting not to probe into the peasants' delusions—for example, not to inquire into the encounter with Shishkin on April 8. For if the peasants were not, in fact, sincerely deluded, then they *were* rebels, after all. Rebels would have to be tried, convicted, confined to prison, or sent into exile. What would the trial and punishment of the thousands of

peasants who had responded to Petrov, or even the hundreds
of inhabitants of Bezdna, do for the newly restored stability
and tranquility of the province? It was prudent, at the very least,
to accept the peasants' penitence and to believe that they were innocent victims of their own naiveté.

Yet the encounter between Petrov and Shishkin, and the peasants' response to it, does suggest that neither Petrov in his mis-
interpreting the statute nor his followers in adhering to him were
honestly deluded. We cannot be sure. We can only wonder whether
they tacitly collaborated in a deliberate fiction, which provided a
seemly pretext for testing the authorities and attempting to "eke out
volia." This strategy would have the advantage, compared to a direct
challenge to officialdom, of opening the way to forgiveness in the
event of failure. Participants in Petrov's movement could claim they
were loyal subjects who, in their simplicity, had been led astray.
This claim would correspond perfectly with the view of most officials that the *muzhik* was stupid and credulous, and forgiveness
would follow. If this was, indeed, the peasants' conscious strategy,
it worked. Apart from Petrov, only five peasants were punished,
and very lightly, for participation in the "riot" at Bezdna.[84]

Of course, many more participants were killed by Apraksin's
bullets. If the peasants did have a deliberate strategy, it did not allow for this shooting. Apraksin, in his inexperience, did not limit
himself to exhortation and a show of force, as officials ordinarily
did when dealing with a mass of insubordinate peasants.[85] Yet if
Petrov's appeal did not depend on prophecy and mystery, if he and
his followers were manipulating the myth of the tsar and their own
reputation for credulity in order to put massive pressure on the
regime, then the conventional official response would not have
worked. Indeed, how could the movement have been turned back
except by shooting? If Petrov was the calculating organizer of a
massive demonstration designed to extort concessions from the
regime, then Apraksin's response was, given his duties, perfectly
correct.

Shchapov

With Shishkin's report, and the hypothesis that the peasants put
forward a myth to suit their own purposes, we have almost come full
circle. The circle passes through a welter of myth-making, self-seek-

ing, fabrication, hypocrisy, dissimulation, and deliberate confusion. These are the characteristics of our sources, and of almost any comparable body of sources on such an incident. Through these sources, the historian must pick his way to the truth; if and when he gets there, he must then resume his operations again and again on other incidents and circumstances, in the hopes of eventually gaining a solid understanding of the major problems for which Bezdna can serve as a case study. This is exacting work.

There is another course. That is to enter eagerly into the making of myths and try to turn the events at Bezdna to positive account. Russian radicals took this course. Reaching out in faith and hope to the *narod*, they identified the *volia* the peasants sought with their own dreams of freedom and converted the conflict at Bezdna into a democratic myth.

The process of affirmative myth-making was constrained by the censorship and the police. When Russia's leading radical journal, *Sovremennik,* turned to the events at Bezdna (under the rubric "On the Question of a Rapprochement with the *Narod*"), the commentary was inhibited and oblique. *Sovremennik* blamed the deaths at Bezdna on the peasants' illiteracy and their estrangement from the educated classes. It was not possible to criticize Apraksin or the other officials involved, but it was possible to criticize nameless opponents who explained away Bezdna by saying, "The peasant is an animal." Beyond that, *Sovremennik* could only point out that the peasants were inspired "by the general mania for living according to one's own lights, [so] they thought they themselves were capable of making arrangements with the *pomeshchik.* . . . [For] they demand pure *volia;* they expected something utterly different from what they were told."[86]

No periodical in Russia could go further than this.[87] But Herzen, writing in London, could speak out clearly and passionately. The events of 1861 helped to dispel Herzen's hopes for the imperial regime and to convince him that what had seemed a "government of progress, of liberal ideas" was irredeemably stained with blood. Despairing of reform from above, he was drawn to the idea of peasant revolution, and in an article entitled "April 12, 1861" he made the peasants killed at Bezdna martyrs in this cause.

> And you, my unfortunate brethren, the schismatics, you who
> have suffered much, but have always stood aloof from the
> Russia of *pomeshchiki,* of hangmen, of those who shoot down

unarmed people, you must fix in your memory the new day of the passion—April 12. The time of Biblical persecutions is at hand. You know from the *Lives of the Saints* how the emperors undertook to massacre the Christians—and you know who triumphed. But triumph does not come without faith, and without effort. Be strong in spirit, and remember the cry of the fallen martyrs of Bezdna,

Volia! Volia![88]

Even in this apostrophe, emotion and calculation are intermixed. Herzen passionately took up the cry of *volia, volia,* yet he also attempted to exploit the supposed adhesion of the peasants of Bezdna to the Schism. He was involved with attempts to convert the schismatics' alienation from the Russian state into active political opposition. "April 12, 1861" was an outburst of indignation, but it was also part of a long-standing design.

There was no such element of calculation in the most celebrated and significant commemoration of the martyrs of Bezdna. This was the requiem service held at Kazan four days after the shooting (and the day before Petrov's execution). Students at Kazan University arranged for the service, which was also attended by students at the Theological Academy and other citizens. The students had no connection with Bezdna and did not know any of the victims.[89] Populist radicalism had taken hold among many of them, however, [90] and others were moved to make a gesture of solidarity with the dead peasants by the unseemly glee with which many *pomeshchiki* in Kazan greeted the news from Bezdna.

On the face of things, the requiem service was an ingenious means of expressing political sentiments. It was pious and innocuous in form, apart from some interpolations into the liturgy by the celebrant priests, who were also students. Officials at Kazan attempted to minimize its significance or to explain it away. The government in St. Petersburg, however, did not find the requiem innocuous, for it was still and all "a demonstration against the nobles." More important, it might undo the benefit of Apraksin's actions.

It is already known in [Kazan] Province that students celebrated a requiem in the city cemetery without interference. From this the peasants draw the conclusion that the victims were indeed innocent; subversive persons have represented Anton Petrov as a martyr, not a criminal, and circulated rumors that a fire shines over his grave, that an Angel dressed in white is visible [there] at night, and that he will soon rise again.

The execution of Anton Petrov instilled terror in the *narod*, but unfortunately this terror is beginning to diminish because of the news of the celebration of the requiem at Kazan. At the present time the *narod* is in such turmoil of mind that any unpunished action which disrupts the tranquility of society or gives nourishment to rumors can have the worst of consequences.[91]

So the celebrants were exiled to distant monasteries and the few students that could be identified as organizers of the requiem were expelled; their action did not go unpunished.

It was not the requiem service but the eulogy delivered just afterwards that concerned the government most. The day after the service, Governor Kozlialinov telegrammed to St. Petersburg that the service had taken place: "Everything was peaceful, but after the requiem Professor Shchapov said something." The reply came promptly back that the tsar himself wished to know, "What did Shchapov say?"[92] Under questioning, Shchapov stated:

I did not say anything inflammatory, hence there was not and could not have been any commotion at the cemetery. I said: Christ our God, who proclaimed true liberty and brotherhood, died on the cross because of Pilate's court and with his blood redeemed us all. You, my friends, were carried away by a false idea of liberty proclaimed to you by a false prophet. Then I spoke briefly about the historical origins of false prophets in Russia, who appeared in the first half of the eighteenth century in Russia and called themselves Christs. [Shchapov was here drawing upon his study of religious sects, one of his specialities as a historian.] From this I concluded that the dead were carried away by a false idea of liberty because we had not explained true liberty to them, we had given almost no attention to their enlightenment. I concluded: In your innocent ignorance, you, the wayward sons of the fatherland, fell victims to our failure to enlighten you, although the enlightenment of the *narod* is our duty. Forgive us. Peace to your dust, and eternal memory.[93]

This version of the eulogy was innocent enough, but it would not stand up, because government investigators interrogated witnesses. Some of those present protested that Shchapov's voice trembled so much that the eulogy was inaudible; it was suggested he was drunk at the time.[94] The investigators were nonetheless able to compile a different version of the eulogy.

The Government's Version of Shchapov's Eulogy[95]

My friends, so inhumanely killed. Christ himself proclaimed redemptive freedom, brotherhood, and equality to the *narod*, in the time of the Roman Empire and the slavery of nations, and through Pilate's court he sealed his democratic teaching with his own blood. In Russia for 160 years, because of a lack of enlightenment, self-proclaimed Christs have been emerging from amidst the village communes, who in their own way proclaimed liberty and emancipation from conditions of slavery and suffering in the State. Since the middle of the eighteenth century these purported Christs have been called prophets, redeemers of the rural *narod*. Now a new prophet has appeared and once again has proclaimed liberty in the name of God, and because of this many innocent victims suffered; they did not understand the limitations of the government's Statute, because enlightenment had not been bestowed upon them. Peace to your dust, poor sufferers, and eternal memory! May God grant rest to your souls. Long live communal freedom, which has been granted to your surviving brethren!

This version was inflammatory, from the government's point of view. Shchapov was summoned to St. Petersburg and placed under arrest en route. In the capital he was interrogated and produced a lengthy deposition. In it Shchapov explained that he had not arranged for the requiem and did not know who had. He had seen the students on the way to church and had followed along. At the church, he had asked the priests to adhere strictly to the liturgical text. But he was caught up in the spirit of the moment, for, "Many of the students and city folk present sang and prayed through tears, and when the entire church, in the image of an ancient Christian *agape*, began to sing 'Eternal Memory,' it was so moving that it seems even a heart of stone would have dissolved in tears."

Shchapov's heart was not of stone. "Moved to tears by the general, noble, Christian-humanitarian sympathy for the unfortunate peasants who were killed . . . I sketched out an outline [of the

eulogy] in pencil on a scrap of paper. . . . In a moment of overpowering, exalted inspiration, the graveside speech welled forth in-
voluntarily from the depths of my feeling." Here is what Shchapov
claimed he said.

Shchapov's Second Version of the Eulogy[96]

Christ, before whose passion Christians will prostrate themselves in
the forthcoming passion week, proclaimed a democratic teaching
and true liberty, and for this he was nailed to the cross by Pilate's
court-martial. You, my unfortunate friends, and your ancestors, not
being enlightened by a rational understanding of Christ's teaching,
in your blundering blindness have ever since the middle of the
seventeenth century believed in your own, democratic, purported
Christs, who emerged from amongst the simple peasants. Since the
middle of the last century, your ancestors began to call these Christs
prophets and redeemers, and from them awaited a mystical democratic liberty, at the very time when the slavery of serfdom was increasing. Now one of these prophets has appeared among you once
again and because of the lack of enlightened teachers, you had
a childlike trust in your own literates from the *narod.* You were
carried away by the false liberty he professed, and for this you were
done to death by armed force. Against the will of the tsar and
despite the wishes of the nobility, this false prophet began to proclaim to you the illusory democratic *volia* you desired, and you fell
innocent victims to this temptation. Woe to us and to the whole
narod, if liberty and land—the land which you and all the village folk
have sown and cultivated for centuries, the fruits of which nourish
us, the land which you sought to reclaim, along with liberty, as
inalienably yours, the land which has now received you into its
bosom as unfortunate martyrs—woe to us, I say, if because of the
blood you shed, liberty and land arouse the agricultural masses to an
uprising against the landowners and bosses. Unfortunately, among
the masses ominous warnings of this uprising are dimly heard. The
sin would be ours!

Standing at the head of the *narod,* serving at the expense of the
narod and enjoying special rights and privileges, charged with the
enlightenment and welfare of the *narod,* we did not enlighten you
or advance your welfare, we did not set forth for you the essence of
true liberty, we did not eliminate in time the moral possibility of

the appearance among you of false-prophet teachers, we did not educate genuine, enlightened, rational teachers for you; the interpreters and exponents of the tsar's will did not explain to you in advance, faithfully, accurately and clearly the Statute on the Peasants. According to your peasant brethren, your blood is on the heads of the bosses, they reproach the wardens and the priests because they read the tsar's Statute but did not explain it.[97]

Enlightened and humanitarian men concur in sympathy for your involuntary transgression and for the unfortunate shedding of blood. Accept our Christian commemoration of your souls. Peace to your dust, and eternal memory! May your blood be requited for the benefit of your children, your descendants and your surviving peasant brethren throughout the Russian land by the establishment and strengthening of communal-democratic liberty, which the government has granted by the creation of village societies and cantons, elective village self-government, village and cantonal assemblies! And, may there be established peacefully, without bloodshed, communal-democratic popular councilship, when the tsar himself summons the whole *narod* to it.

It is obvious that, under the pressure of interrogation, Shchapov confessed to a more seditious version of the eulogy. The very word "democratic" was a red flag to the regime. The expert opinion of the Metropolitan of Moscow was solicited, and he explained that the teachings of Christ were not at all democratic; on the contrary, the Savior was a firm believer in social distinctions and hierarchy. In this version, Shchapov still tried to explain "communal democratic liberty" as a reference to village institutions established by the emancipation legislation. Yet he had, he now confessed, called for *obshchinno-demokraticheskoe narodosovetie*, or "communal-democratic popular councilship" on the national level. *Narodosovetie* was, he explained in parenthesis, a "venerable expression," coined by the eighteenth-century writer Pososhkov. Nonetheless, it meant democratic representative government and an end to the autocracy— when the tsar saw fit to summon the *narod*.

For Shchapov insisted that he was a loyal and dutiful subject of the tsar. "I am convinced that the events at the Kurtino [cemetery] would have passed without consequences, would not have disturbed the authorities . . . if the egoistical enemies of peasant freedom had not exaggerated its significance." It was the *pomeshchiki* and officials who would not submit to the tsar's will, as expressed in the emancipation legislation. The *narod,* and Shchapov himself, on the other hand, had responded with dutiful, joyous gratitude, for they were not the tsar's enemies.

Indeed, the *narod*'s faith in the tsar is strongly emphasized in Shchapov's deposition; it is the cornerstone of the political program which he set forth along with his justification of himself. He attributed the turmoil that had accompanied the abolition of serfdom solely to the tsar's faithless officials. In several villages, he reported, "the peasants heard that the manifesto had been issued and in their joy brought some colts to the wardens, so that they would explain the tsar's decree. The wardens took the colts, and all they would say to the *muzhiki* was, 'Live as you used to, there's your *volia.*'" The peasants had an inveterate hostility to "the boyars and the bosses," but rather than contend with them, "they express the desire to give their collective petitions to the sovereign, in which they want to articulate directly their needs, desires, and the various kinds of injustice and oppression on the part of *pomeshchiki* and officials. Only they despair of getting access to the sovereign."

Narodosovetie, then, was simply a means for the tsar to avail himself of the *narod*'s devotion to him. "The peasants wish that someone—or better, several humane and enlightened men from their area—could say or write for them a word of truth for the tsar. . . . They put all their hopes in the sovereign tsar, whom they love boundlessly as the true father of the *narod.*"

While the *narod* was isolated and silenced, Shchapov did have "access to the sovereign" by virtue of the official investigation of his eulogy. He tried to turn this threat to account by following up his deposition with a letter to the tsar himself. Only at the very end of the letter did he allude to his own fate, calling attention to his sufferings and the purity of his intentions and beseeching "the most merciful sovereign . . . magnanimously [to] grant me forgiveness" and release from confinement. The bulk of this letter, however, was a series of reform proposals, in which he enlarged on the themes of his eulogy. He emphasized "enlightenment" most of all, calling for an elaborate program of popular education, so that the nation could benefit from the stifled genius of the *narod.* He called for freedom of speech and the press, but was careful to provide that "liberal plans and proposals" would not be paraded before the public but would be presented secretly to the tsar. He outlined a network of elective agencies of local administration that was similar to the zemstvo system that would be established in 1864. Unlike the zemstvo, however, Shchapov's agencies of *narodosovetie* would be charged with the special task of supervising the work of the officials sent out to the provinces by the central government. More important, *narodosovetie* would extend to the national level in the form of "central councils or assemblies of the land." The very term he used showed that the idea was not subversive, for the Muscovite tsars had convened *zemskie sobory*. And Shchapov insisted that the "laboring classes" were capable of giving good counsel, for they had intelligence and practical sense. At present, however:

> The poor *narod* despairs of getting through to its only defender, the sovereign, with the truth that cries out to be heard. A peasant once said to me, "Oh, if only God would let someone, even you, say but one word to the tsar for us! Grant it, oh Lord. . . ." How many times, in the provinces, in the face of flagrant injustice, is the proverb repeated: "God is high and the tsar is far off."

In his letter to the tsar, Shchapov not only emphasized the *narod*'s faith in the tsar but sought to show that he shared this faith himself, in all its touching simplicity. His letter was not "a political address— God save me from the very idea—but a forthright letter, loyal and sincere, to the father of the *narod,* whose love is abounding and who asks only of his faithful subjects directness of speech, sincerity of feeling, good intentions and good deeds."[98]

The tsar did read Shchapov's letter, but it only convinced him that Shchapov's detractors were correct. Professions of devotion and faith in himself did not distract Alexander's attention from the substance of Shchapov's proposals. From the official point of view, these were socially disruptive—Shchapov did not conceal his antagonism for *pomeshchiki* and "bosses"—and politically subversive. *Narodosovetie* might be an archaic word, but it still meant the end of the tsar's autocratic prerogatives, and Alexander was not taken in. He wrote in the margin of the letter, "All this shows just what his main ideas are and proves that he is a man who must be closely watched, when We consider it possible to release him from confinement." Shchapov had managed to get "the truth through to the tsar," but appealing to the benevolence of the tsar did not work for him any better than it had for Anton Petrov and his followers.[99]

To be sure, Alexander's suspicions about Shchapov were quite correct. The reform proposals suggested in the eulogy and explained in the deposition and letter were Shchapov's cherished ideals, and he did seek to give a faithful picture of the sentiments of the *narod*—resentment at oppression, hostility to the favored classes, and naive devotion to the distant tsar. The *narod*, he believed, was sincere in this devotion, but for Shchapov it was a matter of hypocrisy and opportunism. He was a radical democrat, hostile on principle to monarchy, but willing to play the role of a loyal subject in order to flatter the tsar into granting concessions. We know his true attitudes from an extensive private letter he wrote shortly thereafter,[100] and, indeed, from the notorious eulogy. Shchapov represented his eulogy as a pious and innocuous effusion of feeling. He gave some ground under interrogation in St. Petersburg and admitted that he had included an appeal for *narodosovetie*. It was hard for officials to determine if he had said anything more culpable and disloyal, because they had to rely on Shchapov's account and on the testimony of his listeners, who were sympathetic to him. There was the outline which Shchapov claimed to have scribbled on a scrap of paper, but he gave it away after the eulogy and it disappeared. However, a brief version of the eulogy, written in Shchapov's own hand and not for the eyes of officials, survived, although it did not come to light in time to affect Shchapov's fate. Here is the text.

Shchapov's Own Text of the Eulogy[101]

My friends, killed for the *narod*!

The democrat Christ, heretofore the mythical God created by humankind in Europe, to whose sufferings men will prostrate themselves in the forthcoming holy week, proclaimed communal-democratic liberty to the world in the era of the yoke of the Roman Empire and of the slavery of nations, and for this he was nailed to the cross by Pilate's court-martial, and so became the redemptive sacrifice for the whole world's liberty.

In Russia, for the past century and a half, among the bitterly suffering, dark mass of the *narod*, among you *muzhiki*, your own Christs have appeared—democratic conspirators. Since the middle of the last century they have come to be called prophets, and the *narod* has believed in them as redeemers and liberators. Once again such a prophet has appeared and you, my friends, were the first to

answer his summons and to fall as the redemptive victims of despot-
ism, sacrificed for the liberty that the *narod* has awaited so long.
You were the first to disturb our sleep, to destroy by your initiative
our unjust doubts that our *narod* is capable of taking an initiative in
political movements. Louder than the tsar and more nobly than the
noble, you said to the *narod:* let thy servant go in peace. The land
you worked, whose fruits nourished us, which you now wanted to
acquire as your property, and which has now taken you into its
bosom as martyrs—this land will summon the *narod* to rebellion and
to liberty. Peace to your dust, and eternal historical memory to your
selfless deed! Long live a democratic Constitution!

From this, the most reliable version of Shchapov's eulogy, we can
make several inferences. It is clear that for Shchapov naive monarchism was a pose, deliberately assumed in the interests of political
goals—both reforms and his own freedom—which the regime did not
seem disposed to grant. He was, to be sure, an educated man, born
of peasant stock and devoted (perhaps naively) to the peasantry,
but still a professional intellectual. Dissimulation and sophistry are
to be expected of intellectuals, especially when they are in trouble.
And yet, having seen how natural and necessary it was for Shchapov
to drape his political ideas and personal plea in naive monarchism,
we have to wonder whether Anton Petrov and his followers indulged
in something like Shchapov's dissimulation. For them, of course,
the pose was convincing. Perhaps it was no pose at all, and they
were sincere where Shchapov was hypocritical. Yet the example of
Shchapov's hypocrisy in a situation similar to theirs, along with
other hints and bits of evidence, makes us wonder how much
naiveté there was in the *narod*'s professions of faith in the tsar.
This text also shows what kind of myth Shchapov tried to distill
from the events at Bezdna. In the outline, as in all other versions of
the eulogy, he drew upon his research into popular religion and
popular rebellion. Yet here he was not the historian, carefully sort-
ing through competing myths. In the eulogy, he entered ardently
into the making of myths. He made of the peasants of Bezdna not
only victims of tyranny but martyrs to a new holy cause. He boldly
identified the *volia* they sought with his own cherished ideals—
revolution and constitutional democracy. In so doing, he asserted
the solidarity and identity of radical intellectuals like himself with
the *narod*. The peasants at Bezdna had, doubtless, never so much as

heard the words "democratic constitution"; Shchapov's myth was even more contrived than Apraksin's reports or Krylov's memoirs, but in making it he was responding to a moral need more imperative than veracity. And Shchapov's myth has proved enduring and powerful, and so acquired an actuality of its own, on a very different level from the interpretations that can be cautiously elicited from dossiers. For Shchapov's eulogy was a benchmark in Russian radicalism. Perhaps the great significance of the events at Bezdna is that they provoked a shy professor, who had never been to Bezdna, to find the courage to make the first public appeal in Russia for a democratic constitution.

Notes

In English, there are brief accounts of the Bezdna affair in Franco Venturi, *Roots of Revolution,* Knopf, New York, 1960, pp. 214–217, and T.L. Emmons, "The Peasant and the Emancipation," in W.S. Vucinich, ed., *The Peasant in Nineteenth-Century Russia,* Stanford University Press, Stanford, Calif., 1968, pp. 56–59. In Russian, see especially P.A. Zaionchkovskii, *Provedenie v zhizn' krest'ianskoi reformy 1861 g.,* Moscow, 1958, pp. 66–71, and M. Naidenov, *Klassovaia bor'ba v poreformennoi derevne (1861–1863 gg.),* Moscow, 1955, pp. 106–123. There are good bibliographies on the Bezdna affair in S.B. Okun' and K.V. Sivkov, eds., *Krest'ianskoe dvizhenie v Rossii v 1857–mae 1861 gg.: Sbornik dokumentov,* Moscow, 1963, p. 697, and A.L. Iampol'skaia and D.S. Gutman, eds., *Bezdnenskoe vosstanie 1861 goda. Sbornik dokumentov,* Kazan, 1948, pp. 148–153, cited below as *Bezdnenskoe vosstanie.*

1. A police agent's report of an overheard conversation; I have translated *nachal'stvo* as "bosses"; quoted in G.A. Kavtaradze, "K istorii krest'ianskogo samosoznaniia, perioda reformy 1861 g.," *Vestnik Leningradskogo universiteta,* 1969, no. 14, p. 61.
2. P.I. Iakushkin, "Bunty na Rusi," *Sochineniia,* St. Petersburg, 1884, p. 45.
3. E.A. Morokhovets, ed., *Krest'ianskoe dvizhenie 1827–1869,* 2 vols., Moscow-Leningrad, 1931, II, p. 20.
4. So the committee charged with overseeing the implementation of the reform pointed out in response to a suggestion that the government issue a digest of the reform legislation in the language of the *narod*; Arkhiv zakonodatel'nykh del, *Zhurnal*

Glavnogo komiteta ob ustroistve sel'skogo sostoianiia, t. I: s 5 marta 1861 goda po 28 dekabria 1862 goda, Petrograd, 1918, p. 59.

5. Eric Hobsbawm, "Peasants and Politics," *Journal of Peasant Studies,* I, 1 (October 1973), p. 13.

6. N.A. Krylov, "Vospominaniia mirovogo posrednika pervogo prizyva," *Russkaia starina,* vol. LXXIV (April and June 1892), p. 93. Krylov's account of this incident is substantiated in a warden's report of March 28, 1861 (in *Bezdnenskoe vosstanie,* p. 11), and in other official sources.

7. Krylov, "Vospominaniia," p. 91.

8. [F.A. Polovtsov], "Skazanie o bezdninskom poboishche v kazanskoi gubernii po sluchaiu osvobozhdeniia krepostnykh krest'ian," *Kolokol,* nos. 122/123–125 (February 15, March 1, and March 15, 1862), p. 1032.

9. Krylov, "Vospominaniia," pp. 96–97.

10. *Bezdnenskoe vosstanie,* pp. 24–25.

11. An investigator for the Ministry of Internal Affairs adduced the official estimate that there were almost ten thousand schismatics in Kazan Province out of a total population of a million and a half, but he did not show that they flourished in the area of Bezdna or prove that Anton Petrov was one of them; *Bezdnenskoe vosstanie,* p. 130.

12. Okun' and Sivkov, *Krest'ianskoe dvizhenie,* p. 350.

13. *Bezdnenskoe vosstanie,* pp. 25–26.

14. E.A. Morokhovets, ed., *Krest'ianskoe dvizhenie v 1861 godu posle otmeny krepostnogo prava,* parts I–II: *Donoseniia svitskikh generalov i fligel'-ad"iutantov . . .,* Moscow-Leningrad, 1949, pp. 66–69.

15. *PSZ,* second series, vol. XXXVI, section 1, no. 36661, article 33, p. 224.

16. This text has *neponimanie,* but Okun' and Sivkov's edition of this report has *nepovinovenie,* which is surely correct.

17. *Prilozheniia k Trudam Redaktsionnykh komissii dlia sostavleniia polozheniia o krest'ianakh. . .: Svedeniia o pomeshchich 'ikh imeniiakh,* 6 vols. in 3, St. Petersburg, 1860, I [part 6: Kazanskaia guberniia], p. 14.

18. See Okun' and Sivkov, *Krest'ianskoe dvizhenie,* p. 342.

19. This incident is mentioned in one other source; see *Bezdnenskoe vosstanie,* p. 54.

20. The original adds *v serebre,* meaning "in silver" here, which makes no sense.

21. The text is given in *Zhurnal Glavnogo komiteta,* pp. 97–100; it

was reproduced verbatim "from the newspapers" in "Sovremenniaia khronika," *Otechestvennye zapiski,* May 1861, pp. 26–29, and in other journals. On the requirement that this communiqué be published "without any abridgement, change or commentary," see Iu.I. Gerasimova, "Otnoshenie pravitel'stva k uchastiiu pechati v obsuzhdenii krest'ianskogo voprosa . . . ," in M.V. Nechkina et al., eds., *Revoliutsionnaia situatsiia v Rossii v 1859–1861 gg.,* fasc. 6, Moscow, 1974, p. 102.

22. "Vypiska iz donoseniia ministru vnutrennikh del chinovnika osobykh poruchenii Sobeshchanskogo," in E. Chernyshev, ed., "Materialy po istorii klassovoi bor'by v Rossii v 60-kh godov XIX veka," *Izvestiia Obshchestva arkheologii, istorii i etnografii pri Kazanskom gos. universitete,* vol. XXXIII, fasc. 4 (1927), pp. 82–83. The full text of this *donosenie* is given in *Bezdnenskoe vosstanie,* pp. 129–145.

23. F.A. to V.A. Polovtsov, May 15, 1861, in I. Kuznetsov, ed., "Sem'desiat' let tomu nazad," *Krasnyi arkhiv,* no. 74 (1936), p. 31.

24. In the event, Bibikov backed Apraksin strongly. "I will not venture to intercede for General Apraksin," Bibikov telegrammed to the tsar, "since he has the pleasure of serving directly under Your Majesty, but I can testify that by his sensible and decisive actions, he has instilled respect for the army in this province," manifest in the peasants' return to work in the fields; rescript to I.G. Bibikov, April 16, 1861, in *Bezdnenskoe vosstanie,* pp. 98–99; Bibikov's telegram to the tsar of May 4 in M.V. Nechkina, ed., "Vosstanie v Bezdne," *Krasnyi arkhiv,* no. 35 (1929), pp. 190–191.

25. Kuznetsov maintains that it was Polovtsov's letter of May 15 that led to his dismissal; Kuznetsov, "Sem'desiat' let tomu nazad," p. 28n. To be sure, Polovtsov was the leading figure on a commission of inquiry into the Bezdna affair, set up by the provincial governor; his closest collaborator on this commission was transferred to a less attractive post. However, an investigator sent from St. Petersburg reached much the same conclusions as this commission, and its recommendations, including the release of the peasants arrested at Bezdna, were upheld; see *Bezdnenskoe vosstanie,* pp. 78–87 and 129–145, and, for Polovtsov's views on his dismissal, F.A. P[olovtsov], "Iz vospominanii 1859–61 godov," *Istoricheskii vestnik,* vol. CX (October–November 1907), pp. 485–486.

26. *Zhurnal Glavnogo komiteta,* p. 57.

27. A.I. Gertsen, *Polnoe sobranie sochinenii i pisem,* 22 vols., Petrograd, 1919–1925, XI, p. 109 (Lemke's note to "12 Aprelia 1861"). For another instance of the Third Section's campaign against Kozlialinov and Polovtsov, see Larionov's report to V.A. Dolgorukov, in Okun' and Sivkov, *Krest'ianskoe dvizhenie,* pp. 369–370. Polovtsov was not, apparently, aware of this campaign, but in his anonymous report to *Kolokol* he did cite his own dismissal and the "gang of spies" hanging around the taverns of Kazan to illustrate the political climate in the province; [Polovtsov], "Skazanie," p. 1018.

28. [Polovtsov], "Skazanie," pp. 1032–1035.

29. [Polovtsov], "Iz vospominanii," p. 474.

30. [Polovtsov], "Skazanie," p. 1035; [Polovtsov], "Iz vospominanii," p. 474.

31. [Polovtsov], "Skazanie," p. 1034; see also [Polovtsov], "Iz vospominanii," p. 483.

32. [Polovtsov], "Skazanie," p. 1034; *Bezdnenskoe vosstanie,* p. 65.

33. [Polovtsov], "Skazanie," p. 1035.

34. [Polovtsov], "Iz vospominanii," p. 475; compare *Bezdnenskoe vosstanie,* pp. 85–86.

35. [Polovtsov], "Skazanie," pp. 1017–1018. It seems that Polovtsov's success was due in some part to a previous visit to this estate by a company of troops under Major Verzhbitskii, which had terrified the peasants; see Kuznetsov, "Sem'desiat' let tomu nazad," p. 29, and "Raport kazanskogo gubernskogo prokurora," May 8, 1861, in Nechkina, "Vosstanie v Bezdne," p. 202.

36. F.A. to V.A. Polovtsov, May 15, 1861, in Kuznetsov, "Sem'desiat' let tomu nazad," p. 31.

37. Apraksin to Alexander II, May 14, in Morokhovets, *Krest'ianskoe dvizhenie v 1861 godu posle otmeny krepostonogo prava,* p. 75. Apraksin's words were incorporated verbatim into the Journal of the Main Committee; *Zhurnal Glavnogo komiteta,* p. 171.

38. [Polovtsov], "Skazanie," pp. 1032–1033.

39. On the movement of troops to Bezdna, see Kozlialinov's reports to the minister of internal affairs reproduced on pages 37 and 64, and "Raport . . . Sobeshchanskogo," *Bezdnenskoe vosstanie,* p. 139. The dispatches of the commanders of the units on their way to Bezdna are reproduced in *Bezdnenskoe vosstanie,* pp. 22–24, but since they were sent to Kozlialinov at Kazan, they cannot have influenced Apraksin's decision.

40. [Polovtsov], "Skazanie," p. 1043.

41. Morokhovets, *Krest'ianskoe dvizhenie v 1861 godu posle otmeny krepostonogo prava*, pp. 71–73.
42. *Svod voennykh postanovlenii*, part 5: *Ustav voenno-ugolovnyi* (1859), article 609.
43. Okun' and Sivkov, *Krest'ianskoe dvizhenie*, pp. 365–366 and 545, n. 272.
44. *Bezdnenskoe vosstanie*, pp. 80–81; see also Okun' and Sivkov, *Krest'ianskoe dvizhenie*, p. 544, n. 266.
45. *Bezdnenskoe vosstanie*, p. 86.
46. *Bezdnenskoe vosstanie*, pp. 36, 47.
47. [Polovtsov], "Skazanie," pp. 1042–1044.
48. [Polovtsov], "Iz vospominanii," pp. 476–477.
49. Polovtsov's memoirs accord with Krylov on the composition of the council but hold that he advised Apraksin that "at most it will be necessary to beat a couple of dozen *muzhiki* . . . and the whole riot will be over"; [Polovtsov], "Iz vospominanii," p. 473. A letter in *Kolokol* reported, "Two of the governor's adjutants struggled in vain to dissuade" Apraksin, but this letter was almost certainly written by Polovtsov after his change of heart; see "12 Aprelia 1861," *Kolokol*, no. 101 (June 15, 1861), p. 849, and A.I. Gertsen, *Polnoe sobranie sochinenii v tridtsati tomakh*, vol. XV, Moscow, 1958, p. 363.
50. "Martirolog krest'ian," *Kolokol*, no. 100 (June 1, 1861), p. 838. The same report appears in a private letter by N.N. Bulich, but he was responsible for the report in *Kolokol*; Kuznetsov, "Sem'desiat' let tomu nazad," p. 27, and the index to the facsimile edition of *Kolokol*, p. 62.
51. See also Tatarinov's third-hand rendering of Polovtsov's initial impressions in "Materialy po istorii russkoi literatury i kul'tury, II: Krest'ianskii bunt v s. Bezdne . . .," *Russkaia mysl'*, April 1911, p. 104.
52. [Polovtsov], "Iz vospominanii," p. 473. Polovtsov's change of heart may have been prompted by his disgust at the way the nobles of Kazan celebrated the events at Bezdna; see his letter of April 19 in Kuznetsov, "Sem'desiat' let tomu nazad," pp. 28–29.
53. Chernyshev, "Materialy," pp. 79–80.
54. *Zhurnal Glavnogo komiteta*, p. 368.
55. In his letter of April 19, Polovtsov explained to his brother that "Kozlialinov acted absolutely correctly" but that he was fearful that the governor would be blamed "simply because there were uprisings"; Kuznetsov, "Sem'desiat' let tomu nazad," p. 29.

56. Gertsen, *Polnoe sobranie sochinenii i pisem*, ed. Lemke, vol. XI, p. 109n.

57. Letter of April 22, 1861, in *Russkaia mysl'*, April 1911, p. 106; Kuznetsov, "Sem'desiat' let tomu nazad," p. 26.

58. *Zhurnal Glavnogo komiteta*, p. 99; Morokhovets, *Krest'ianskoe dvizhenie 1827-1869*, vol. II, p. 9.

59. Krylov's reckoning of the dead was published only in 1908 by I.I. Ignatovich, in "Volneniia pomeshchich'ikh krest'ian ot 1854 po 1863 g.," *Minuvshie gody*, 1908, no. 8, p. 202n. In May 1861, the sheriff of Spassk District reported to the governor that 61 peasants were shot dead on the spot and 41 more died of wounds; the governor, in turn, reported to the minister of internal affairs five days later that a total of 91 peasants had died, and that of the 87 undergoing treatment, 29 had already recovered. Neither attempted, for official purposes, to estimate how many peasants fled wounded and died elsewhere, fearing to seek treatment because their wounds were proof they were "rebels"; *Bezdnenskoe vosstanie*, pp. 60, 64; see also p. 139.

60. Krylov, "Vospominaniia," p. 624.

61. Krylov, "Vospominaniia," pp. 622-623.

62. Krylov, "Vospominaniia," pp. 624-625.

63. Morokhovets, *Krest'ianskoe dvizhenie v 1861 godu posle otmeny krepostnogo prava*, pp. 62-66. This letter was sent on to the Ministry of Internal Affairs, perhaps by Ermolova.

64. Krylov, "Vospominaniia," p. 619.

65. Krylov, "Vospominaniia," p. 620.

66. The commission of inquiry set up by the governor of Kazan found that Petrov's teaching "passed among the *narod* in a form wholly different from what Anton said"; *Bezdnenskoe vosstanie*, p. 81. Compare Venturi, *Roots of Revolution*, p. 215.

67. Quoted in Ignatovich, "Volneniia," p. 205.

68. "Vypiska iz donoseniia . . . Sobeshchanskogo," Chernyshev, "Materialy," p. 82.

69. Krylov's memoirs indicate that in his mature years he combined Russian nationalism with a liberal's hostility to the bureaucracy; these tendencies were compatible with a sentimental and patronizing conception of the *narod*. Apart from the memoirs already quoted, see his "Nakanune velikikh reform (Lichnye vospominaniia)," *Istoricheskii vestnik*, vol. XCIII (September 1903), pp. 786-823.

70. Okun' and Sivkov, *Krest'ianskoe dvizhenie*, pp. 358-360.

71. For Tarasov's deposition, see *Bezdnenskoe vosstanie*, p. 93.

72. For the text of the sentence, see Morokhovets, *Krest'ianskoe*

dvizhenie v 1861 godu posle otmeny krepostnogo prava, pp. 70–71.

73. The collective depositions are translated from V. Leikin, ed., "Bezdnenskoe vosstanie 1861 g.," *Krasnyi arkhiv,* no. 36 (1929), pp. 180–182. On the deaths of peasants from these villages, see *Bezdnenskoe vosstanie,* p. 64.

74. *PSZ,* second series, vol. XXXVI, section 1, no. 36662, article 189, p. 261.

75. Okun' and Sivkov, *Krest'ianskoe dvizhenie,* p. 360.

76. Okun' and Sivkov, *Krest'ianskoe dvizhenie,* pp. 363–364.

77. *Bezdnenskoe vosstanie,* pp. 17–19.

78. In fact, two reports, published in *Bezdnenskoe vosstanie,* pp. 13–14. Shishkin initially came to Bezdna in response to a complaint that the peasants refused to do *barshchina,* and only later did he discover that the peasants were inspired by Petrov's interpretation of the emancipation legislation.

79. The published text has *s* ("with"), but surely *za* ("for") is correct.

80. *Bezdnenskoe vosstanie,* p. 19.

81. Krylov, "Vospominaniia," pp. 615–616. The deposition of Andrei Matveev mentions a conversation through a window between Petrov and Shishkin, apparently the conversation of April 7; Okun' and Sivkov, *Krest'ianskoe dvizhenie,* p. 356.

82. Shishkin's list is reproduced in *Bezdnenskoe vosstanie,* pp. 70–71. By his reckoning, 19 villages in Spassk District were entitled to the tsar's thanks, and 75 were not.

83. [Polovtsov], "Iz vospominanii," pp. 483–484.

84. Okun' and Sivkov, *Krest'ianskoe dvizhenie,* p. 544–545.

85. See Daniel Field, review essay on Okun' and Sivkov's *Krest'ianskoe dvizhenie,* in *Kritika,* III, 3 (Spring 1967), pp. 34–55.

86. Piotrovskii, "Pogonia za luchshim. Kriticheskie ocherki, IV: K voprosu o sblizhenii s narodom," *Sovremennik,* vol. 88 (August 1861), p. 245.

87. Indeed, an official of the Main Censorship Administration expressed his astonishment that a censor could have passed the article for publication; Gerasimova, "Otnoshenie pravitel'stva k uchastiiu pechati," p. 102. The contorted, cautious observations in "Sovremennaia khronika," *Otechestvennye zapiski,* June 1861, pp. 33–37, represent the limit of permissible comment.

88. [Alexander Herzen], "12 Aprelia 1861," *Kolokol,* no. 101 (June 15, 1861), p. 849.

89. Two students went to Bezdna after the shooting, but they

were promptly picked up by the police and sent back to
Kazan; *Bezdnenskoe vosstanie*, pp. 34–36.

90. For example, radical students dismissed Professor Bulich as a
hypocrite when he expressed emotional sympathy for the peasants killed at Bezdna, yet Bulich was a celebrated liberal, the
idol of the students only a few years before, and a collaborator
of Herzen's. Indeed, he provided Herzen with his first reasonably full account of Bezdna (see n. 50, above); G.N. Vul'fson
and E.G. Bushkanets, *Obshchestvenno-politicheskaia bor'ba
v Kazanskom universitete v 1859–61 godakh,* Kazan, 1955,
p. 76.

91. *Zhurnal Glavnogo komiteta,* pp. 171–172. Here again,
the committee quoted General Apraksin; compare his report
of May 14 in Morokhovets, *Krest'ianskoe dvizhenie v 1861
godu posle otmeny krespostnogo prava,* p. 75.

92. G.A. Luchinskii, "A.P. Shchapov, Biograficheskii ocherk,"
Sochineniia A.P. Shchapova, vol. III, St. Petersburg, 1908,
p. xxxviii.

93. For Shchapov's first deposition, made to the Archbishop of
Kazan (Shchapov taught in the theological academy as well as
the university), see "Opredelenie Sv. sinoda . . .,"
Bezdnenskoe vosstanie, pp. 105–106.

94. F. Kudriavtsev, ed., "K istorii demonstratsii-panikhidy . . .,"
Krasnyi arkhiv, no. 17 (1926), p. 184; Okun' and Sivkov,
Krest'ianskoe dvizhenie, p. 368.

95. *Zhurnal Glavnogo komiteta,* 369–370; compare *Bezdnenskoe
vosstanie,* pp. 112–113. It is not clear why the government
used this text in its bill of particulars against Shchapov and
the students, since it had elicited from Shchapov the more incriminating version reproduced on pages 97–98.

96. The deposition of which this version of the eulogy is a part is
in Chernyshev, "Materialy," pp. 84–87.

97. In his deposition, Shchapov interjected here: "'They didn't
make any sense,' as the Kazan peasants put it."

98. A. Sidorov, ed.,"Pis'mo A.P. Shchapova Aleksandru II v
1861 g.," *Krasnyi arkhiv,* no. 19 (1927), pp. 151, 160–161,
164, 165.

99. The tsar's comment is published with Sidorov's text, "Pis'mo
. . .," p. 151. On October 30, 1861, Shchapov was sentenced,
apart from the dismissal and incarceration he had already
undergone, to confinement in a monastery "for reflection
and exhortation." He was pardoned in 1862, however;
Luchinskii, "A.P. Shchapov," p. lii.

100. See Shchapov's letter to P.P. Viazemskii of October 8, 1861, ed. M.V. Nechkina, *Literaturnoe nasledstvo,* no. 67 (1959), pp. 645–668, especially pp. 657, 661.

101. Okun' and Sivkov, *Krest'ianskoe dvizhenie,* pp. 364–365, reproduce the outline with Shchapov's excisions and emendations; this translation corresponds to what appears to be the final and most coherent wording. Vul'fson has recently pointed out that this text cannot be the outline Shchapov claimed to have jotted down on the spot; it is written in ink, and there would have been no inkwells in the cemetery. Because it is in ink and is full of corrections and additions, Vul'fson cites it as evidence that Shchapov, together with the students who organized the requiem, planned the eulogy in advance. His contention would be stronger if he could demonstrate that this text was a preliminary draft, not a retrospective reconstruction. Since he believes that Shchapov pretended to have improvised the eulogy in order to make it seem less subversive, Vul'fson implicitly holds that the outline jotted on a scrap of paper never existed. He has, however, discovered and published a thirty-six-word summary of the eulogy in Shchapov's hand which might be the long-lost outline; G.F. Vul'fson, *Raznochinno-demokraticheskoe dvizhenie v Povolzh'e i na Urale v gody pervoi revoliutsionnoi situatsii,* Kazan, 1974, pp. 244–247.

Chigirin District, Kiev Province (1870s)

Legend:
- Towns
- Villages
- Main highway
- Railroad

Miles
0 — 20

POLTAVA PROVINCE

KHERSON PROVINCE

CHIGIRIN DISTRICT

CHERKASSY DISTRICT

Krylov

Ratsevo

Tarasovka

Adamovka

Shabel'niki

Mordva
Rossoshintsy

Chigirin

Borovitsa

Mudrovka

Novoselitsa

Medvedovka

Sagunovka

Khudiaki

Cherkassy

Smela

Dnepr River

Tiasmin River

Tiasmin River

River

We cannot honestly take up the role of Attila, nor even the role of Anton Petrov. To do so, we would have to deceive others or ourselves. We would have to answer for this lie before our consciences and before those who are close to us in spirit.

Herzen, "To an Old Comrade"

3

The Chigirin Affair

The conflict between the imperial government and the peasants of Chigirin District, Kiev Province, had two distinct phases. The first phase was a struggle, lasting several years, over land and the institutional forms of land tenure. Characteristically, the recalcitrant peasants avoided even the threat of violence against the authorities, but they were unusually stubborn. To impose its will, the government had to invoke the full machinery of coercion: exhortation, prosecution, imprisonment, the quartering of troops, and the confiscation of property. By 1876, the government had brought the Chigirin villages to heel and secured at least the semblance of compliance. There were, however, peasants who still refused to recognize the officially sponsored system for the allocation and tenure of land. In the second phase, these obdurate peasants undertook to recruit their fellow villagers into a secret society. This society was pledged to secure *volia*, not just a new pattern of land tenure, and to take up arms against nobles and officials. The society grew rapidly during 1877 and, at the time of its exposure and destruction, had at least a thousand members.

There are obvious differences between this sequence of events and the confrontation at Bezdna. The Chigirin affair was not a matter of days, but of years. It entailed conflicts within the peasantry as well as between the peasants and officials. The most important difference lay in the leadership. Anton Petrov was a local peasant whom

circumstances—including his personality—thrust into prominence.
Much the same could be said of the leader of the Chigirin peasants
in the first phase, but in the second phase, the peasants' acknowledged leader was a radical intellectual. If he had a counterpart in
Kazan Province fifteen years earlier, it was not Petrov but Shchapov.
We are still three decades away from the revolutionary era, with its
confluence of articulate radicalism and popular upheaval. Yet we
have moved past the time when radical intellectuals had no relationship with the *narod* beyond their own feelings of sympathy and
identification.

Despite these differences, Bezdna and Chigirin are akin because of
the central importance of the myth of the tsar. In both phases, the
Chigirin peasants responded to leaders who invoked the tsar's name
and, indeed, claimed to have had promises of favor from the tsar
himself. In Kiev Province in the 1870s, as in Kazan Province in 1861,
the government stimulated the peasants to activity by initiating a reform, but the peasants' aspirations went beyond the confines of
statutes and regulations. What they wanted was not reform, but
rather *volia*.

In the autumn of 1877, the Russian government was shocked to discover that the peasants of Chigirin District were involved in an insurrectionary conspiracy. Peasant discontent was an old problem
for the regime, in this district as in others, and peasant rebellion was
a persistent anxiety. What was particularly ominous about the
Chigirin conspiracy was its form and inspiration: a young revolutionary named Iakov Stefanovich had recruited about a thousand
peasants into a secret society, and this society was pledged to rise in
arms against "officialdom" and the nobility. This was the first
significant conjunction between the emerging revolutionary movement and a large number of peasants.

For Stefanovich's fellow revolutionaries, the Chigirin affair was a
matter for debate. They could not but be impressed with the scale of
Stefanovich's organization, particularly in light of the fiasco their
movement had recently suffered in "going to the people." In 1874,
hundreds of young radicals had attempted to leap across the gulf
between educated society and the common people by going out into
the villages to talk to the peasants, to learn from them, and to spread
socialist propaganda. The radicals found the peasantry less receptive
than they had fondly hoped; more important, they were quickly and

systematically arrested by the police. The story of this "movement to the people" is more complex than it is usually represented to be, but there is no doubt that both the authorities and the revolutionaries regarded it as an utter failure. The gulf between educated revolutionaries and the common people they wished to serve seemed as broad and deep as ever, and the sheer number of peasants enrolled in Stefanovich's organization was correspondingly impressive. However, the means Stefanovich had used raised questions of revolutionary morality. Far from rallying the Chigirin peasants against tsarism, Stefanovich had represented himself as the tsar's agent and claimed that the tsar himself wanted his beloved peasantry to organize a rebellion against their oppressors, beginning with the tsar's own perfidious officials. It was this exploitation of peasant monarchism to revolutionary ends that preoccupied both the government and the radicals. The government feared the fraud might be reenacted elsewhere with more serious results. The radicals, for their part, wondered whether it ought to be reenacted. For thirty years or more, the Chigirin affair would be a constant theme in discussions of revolutionary strategy and revolutionary morality.

From another vantage point, however, Stefanovich's conspiracy was simply one stage of a stubborn struggle waged by a particular body of peasants for immediate goals. Chigirin District (the Ukrainian form is "Chyhyryn") lay between the Dnepr and the Tiasmin rivers, to the southeast of Kiev, which was the administrative center for the province. The peasants of the area were Ukrainian, distinct from Great Russians in culture and social organization. They spoke what was then slightingly termed the "Little Russian dialect" or what we call the Ukrainian language. Hence they were doubly remote from the culture of the official world and the upper classes, where even those who were of Ukrainian origin were scarcely distinguishable from their colleagues.

As Ukrainians, the Chigirin peasants were the heirs to the cossack . tradition. Today the cossacks are remembered as an irregular cavalry force that zealously suppressed the domestic enemies of the tsarist regime. For nineteenth-century Ukrainians, however, the image of the cossack was very different. According to this mythology, which had its roots in the historical reality of the sixteenth and seventeenth centuries, the cossack was the freest and least submissive of men, a horseman untrammeled either by the agricultural cycle or the mundane exactions of governments. We can conjure up something like this image by combining our most idealized notions of the cowboy, the buccaneer, and the American Indian. When the Chigirin peasants proved to be tenacious in their resistance to the demands of the government, the provincial governor laid some of the blame on the cossack tradition. They are descended, he observed, "from those who belonged to the cossack caste, and have retained an ungovernable streak in their character; they are not very respectful, bold in their speech, and insolent to a fault."[1] To be sure, it suited the governor to explain the disorders in his province in terms of the unreachable past, rather than blame the shortcomings of his own administration or the very structure of state and society. Yet we shall see that radicals also believed that the cossack tradition had a real vitality.

Finally, Ukrainian peasants had a distinctive system for the tenure and use of land. In Great Russia, peasant land was controlled by village communes. A commune would allocate and reallocate plowland among the households of the village according to the number of "souls" (male peasants) in each household. Although there might be a considerable range of prosperity and poverty within a communal village, the system did make for economic equality. In most parts of the Ukraine, the commune was unknown. Tracts of land were held by households and passed from father to son; the village had no direct control of the plowland within it, and there was no regular system for adjusting landholdings to the needs of families. Some households might hold several standardized tracts (*uchastki*), while others would have only a kitchen garden and still others, the so-called "orphans," had no land of their own at all. The Ukrainian household tenure system had the sanction of both custom and law, and was reinforced by the reform legislation of the 1860s.

The particular peasants with whom we have to deal were remarkable chiefly for their poverty. The right bank of the Dnepr River was the northeast boundary of Chigirin District. Many peasant families had allotments along the bank that were so sandy that they were hardly worth cultivating. To support their families, pay their taxes, and meet the charges for these allotments, peasant men took jobs on the river as boatmen and fishermen. Many more, however, went off every spring to seek wage work in other provinces. This practice of "going out" (*otkhod*) was quite common in northern Russia, but was otherwise unknown in the Ukraine. While the district was surely a backwater—a "bear's corner," as the Russian expression has it—the men of the riverbank villages had whatever sophistication and worldly experience that travel to distant places can provide. The point is worth remembering because the naiveté of the peasantry was one of the major points at issue in the Chigirin affair, and because it was the riverbank villages that took the lead throughout the protest movement.

The protest movement in Chigirin District was precipitated by a two-pronged initiative from the central government. There were in the district about fifty thousand former state peasants—that is, peasants who had always been administered directly by the government and had never been serfs. In 1867, the government ruled that state peasants must redeem their allotments; since the provisions of the statutes abolishing serfdom had been extended to them, they had rented these allotments from the state. In connection with this change, the government ordered a lustration of the lands held on household tenure. (The word *lustration* is about as esoteric in English as its counterpart *liustratsiia* in Russian; the OED defines it as "inspection," "review," or "survey" and cites the nineteenth-century usage.) The lands were to be surveyed, appraised, and the redemption payments due from each household were to be adjusted (they were based upon the old rental payments) in accord with the findings. While the household-tenure system was to be retained and the richer households left with the tracts that were properly theirs, the lustration did provide an occasion for some adjustments in favor of peasants with little land. However, the majority of the former state peasants of the Chigirin area seized upon this pretext to demand a thoroughgoing overturn in the allocation of land, a re-allocation of land on a per capita basis, "by souls." In behalf of this demand, they waged a struggle extending over more than seven years, tenaciously obstructing the lustration and the implementation of the redemption system and resisting those who tried to impose them. Among the latter were their richer fellow villagers. Those who were satisfied with the present arrangement and wanted to consolidate it cooperated sedulously with the authorities and accepted the acts of lustration. Hence they became known as *aktoviki*, in contrast to the *dusheviki*, those who insisted on a reallocation by souls (*dushi*). The bitter conflict between the two groups was an important element of the Chigirin affair, for it was very unusual for a village to take a stand against officialdom unless it could do so as a community; a divided village could not ordinarily withstand pressure from without. For their stubbornness, the *dusheviki* suffered beating, imprisonment, exile, and the devastation of their homesteads; the punishments imposed on them for involvement in Stefanovich's organization would prove to be a relatively minor component of this repression, as we shall see.

What did the Chigirin peasants mean by "allocation by souls," and why were they so tenacious in seeking it? The question is complicated, but we can begin to answer it by examining their own full and formal, although somewhat disingenuous statement of their position. In 1875, after various other means had failed, the government tried to break the resistance of the *dusheviki* by seizing the ringleaders and putting them under police custody in various administrative centers of Kiev Province. Eight of them, all residents of the canton of Shabel'niki, tried to win their release with this petition.

A Petition to the Minister of Justice
May 12, 1876[2]

About six years ago there was proclaimed to us a most gracious order by the Sovereign Emperor about the allotment of land to us in return for a fixed payment. In response to this, we at once declared our desire that the land be allotted *per soul*. After this surveyors came, measured the land and assigned allotment tracts to some peasants, but we were not assigned any land; then, in 1873 or 1874, the arbiter of the peace came along with the surveyors and proclaimed that we should accept the acts of lustration on the allocation of land.

Since we absolutely did not understand and still do not understand the meaning and significance of "acts of lustration" and this was not explained to us, and furthermore they demanded that we immediately pay some [*tax*] arrears, of which we knew nothing, to the amount of 500 rubles, we could not immediately agree to accept the acts, which we could not understand, and so we asked the authorities to allot land to us by souls.

Then in April, 1875, we were again asked to accept the acts of lustration; through our spokesmen we made a request for allocation of land by souls.

We proclaim that any decision of the Sovereign Emperor's is holy for us and we will submit to it unconditionally. We ask only one thing, that we be allotted land *by souls* and that government surveyors divide the land for us. Our request was not heeded. They

demanded that we accept the acts on household allotment unconditionally, and furthermore, that we divide the land ourselves, without
participation by the authorities. We were beaten with birch-rods
several times, put in jail, soldiers were sent to make exactions from
us, and finally we were sent to Kiev, where we have been for almost
a year, without a place to live (we spend the night in the police station) or food or clothing or work.

In the month of March of this year we appealed to the Kiev procurator; we explained our situation to him and asked him to take an
interest in our fate and explain to us what criminal act we have
committed. Why are we kept in Kiev under police supervision? Are
we the objects of a judicial investigation? If so, where, and by whom,
and will it be concluded soon? If not, then what must we do to return to our homes and bolster our households, which have gone to
ruin in our absence, and help our families, which have been reduced
to destitution?

The procurator informed us that he cannot help us at all. Therefore, not knowing at all why and how long we will be detained at
Kiev, we have ventured to seek Your Excellency's protection, and
humbly request your attention to our situation. We are not aware
that we have *deliberately* been insubordinate to the established
authorities, still less to the Imperial will.

While we did not accept the acts of lustration, *it was only because
then as now we did not understand their meaning and force;* we
cannot accept an allocation of land to the whole community or by
households because allocation by households is very unequal; it
would reduce some to poverty and enrich others. For example, it is
very advantageous for a household with two revision souls *[i.e., two
males]* to have an allotment of 10 *desiatiny,* while the same 10
desiatiny would not provide even a bare ration of bread to a household with ten souls. So it is that *allotment by households would
multiply kulaks and paupers in our villages.*

This cannot happen with allotment by souls, because then every
soul is provided with the same amount of land. This is our desire,
and it cannot be called criminal! We have committed no other offense. We formally declare that we hold sacred the monarch's will
that we should be allotted with land in return for a fixed payment,
and accept his decision with full and deep gratitude.

We ask to be allotted with land by souls, and not by households,
and that the land be divided by a government surveyor, for if we
divide it ourselves, then our village and canton constables and rich

men generally will seize large amounts of the best land for themselves, and the poor will be left with nothing.

We undertake to render fully and punctually the redemption payments in the amount established by the tsar's order!

From this Your Excellency may see that the only reason we are held under arrest and under police supervision is the fact that we request allocation of land not by households, but by souls. If we are charged with some criminal activity, we ask Your Excellency to order the appropriate person to declare to us who is conducting the investigation and where, and what we are accused of, for no one so far has summoned us for interrogation. Then, Your Excellency, order us to be set free and allowed to return home; our remaining in Kiev can only entail even greater ruin and destitution for our families, which must be experiencing hunger even now.

May 12, 1876
Stepan Parkhomenko, Kirill Prudkii, Grigorii Tannenik, Sergei Datsenko, Stepan Mirkotan, Lazar' Timoshenko, Kuz'ma Prudkii, Anton Komarenko, Grigorii Mirkotorenko, Foka Kravchenko. And, since they are illiterate, the townsman Luka Semenov Tatsenko, a resident of Skvira, has signed for them.

We must thank the townsman Tatsenko for the officious language of this petition, but the petitioners were responsible for the substance and tone, the ostentatious naiveté in particular. Naive or not, the petitioners were less than candid with the minister. They could, as they knew, return to their village if only they would formally accept the new allocation of land and renounce the communal system. On the other hand, their legalistic emphasis was appropriate, since, as an official who had dispatched some of them to Kiev privately conceded, there was no basis for criminal charges against them.[3] The authorities were attempting to bring Shabel'niki and its neighbor villages to heel by removing the most influential *dusheviki* and holding them in the district towns of Kiev Province. Theirs was a loose confinement, for while they were locked up in police stations at night, they were sent out into the streets by day to earn their keep. This system had the merit of economy. Fearful though it was of subversion and disorder, the regime's resources were limited; when the leader of the Chigirin peasants was captured in 1875 after a major manhunt, the governor of Kiev Province himself did not have the funds to pay the modest reward promised to his betrayer. Still,

Kiev was only second to St. Petersburg as a headquarters of young radicals; since the Chigirin peasants were, as officials realized,[4] a natural focus for the efforts of these radicals, it was not prudent to take the most disruptive peasants from Chigirin and set them to wandering the streets of Kiev.

The petitioners also tried to mislead the minister of justice about the character of their resistance. The *dusheviki* had not, with one marginal exception, offered violence against any state official. But they had used force and threats of force against their fellow villagers. There were also instances in which Chigirin peasants attempted to seize by force the documents in which the new allocation of land and dues was set forth. More frequently, they simply refused to accept the lustration or allow it to be implemented. Unauthorized village assemblies convened and passed resolutions such as this, to which 310 peasants subscribed.

Resolution of Lipovo Canton[5]

On May the 5th, 1875, we the undersigned state peasants of the villages of Lipovo, Kalaborka, Vetrovka, and Andrusovka in the canton of Lipovo hereby attest that we did not and do not desire to accept the acts of lustration, and all unanimously desired and do desire to hold the land by souls according to the *ukaz* of His Imperial Majesty, and therefore resolve to return these acts to the authorities and request them to allot us with land not according to the tract or lustration system, but by souls, to which we here subscribe.

Resolutions like this were designed to give a legalistic color to resistance since, as frustrated officials insisted, the new system had the force of law and the peasants were required to accept it.

A more significant form of resistance was refusal to pay taxes or redemption payments according to the new schedules. It was this, as we shall see, that brought the full weight of official wrath on the Chigirin District in the summer of 1875; then and after, the level of tax arrears served as the measure of acquiescence or resistance by each village and each household.

Yet the peasants represented themselves as the most loyal and devoted of the tsar's subjects. The petition is emphatic on this point, and even in the short resolution just quoted, the Lipovo peasants invoke an "*ukaz* of His Imperial Majesty." What did they have in mind? Perhaps it was a government ruling of 1870 holding that villages could, under certain conditions, shift from the tract to the communal system of land tenure. Yet when Chigirin peasants were closely questioned about the rationale of their movement, they would speak of a much more lavish and wholly imaginary *ukaz*. Rumor had it that the tsar had ordered a general repartition of land, granting to the peasantry land held by the nobility and the state itself, and that this *ukaz* had been concealed by corrupt and selfish officials. Rumors of this kind circulated all over the empire in the 1870s. They represented a natural conjunction of peasant poverty and peasant monarchism. They were particularly vigorous in the Chigirin District, thanks in part to the efforts of Foma Priadko.

Priadko, a retired soldier from the nearby village of Sagunovka, was the most important leader the peasants had during the first phase of the Chigirin affair. In 1872, he had been one of a group of emissaries the Chigirin peasants had sent to the tsar in St. Petersburg. All the others had been intercepted by the police and sent home, but Priadko had managed to reach the capital. According to a report published in a radical journal, Priadko claimed to have seen the tsar himself and to have won his sympathy:

> As soon as he returned home, he zealously undertook to strengthen the peasants' conviction that they must be as insistent as possible in demanding an allocation of the land by souls. To achieve his end more quickly, [Priadko], the peasants say, somewhere got hold of a piece of paper with some kind of seal on it; going secretly from one village to another, he related how this paper had been given to him by the tsar-*batiushka*, who wrote in it that the officials, those dogs, had deceived him, since it appeared from their reports that allotment by souls had been achieved in [the Chigirin area]; that soon he, the tsar, would get hold of these treacherous officials, remove and punish them all and give his brothers the peasants the allotment they wanted. Word about the paper from the tsar spread like lightning . . . and, while on the one hand this rumor increased the peasants' faith in the tsar, on the other hand it aroused them more and more against the officials and enhanced their desire to achieve allocation by souls whatever the cost.[6]

There are similar stories in other radical periodicals. The official record confirms them only indirectly at best, but does provide evidence of a minor hoax that Priadko arranged, designed to convince the peasants that the tsar's son and heir was coming to Chigirin to aid them.

It is certain, at any rate, that Priadko encouraged the peasants' hopes in the tsar and that he did so in part by deception and fraud. He owed some of his influence to his supposed contact with the tsar, and some to his seemingly magical ability to avoid arrest. He was able to move through the villages agitating among the *dusheviki* and slipping through the snares of the police until he was finally captured in his native village in November of 1875. Even his entrapment has the quality of legend. A treacherous neighbor invited Priadko to his house to read psalms at the bedside of a sick child; while Priadko was detained, the neighbor's confederate, a Jew, ran through the night to bring the police.[7] Priadko was arrested, imprisoned, and eventually sent into Siberian exile. While at large, he had stiffened the Chigirin peasants in their resistance to the regime and confirmed their devotion to the tsar. And his activities, or his legend, may have provided Stefanovich with the basic principle for his conspiracy, as we shall see.

The Chigirin peasants, then, professed their devotion to the distant tsar even as they resisted his officials on the spot. Yet their positive demand, allocation of land by souls, "cannot be called criminal," as the peasants observed in their petition. "Allocation by souls" seemed to mean the communal system that law and custom alike imposed upon the peasantry of the Great Russian provinces; indeed, one official fondly supposed that the Chigirin peasants wanted to shift to that system out of admiration for Great Russians.[8] And allotment by souls had the merit, as the petition points out, of retarding the polarization of villages between the rich and the very poor. Yet this, from a certain point of view, was no merit at all. The case against the extension of the communal system to the Ukraine was most forcefully made very early in the controversy by A.M. Dondukov-Korsakov, governor general at Kiev. He was undismayed by the prospect of the polarization of the village and an ever-growing proportion of landless peasants. For:

> Nothing could be more harmful than a general equalizing of land and dues among all the peasants. Through such a general leveling, those on whom nature has bestowed capacity, the eager and the industrious, will face insurmountable barriers to escaping from the general level of mediocrity. If all the

peasants are to be uniformly allotted with small plots of land, scarcely adequate to feed them and pay their taxes, then they will always comprise a separate class, with nothing in common with the other small proprietors, who hold their land by full property right rather than communally. The interests of the former and the latter will always diverge. The peasant estate, debased to one common level, but firmly united by its common interests, strong only in numbers but not in moral and material resources, will always envy the other estates of the realm, which can freely develop to the extent of their capacities and effort. This situation holds the peril of great calamities.

Dondukov-Korsakov was careful to insist that his remarks were not meant to apply to the communal system in Great Russia, but he went on to praise the household-tract system as "rational" and "natural" and to maintain that the debate between the two systems was "sustained by the groundless theories of the communists."

At the heart of his argument was a positive affinity for the "industrious" peasants who held fairly generous tracts of land. If the household tract system was not maintained, he predicted:

The prosperous peasants who have an adequate amount of cattle to work their lands . . . will be ruined; they will sell some of their cattle and, being left without their usual occupation, will have to seek work on the outside, to which they are not accustomed. Is it possible calmly to permit the ruin of these peaceable and tranquil toilers to satisfy the claims of men who never had land or else, because of their laziness, lack of foresight, or lack of means, yielded it to others?[9]

Dondukov-Korsakov is voicing the affinity which public officials tend to have for the more prosperous segment of the population under their charge—in this instance, for the peasants who held one or several household tracts and would, as the controversy developed, comprise the *aktoviki.* Lower-level officials shared this affinity, and so did the central government. It did not, as Dondukov-Korsakov advised, forbid any transfer to communal tenure. In a decree of 1870, the government ruled that Ukrainian peasants could shift to communal, repartitional tenure; however, a village assembly could not make any disposition of the tracts belonging to households that did not desire to shift to "allotment by souls"; furthermore, it could not exclude from the share-out those souls in the village who presently had no land at all. And the peasants who did shift would not be eligible for any additional allocations of land that might be made as a result of the lustration, which was then about to begin. In short, the prosperous peasants were secure in the enjoyment of their present holdings, but the poor and the utterly destitute were permitted to pool and redivide their poverty. The option was so unattractive that officials hostile to communal tenure hoped that a few villages would accept it, so that their example would disabuse the rest forever.[10]

This ruling did not satisfy the *dusheviki,* who, in the name of allotment by souls, resisted and obstructed the local authorities for several years. The recurrent conflict gave officials ample opportunity to probe what the peasants understood by "allocation by souls." The term simply denoted the Great Russian communal system. It came to light, however, that the *dusheviki* had no interest in the periodic repartition of plowland, which was the essence of the communal system. Once the land had been reallocated "by souls," they would have it pass from father to son as before, under the household-tract system. What was important for them was that all allotments should be of equal size; they were not at all inclined to respect the property rights of their fellow villagers with large tracts, or with several. What they aspired to, then, was not a different form of land tenure but more land. When the peasants were pressed, they invariably put this aspiration in precise form: five *desiatiny* (or about thirteen and a half acres) per soul. Now, the average allotment held by the state peasants in Chigirin District was 2.34 *desiatiny.*[11] It took no elaborate calculation to appreciate that granting a five-*desiatina* allotment would entail more than encroaching on the holdings of the minority of prosperous peasants: it would require a massive distribution of lands belonging to nobles and to the state. Behind the request, "which cannot be called criminal," for a more egalitarian form of tenure lay a radical demand for a general redistribution of land.

No law or decree provided any basis for the association between allotment by souls and a new grant of land. The concepts were linked only by faith and hope, against which the most authoritative official pronouncements were powerless. In May of 1875 the provincial governor himself came to the village of Chaplishche and patiently explained that the lustration and the payments it imposed really were the tsar's will; a retired soldier replied that "it could not be that the sovereign emperor would sell state lands to peasants, and it is inconceivable that the sovereign needs pennies so much that he'd exact them in return for sandy land; surely he would give this land for free." And all but thirty of the assembled peasants agreed, the governor reported; "they refused to make redemption payments or accept the acts of lustration, stating that they desire allotments according to His Imperial Majesty's *ukaz.*"[12] The reference to the imaginary *ukaz* indicates again that the peasants' faith and hope were inspired by the persistent rumors that the tsar would favor his faithful peasants with a general repartition of land. The struggle of the Chigirin peasants was founded on a wishful myth.

The myth provided a further reason for resisting the lustration. The lustration would consolidate peasant allotments in their present form of tenure and, by and large, in their present size. But the *dusheviki* also maintained that if they allowed their names to be inscribed on the rolls of the lustration, this would signify a lack of faith in the tsar, for which he would exclude them from the redistribution to come. The *dusheviki* avoided any formality which might conceivably be interpreted as acceptance of the new system. Some of the seals used by village administrations wore out at this time; the peasants blocked official attempts to replace them, fearing that to accept new ones might somehow mean acceptance of the lustration. Because the workings of bureaucracy were mysterious and bureaucrats were so cunning, it was impossible to know what fateful and secret significance might be attached to forms and symbols. And so a spirit of quarantine prevailed among the *dusheviki;* they avoided all dealings with officials to avoid being enrolled unawares with those who had lost faith in the favor of the distant tsar.

A picture emerges of a naive, superstitious, and stubborn peasantry confronting the rationalistic bureaucracy. Yet the contrast is not absolute. The peasants may have been inspired by a myth, but their demands and their tactics were utterly mundane. They did not depend on the signs, wonders, and inspired prophecy that was supposed to have sustained the peasants at Bezdna. To be sure, in August of 1875, after months of suffering and struggle, a woman named Nastasiia Likhosherstova claimed to have been sent by God to encourage the peasants to stand fast for allotment by souls. The peasants arrested by the police, she said, were "sufferers for the truth" and the *dusheviki* were "defending the New Jerusalem"; those who did not follow them would perish. Likhosherstova was arrested, released by an angry mob, successfully rearrested, and there the matter ended.[13] This one incident was the only supernatural element in a long struggle for remote but eminently wordly goals. Apart from the central myth, then, the peasants' conduct was rational enough, unless it is irrational to struggle for what authority does not want to grant.

Furthermore, the officials involved were very far from attaining the ideal of bureaucratic rationality. Consider, for example, the actual process of the lustration. This was a series of routine bureaucratic operations: surveying, assessing, appraising, verifying titles, modifying property lines, and allocating taxes. In Chigirin District, it was carried out with a fabulous degree of incompetence, malfeasance, and corruption. Marshes and sandbanks were reclassified as arable land and levied with high redemption payments. Peasants with large allotments (and therefore, presumably, the resources to make an attractive bribe) were assigned still more land, while some *dusheviki* lost their allotments or were shifted onto worthless land. The spoliation was so crude that some of the surveyors simply arrogated peasant land to themselves. Peasant appeals were initially ignored and later rejected on the ground that they were filed too late. The process is very hard to reconcile with the concept of bureaucratic rationality.

The officials of Kiev Province found this pattern of abuses, which came to their attention only as a result of peasant resistance to the lustration, could not be reconciled with their own standards of bureaucratic procedure. And, having previously assured the Chigirin peasants that the lustration had all the force and sanctity of law, they undertook to have it done all over again on a more equitable and honest footing. This concession allayed the discontent of some Chigirin peasants, but it could not satisfy the principal aspiration of the *dusheviki*. For they had not been protesting against the abuses of the lustration, but against the lustration as such, as a consolidation of the present pattern of landholding. A new lustration could not satisfy their hunger for more land, and a new lustration was about as much of a concession as the regime was willing to make.

So it was that repression was the government's principal means of ending their resistance. In April of 1875 the governor general decided that the police of Chigirin District could not cope with the situation and ordered two companies of dragoons to Shabel'niki and another company to the village of Borovitsa. This fact may mislead us; the resort to troops suggests a high level of violence on both sides. Yet the peasants were relying primarily on stubborn, inert pressure, and the presence of troops permitted the government to exert the same kind of pressure in response. There was some violence, but nothing like a clash of arms between insurgents and troops. Rather, with the troops on hand the government could apply its usual techniques for dealing with recalcitrant peasants.

First of all, various *dusheviki*—the supposed leaders, or simply those who made the most noise—were arrested and sent away; in the absence of troops, it was almost impossible to arrest a *dushevik* because the others would not allow it. Some *dusheviki* were beaten in the presence of the whole village. Two peasants, according to one report, died from the beating.[14] While these deaths would not have been deliberate, they could only have enhanced the effect intended: to humiliate and demoralize the peasants and impress them with the authorities' power and determination. The authorities had better intelligence than they would usually get in a village, since the *aktoviki* identified the most active and influential *dusheviki*. In return, *aktoviki* were installed as cantonal officials, for the elected officials tended, like most of the villagers, to be *dusheviki*. More important, the *aktoviki* could, with the protection of the troops, cultivate the extensive lands the lustration had assigned to them. The *dusheviki* had made it clear that they would not permit any peasant to work an allotment larger than the average; the introduction of the troops at the beginning of the growing season forestalled this threat and as a result upheld the authority of both the lustration and the regime itself.

The most widespread and vexing form of resistance practiced by the Chigirin peasants was nonpayment of taxes and other dues. The government had a tried and true method for delinquent peasant taxpayers: the seizure and sale of cattle and other portable forms of property, with the proceeds of the sale applied to the tax arrears. Backed up by the dragoons, the authorities were able to proceed in this manner against the willful delinquents of Shabel'niki and neighboring villages. Even so, there were problems. No buyers could be found in the immediate area; the *dusheviki* would not buy and apparently the *aktoviki* doubted they would be able to enjoy their purchases once the troops were withdrawn. The goods had to be carted to the town of Chigirin, where they were sold to outsiders and soldiers for a fraction of their value. The peasants' solidarity pushed the price down and so increased their sacrifice, since a good deal of property would have to be sold to cover a small sum of arrears. Yet one village underwent the whole process rather than pay a mere seven rubles.[15]

In cases of this kind, the police were instructed to seize tools and draft animals only as a last resort, when the proceeds from the sale of other goods did not cover the amount due. Yet few peasants in the Chigirin area owned anything else that could be sold. And a peasant household that lost its horse or ox, even by natural causes, faced utter destitution; without beasts to pull the plow, it would be unable to work its own allotment, so it could not feed itself and meet its other obligations. The upshot was likely to be degradation to the status of day laborer.

The time-tested techniques of pacification and exaction had their effect. They were reinforced by exhortations from the provincial governor and the governor general himself. One community after another solemnly repented its insubordination and renounced the idea of allocation by souls. To be sure, peasants are not encumbered with chivalric pride and think little of performing a ceremony of abject submission to mollify a visiting dignitary. More important, however, even those villages where the *dusheviki* were strongest and which had been earliest and most stubborn in their resistance began to pay up their taxes and dues. By January of 1876, the sheriff could report to the provincial governor that six cantons had paid up in full, and that three more would have done so if the harvest had not been so bad.[16] Since the peasants had chosen nonpayment of taxes as their means of resisting the inventory and the household-tract system, this was progress indeed.

Only Shabel'niki was stubborn. This canton had not been the first to resist, but it was much the slowest to submit. Instead of placating visiting dignitaries, it had greeted the governor general with what His Excellency had found intolerable insolence. And it was primarily to Shabel'niki that the dragoons had been sent. The regime could scarcely do anything crueller to a refractory village than quarter troops there. Supporting an army of occupation was enough to bring even a village far more prosperous than Shabel'niki to ruin. The soldiers were not remarkably brutal; indeed, their officers were anxious that they were all too sympathetic to the peasants. They simply moved into the peasants' households—in Shabel'niki, they were installed only in the houses of the *dusheviki*—and made free with what little was there: the house, the vodka, the food, and the women. It took very little of this enforced hospitality to bleed a village white. To get the soldiers out of their houses, the peasants had only to play out a ceremony of submission; the governor ruled that the troops would be removed if the peasants would ask it "as a favor." Yet all they would do was notify the authorities that their resources were exhausted and they could not feed the soldiers any more. The sheriff was obliged to agree and, rather than involve the soldiers in the suffering the peasants were undergoing, he first began to feed them at government expense, then reduced the complement, and finally, after nine months, withdrew it entirely. This was a moral victory for the Shabel'niki peasants, achieved at the cost of their own ruin.

The events in the Chigirin area were bound to attract the attention of Russia's radicals, for their own cherished ideals seemed to be at issue. For the movement we now call "populism," it was axiomatic that the Russian peasantry had a great revolutionary potential which radicals must elicit or stimulate. And for the populists, the peasant commune was a cherished ideal as proof of the Russian peasantry's primitive virtue and as the foundation of the future socialist order. The Chigirin peasants were engaged in a persistent, if largely passive, struggle against the regime, and they seemed to be doing so in behalf of the commune. Furthermore, this happy combination of circumstances came to light at a time when the fortunes and morale of the populists were at a low ebb. In 1875 and 1876, the movement "to the people" was past, while the orientation to terrorism, which would culminate in the assassination of the tsar, was still to come. There were some populists who, determined to avoid the mistakes made by the propagandists who had "gone to the people," settled in villages and pursued normal rural occupations, hoping gradually to acquire the confidence of their peasant neighbors and only then undertake to spread socialist propaganda. This kind of caution diminished the likelihood of attracting the attention of the police or of provoking the suspicious hostility of the peasantry. Yet it required a patience and self-effacement which many ardent young revolutionaries could not attain. The populists of the Ukraine, in particular, were brash and impulsive and inclined to the variety of populism known as *buntarstvo.* Inspired by the writings of Bakunin, the *buntary,* or "rebels," held that a revolutionary's sole and immediate task was to provoke a popular rebellion. It remained to discover how this was to be accomplished. While they cast about for a solution, the "rebels" languished in idleness and apathy. They wandered around the Ukraine, scrounging money from sympathizers and laying grandiose plans. Some settled in villages, but the lure of city lights proved overpowering, and they found themselves congregating in towns, bickering and target-shooting with pistols. The pistols were their badges as "rebels," and they were contemptuous of the more bookish and cautious populists of Moscow and St. Petersburg. Having "gone to the people" in 1874, they now found themselves deliberately isolating themselves from the people, for fear of exposure and arrest. Their frustration found its outlet in derisive remarks about the peasantry, with whom and for whom they wished to rise in rebellion.

Stefanovich

It was at this point in the development of the movement that Iakov Stefanovich discovered the Chigirin peasantry. He had "gone to the people" in 1874 and, narrowly escaping arrest, had fled to Switzerland. There he read in a Russian émigré journal a dramatic account (already quoted on page 122) of the struggle of the Chigirin peasants and the repression visited upon them.[17] He was inspired to return to Russia and fish in these troubled waters.

Stefanovich produced three accounts of his experience with the Chigirin peasants. The first was the deposition he gave when he was arrested in 1877, and the last, which has not been published in full, was another deposition given in 1881. The second, which he wrote for an underground periodical in 1880, is the longest and most rewarding; it is also the most important, since it provided the framework for subsequent debate. It is reproduced here, with some interpolations from his first deposition and other sources.

The Chigirin Affair
The Peasant Society "The Secret Druzhina"
(An Experiment in
Popular-Revolutionary Organization)[18]

I will not go into a detailed exposition of the economic situation of the peasants of Chigirin District; compared to most areas of our native country it is nearly unique, while, on the other hand, the purpose of this note is to describe my mode of action in attempting to create a revolutionary organization among the people. As is known from the trial of June 17, 1877 (see the article "The Chigirin Affair" in the newspaper *Kievlianin*), in the early 1870s the Chigirin peasants began to rise up in behalf of a demand for an allocation of land by souls, instead of the former tract system. The lustration commissions, which the government established to straighten out the peasant question, only provided the impetus to strengthen this uprising. Arbitrary delineation of tracts, complicity with Shusherin (an arbiter of the peace, well-known for stealing village lands), an effective ban on resettlement (only *bobyli*, that is, those with no land, are allowed to move away, and strictly speaking there were no *bobyli* in the area) and, most important, the imposition on all peasants of the tract system—all these provoked the greater part of the peasantry to renounce the acts of lustration compiled by the commissions. Among the peasantry there spread the deep conviction that the actions and decisions of the commissions were contrary to the will of the tsar, who was credited with intentions absolutely identical to the peasants' desires. At first these desires did not go further than reallocation by souls of those lands which lay within the boundaries of the recalcitrant villages. Little by little, however, thanks to rumors spread by religious pilgrims and other chance passers-by *[This is Stefanovich's equivalent of the official view that outside agitators must have aroused the peasants.]* the peasants began to doubt strongly that the rental payments were legal and to believe in the existence of an *ukaz* from the tsar which had not been put into effect and which would take away all the *pomeshchiks*' land and hence increase the allotment for each soul to 15 *desiatiny*. *[A fifteen-*desiatina *allotment for each male among the former state peasants in Chigirin District would amount to substantially more than the total area of the district, or almost six times as much as they presently held. Official sources uniformly indicate that the peasants expected a five-*desiatina *allotment.]*

Among the legends circulating among the people, the following enjoyed special popularity: the tsar had an argument with a minister (it is not known with which one). The former maintained that a majority of peasants want landholding by souls (communally), and the latter—that they want landholding by tracts. To prove he was correct, the minister proposed to make a poll of those who want the one or the other system of land allocation, and if he, the minister, proved to be right, the tsar would be obliged to give him all those who want tracts. The story set forth in this legend has acquired such authority that the peasants told the governor who came on account of the uprising in the village of Shabel'niki, "We are the tsar's and do

not want to belong to the minister, for we know what it was like to
be under the squires *[i.e., under serfdom]*." At first the peasants
awaited the governor's coming in the expectation that he would decide the matter in their favor, but eventually they became convinced
of the opposite and decided to appeal directly to the tsar himself
with a complaint about the illegal behavior of the authorities (the
cantons involved were Shabel'niki, Borovitsa, Adamovka, Mudrovka,
Chaplishche, Tsvitpa, and Novoselitsa). Chief among the seven emissaries was the famous Foma Priadko *[whom the radical émigré press
had represented as a hero]*, about whom the legends do not at all
correspond to his personal qualities, as I came to realize when I was
in prison. The emissaries were intercepted on the way (except for
Priadko, who managed to hide) and brought home under guard. This
strengthened still more the belief that officials are offering the tsar
false information about the supposedly flourishing condition of the
peasants and preventing him from coming into direct contact with
them. The peasants became more stubborn than ever; they would
not make rental payments, and when the governor came (in May of
'75) at the head of the punitive squads, they flatly refused to sign
up for the tracts allotted to them. A comparatively naive minority
yielded to a trick: the arbiter of the peace read them a statement
from the minister *[of state property?]* and declared that you have
only to hear a document like that to realize that a renunciation of the
tracts can have no effect; the majority dispersed, but those who remained at the meeting yielded to this argument and signed. Or so
some of the other group tell it. The agitation of Priadko, who held
that their desires and the tsar's will are identical, had considerable
effect on the peasants, and so did the rumors circulated by passers-
by about an *ukaz* of the tsar, supposedly already issued but hidden
by the squires, ordaining that all land must be taken away from the
pomeshchiki and allotted by souls among all the peasants. In the
area there also appeared inspired fanatics, who held forth in public
about their divine visions which testified to the justice of their cause;
such, for example, was Nastasiia Likhosherstova *[see page 126]*. In
the month of May, as I have said, a punitive force was finally sent.
(It was sent only to the canton of Shabel'niki, to the villages of
Shabel'niki, Mordva, and Pogorel'tsy.) This was indeed rough justice
in the Turkish style. The governor would call out each person and
ask if he would sign for his tract allotment; after the refusal he
would order him knocked on the ground and beaten. Two were

beaten to death. The first beatings were so painful that many
wavered and yielded, but the majority stood firm. The punitive expedition went further; it undertook the seizure and forced sale of
property to cover the accumulated arrears. In the nearby villages
there was no desire to buy up the goods stolen from the peasants;
it was necessary to arrange the sale far from the area of the uprising—
in the settlement of Smela, for example. The canton of Shabel'niki
was utterly devastated; the soldiers who were quartered there in
[i.e., until] January of 1876 for final pacification brought the ruin
to its culmination. About one hundred heads of households were
sent to various prisons. Linked to these evils is the implacable hostility, which existed even before the punitive expedition, of the two
factions: the *dusheviki* and the tract-holders (or *aktoviki*—those
who signed the acts of lustration). The *dusheviki* refused to accept
land if the government would not permit its allocation by souls;
therefore all the land that the *dusheviki* had held was divided into
tracts and turned over to those who signed the acts of the lustration
commission. In light of this, the hostility of the *dusheviki* to the
tractholders is understandable.

One must note that in the matter of the uprising the peasants
were guided by considerations of a purely realistic kind. Thus the
families in favor of allotment in tracts (of at least 12 *desiatiny*)
were those with a modest number of male souls, so that allotment
by souls did not hold any quantitative advantage for them as a group.
Families with four, five or more male souls favored allotment by
souls. The arbiter of the peace deprived the *dusheviki* of the vote at
village meetings. The *aktoviki* (tractholders) spied on the *dusheviki*
and reported to the authorities what they were doing; incited by the
warden, they set up nighttime patrols in order to discover whether
the *dusheviki* were assembling or reading documents, what they were
saying, and so on. The hostility reached such a level that in church
the *dusheviki* (or communards) stood apart from the tractholders,
and their encounters on the street did not pass without arguments
and fights. The discord between the two parties is emphatically clear
from the following: Entering Shabel'niki towards evening, in the
winter of 1875, and wanting to know where the cabin of L[azar'].
T[enenik]. was, I asked the first little boy I met, who was six or
seven. He looked at me suspiciously and asked, "What do you want
Lazar' Tenenik for?" (He was an ardent *dushevik* and under arrest.) I
called myself his relative. "How are you related to him?" I told him

and said I was from a village where Lazar' Tenenik did have relatives.
"So you're his nephew," the boy exclaimed. "Listen," he began to
whisper, "don't go through this part of the village, though it's quick-
er that way, because there are tractholders and if they see you they'll
surely go to the police. Go by this path, along the fences, and you'll
come out where the *dusheviki* live, there anyone can show you the
way." And he led me to a path through the reeds, along the bank
of the Dnepr.

*[Throughout his narrative, Stefanovich refers to Lazar' Tenenik and
the other peasants he dealt with by their initials only. In this translation the full names are supplied when they can be ascertained. He
made an exception only for Andrei Prikhod'ko, whom he thought
had betrayed him. This use of initials creates the impression that he
was protecting these peasants from official retaliation. The impression is false. Although he and his collaborators, Deich and Bokhanovskii, agreed in advance to provide no information to the police if
arrested,*[19] *Stefanovich wrote a lengthy deposition in which he freely
gave the full names of his peasant followers, beginning with Lazar'
Tenenik. He did, however, go to some lengths to avoid implicating
his comrades from the intelligentsia.]*

Although the peasants were plundered and ruined by the punitive
expedition, their spirits were still high; they were firm in the hope
that somehow or other the tsar would learn how illegally they had
been treated and then, obviously, he would make amends for all the
offenses of the authorities. They deeply regretted that they did not
have the resources or men to fit out another party of emissaries to
the tsar; the best peasants were in jail, and their families, deprived of
their menfolk, were so impoverished that they lived by begging
(they already were in 1876); the children were "puffy from hunger,"
as the peasants put it. All the same, the slightest hopeful rumor, a
word said in secret, would revive their courage and determination to
hold out, not to sign for tracts, and not to pay rent. The faith held
firm that the tsar himself would surely visit the aggrieved cantons
and punish the lawless officials. The authorities understood how
much influence rumors brought by travelers have on peasants and
therefore, for example, in Shabel'niki and Borovitsa any traveler was
dragged to the police station and searched "to verify his identity."
   Under these circumstances, there was no possibility of establishing
one of our people *[literally, "our brother"]* in any of the rebellious

villages, so that he could directly observe the course and character of
the movement and influence the peasants in the direction of our
goals. All that was possible was encounters with the peasants in nearby factories, in monasteries, or simply in the steppe. The peasants
were so stubborn in their confidence that the tsar's intentions unfailingly correspond to the desires of the common people that I was
compelled in advance to admit the utter pointlessness of trying to
prove the opposite. Often I would hear, "Let the tsar come here and
order us to take the tracts and we will not go against the tsar's word,
but we are holding out for *[allotment by]* souls because we know
that such is the tsar's will." The natural quest for some support for
the hope that their cherished wishes would be realized, abetted by
the sequence of events in the present reign, has led the common people into this train of reasoning: the tsar summoned the common
people out of their captivity to the squires; for this the squires made
three attempts on his life. The tsar would not have evoked the
nobles' wrath for nothing, which means that he is for the peasantry,
and that means that he did not want to give only *volia*, but also
granted land in the amount the people want, and without any payment for it. This conviction has kept the peasants' protest passive
and made them unwilling to cross the boundary of legality. "Show
us," they say, "a real law with the tsar's seal on it and we will submit without a murmur, but if you can't, do what you like with us,
we will bear it all. But you," they add, "will get the punishment
you deserve from our intercessor, the tsar."

The stubbornness of the peasants was largely sustained by those
of them, numbering about a hundred, who were confined in the district towns in the custody of the police departments; however, they
did have some liberty; in the daytime, they had the right to look for
work in the city and then reported in to the police stations for the
night. (Priadko was kept in a fortress under maximum security.)
They were not given any government rations and it was not always
possible to find work, so that frequently they wandered about the
city begging for alms. And how was it for their families, deprived of
their property, their land, and their principal manpower, the head of
the house! Yet all the same they refused to respond to the insistence
of the police authorities that they "sign up" (for tracts) and go
home. In a few districts, however, the authorities were so humane
that they released the peasants to their families "without a signature,"
putting them under the supervision of the local Chigirin police,

without the right to travel beyond the boundaries of their district. On the other hand, the overseer of the prison at Skvira (several men were confined at Skvira) used the peasants as draft animals; D. G. and S. Sh. were harnessed to a plow and plowed his fields. In Kiev they (nine men) asked the governor to let them go home or at least to provide them with government rations, and received this answer: "Until you sign you can rot in Kiev, and no government rations are allotted to rebels; a rebel is worse than a bandit." "We won't sign even if you drown us in the Dnepr," the peasants said. They believed that before things got to the point of drowning in the Dnepr, the tsar would learn of them and rescue them from their misfortune. And this is the sum and substance of the Chigirin people's resistance to the authorities.

The primary task I set myself was injecting a revolutionary element into this dumb protest, arousing a consciousness of the necessity of real action, and encouraging them to count not on outside help but solely on their own efforts. In short, on this ground that was already prepared to a significant degree, I intended to try and create a revolutionary organization, on the banner of which would be inscribed the people's desire, "Land and Liberty," a desire to which for the moment we had nothing to add. The ultimate goal of this secret peasant society was to be an insurrection.

It was possible, in my opinion, to have some hopes of accomplishing the task only by following this rule: to adapt to the character of the peasant world view in one's form of action, not to introduce anything that would turn upside down the fundamental principles to which the common people are attached and accustomed, and, so to speak, to be a radical insofar as a peasant could be a radical. Proceeding from this general proposition, I had to take heed of those local peculiarities which I had discovered by observation; these local conditions themselves necessarily outlined for me the general program for action in pursuing my goal.

At the end of 1875 the most pressing issue for the peasants was how to let the tsar know about themselves.

The most influential of the peasants were dispersed among the district towns; it was necessary first of all to acquire their confidence. In Kiev there were eleven of them under the authority of the police; among them was a certain Lazar' Tenenik, about whom I had heard earlier. This was one of the richest peasants, a former cantonal judge, and a man of some age. In his family only two male souls were registered, and this circumstance, it would seem, meant that standing for allotment by souls did not hold any personal profit for him, especially since, as the head of a rich and influential household, he could always get a tract of twenty or more *desiatiny;* there were many examples of this. However, Lazar' Tenenik was one of those who held out with special stubbornness for allocation by souls and, since he was a judge, he exerted no little influence on the firm stand of the whole canton of Shabel'niki.

It was in the guise of a peasant from Kherson Province that I first became acquainted with him. *[In his deposition,*[20] *Stefanovich said that he located Tenenik in December 1875 by inquiring at the police station.]* After several meetings with him, I let him know that I had something important to impart. His interest caught, he asked, "Tell me, good fellow, is it good or evil you bring for us?" I explained that I was acting in behalf of my fellow villagers and was empowered by them to take a petition to the tsar. Furthermore, I insinuated the idea that if as many emissaries as possible appeared before the tsar with petitions, his concern for the peasants would be aroused so much the sooner. Therefore I proposed that their emissary should join me. *[According to his deposition, Stefanovich was not so diffident, but volunteered at once to represent Shabel'niki before the tsar.]*

Lazar' was extremely interested in my proposal and hastened to communicate it to the others *[that is, to the other Chigirin peasants being held at Kiev; most of the peasants with whom Stefanovich parleyed had signed the petition reproduced on pages 118-120.]*[21] By no means all of them, however, responded to me as trustfully as Lazar' did; quite simply, they suspected that I was a policeman in disguise, sent by the authorities to discover their intentions. But my urgings not to yield by "signing up" and to be firm in the hope for a favorable outcome allayed their suspiciousness. However, some of them continued to think my proposal was some kind of trick by the squires, and, as proof that I was not lying, demanded that I show them my commission from the community *[that is, from the village in Kherson Province that Stefanovich pretended to represent]*. Satisfied on this count, the peasants became more forthright. They did not know the real situation at home (this was in December of 1875 and they had been taken away from their homes in May of the same year) and their relatives had not visited them for a long time. Hence they did not know whether a man suitable for the role of emissary

and the necessary resources *[for his trip]* was to be found in Shabel'-
niki. I said that before I went to Peter *[St. Petersburg]* , I had to go
home again; the peasants pleaded with me to go by way of Shabel'-
niki and see some of the *dusheviki.* Among them, they thought, there
ought to be a volunteer to go with me to the tsar. I agreed and set
out to Lazar's wife in Shabel'niki.

I was struck by the woman's astonishment that I had managed to
get through without being noticed by the *atkoviki,* which invariably
entailed being taken to the police station. This happy fortuity was
due first of all to my arriving in the evening without any baggage,
which gave me the appearance of a local resident, and then to the
little boy, who explained how I could avoid the police net of the
aktoviki. The family received me with trust and joy because I bore
news and greetings from the head of the family. The wife at once
ordered her children to stand guard so that there would be time to
hide me in the event that some of the authorities approached the
house. She knew all the details of the public affairs of her village,
and was so engrossed in them that I thought it possible with scarcely
any delay to tell her the real reason for my visit. In her opinion,
there was no one in the village suitable for the role of emissary. Anyone of any significance, including those on whom the peasants in
Kiev had been counting, had been arrested. All the same, she wanted
to hold a discussion with someone and pass along the results when I
came by again on my return trip from home to Kiev.

That visit took place two weeks later. I was received with the same
secrecy as before. Late in the evening, when all the children were
already asleep, the woman brought in two peasants with whom I
was supposed to chat. They confirmed what she had said: there
was no one in the village willing to take responsibility for the petition, and finally, there was no one from whom the money necessary
for this affair could be collected. (It is well known that peasants cus-
tomarily conceive any kind of petitioning to entail significant expenses. Incidentally, the celebrated Priadko was by no means scrupulous or selfless when he represented the community.) Eventually the
peasants began to ask if I would put in a word for them—it would
be all the same, after all, since I would see the tsar, and they promised "to pray to God til the end of time" for me. Naturally, I did not
refuse, and the next day I was led out of the village by obscure paths.
This time, however, the tractholders did detect that I had visited
Lazar's wife; they let the police know and the authorities were not

slow to inquire who had come and where he had gone. Lazar's wife said that some "traveling man" had stopped to spend the night, and, thanks to the fact that she indicated the opposite direction from the road I had taken, my pursuers did not catch up with me.

The peasants in Kiev responded with chagrin to the news I brought; I did not tell them that two Shabel'niki peasants had asked me to intercede for them before the tsar, and waited for them to request it themselves. But obviously they could not bring themselves to ask it, solely because they did not hope that I would take on so important a mission without compensation. It was only after I explained how important it was for me personally that the tsar should see supplicants from many villages and not just from mine, that they "humbly" asked me to write a petition for them, too, describing in it the brutality of the punitive expedition and telling how the authorities were coercing them to accept the acts and had hidden from them the tsar's real *ukazy*. Among other things, they asked me not to fail to include in the petition the words the governor had said to an assembly of all the peasants: "the land is not the tsar's but the squires'." They were satisfied with my wording of the petition and, promising to return in the month of May, I set out for Peter. This was in February 1876.

So it was that a significant part of my goal was attained. But this success was far from easy to achieve. Frequently the peasants' confidence, which I had seemingly acquired, would give way to mistrust; there were two stubborn skeptics among them, who generally did not even come to the meetings with me, and they frequently kept the trustfulness of the rest in check. Finally, I realized that for the success of the cause it was necessary, insofar as possible, not to reveal anything about me that was alien to the peasantry, at least initially, when their trust was wavering frequently. This circumstance, putting me as it did in a position of strain, made my prolonged conversations with the peasants extremely wearisome; for example, it was impossible not to join the peasants in their fervent prayers to God to grant them success in their important undertaking. *[A strange complaint for Stefanovich. Perhaps, as a priest's son, he did find it painful to join hypocritically in religious ceremonies; perhaps he is trying to impress his readers with the delicacy of his scruples. Other atheist revolutionaries, including Stefanovich's friend*

Deich, who was born a Jew, eagerly joined peasants in their devotions in order to gain their confidence.]

Now it was up to me to bring "from the tsar" the plan for the revolutionary organization and put it to the peasants. All my observations confirmed my idea that only the authority principle could guarantee that the organization I had conceived would be accepted, and the authority principle in this instance could only mean the name of the tsar Alexander II. *[The "authority principle" was the radicals' euphemism for the idea of exploiting the peasantry's deference to authority by issuing revolutionary appeals in the tsar's name.]* Because the peasants lacked an ideological attitude to the affair, I resorted to an oath as a means of binding every member of the future society to the organization; in a certain setting, the ceremony of the oath would have a persuasive effect on a peasant. Of course, the strength of the organization would be largely premised on its intelligent design, in conformity with the conditions of peasant life, and also, to no lesser extent, on the influence that outstanding individuals and I myself could exert; it was because these conditions were not met, as would soon come to light, that the affair did not have the desired results.

Upon my return from Peter I was to present the peasants with, first of all, "The Secret Imperial Charter" and, second, with the "Code of the Peasant Society 'The Secret Druzhina.' " *[The text of both documents is given on pages 172-178; Stefanovich goes on to describe them for an audience which could not have seen the originals.]*

The charter consisted of an appeal or, more exactly, an order to the peasants in the name of the tsar; they were ordered to unite in secret societies for the purpose of an insurrection against the nobles. The idea was developed as follows: From the very beginning of his reign, the tsar had been concerned about the welfare of the peasantry, but always encountered stubborn resistance from the nobles. In the Manifesto of February 19, 1861 *[abolishing serfdom]* he had granted to the peasants not only personal freedom, but also all the land for their own use, making all the estates of the realm equal in the amount of their allotment (the nobles should retain their houses and grounds—such is the opinion of the *narod*). But the squires did not permit the tsar's will to be put into full effect, and by means of all kinds of cunning and deception they left the peasants almost in the same position as before. Finally, the tsar, lacking supporters even in his own family (the heir was for the nobles) and everywhere surrounded by enemies, reached the conclusion that solely on his own authority he was utterly powerless to do any good for the peasants and proposed to the peasants that they should struggle for their interests themselves. And to this end ordered the whole peasantry to unite in secret societies, called "Secret Druzhiny," and prepare their forces for an armed insurrection against the heir to the throne, the grand princes, the nobles, the bureaucrats, and the priests.

The secret societies were to be organized on the model of the charter, which the tsar had ratified. At the head of the Secret Druzhiny of a given area stood commissars, who comprised the "Council of Commissars," the center of the revolutionary leadership. The tsar declared that even after his death the peasant cause should be maintained and pursued to the end.

That is the essence of the "Imperial Secret Charter." It was printed on a large sheet of Bristol board with a gold seal *[inscribed]* : "Emperor Alexander II."

The Code of the peasant society "The Secret Druzhina" was composed of six chapters. Here briefly is their contents. (1) The obligations of the commissar consist of directing and supervising the course of affairs of a Druzhina for a given area, providing them *[sic]* with subsidies and issuing supplements to the charter, which are to be drawn up together with the council of elders and have compulsory force for the Druzhina. (2) The obligation of each member of the Secret Druzhina: Each member joining the Secret Society takes an oath of fidelity to it and is accepted only with the guarantee of two *druzhinniki [members]. Druzhinniki* are obliged to help each other in need; everyone should have his own pike and keep it until the time of the insurrection; should contribute 5 kopecks every month to the treasury of the Druzhina, and should strive tirelessly to recruit new members. Twenty-five *druzhinniki* comprise an Eldership and elect an elder from among themselves. (3) Obligations of the elder: The elder supervises the affairs of his Eldership, collects the cash dues, administers the oath to new members, and sees to it that the existence of the society is kept strictly secret. The elder is elected for three months. (4) The Council of Elders: Twenty Elderships comprise an *Atamanstvo*. All the Elderships of the *Atamanstvo*[22] form an administration or Council. (5) Obligations of the ataman: The ataman is elected by the council from among the elders. He is the intermediary in the Druzhina's relations with the commissar. He, so to speak, is the executive authority, while the council is the legislative. (6) The Treasurer is also elected by the council only from among the elders and is in charge of the society's funds.

At the end of the charter is the text of the oath and the ceremony for its administration: "before the icon of the Savior, the Bible, a burning candle, and two pikes or knives arranged in the form of a cross." In most copies of the Code the Charter is also included, at the beginning. *[But these copies did not circulate among the peasants until just before the Druzhina was destroyed; see page 188.]* The seal of the Council of Commissars is affixed to the Code; its design represents a crossed pike and axe. Such was the Code. The text of the oath was also printed on separate sheets.

I was able to return from Peter only in November of 1876, while I had promised the peasants to return in May, no later. *[The delay was due to difficulties in arranging for the printing of the Charter, Code, and Oath; as we will see, Stefanovich did not think the peasants would accept handwritten documents as genuine.]* The peasants, of course, might have thought that I had suffered the usual fate of peasant emissaries, and forgotten my existence; therefore, as early as June a letter from me was brought to Shabel'niki (where there were already many who knew where I had gone and why), informing them of the favorable outcome of the commission laid upon me and hinting that I would bring very important papers.* Relatives brought this letter to the peasants in Kiev as well. It brought their expectations to a high pitch, and when I arrived in Kiev the peasants greeted me with enormous joy.

At a meeting with the peasants (there were still nine of them, three had gone home) I announced that I had seen the tsar and received a document from him, which I promised to read to them, but only provided they would give me an oath to keep secret everything they would learn from it. They eagerly agreed; I unrolled then the great sheet of the Secret Imperial Charter and read it, explaining each idea. Then I proposed that they organize a secret society for the purpose of insurrection, since that was the only means of attaining their wishes.

[Stefanovich's note:] This letter was brought to Lazar's wife. The *aktoviki* saw that a man came to her and read "a paper" (the letter); a few minutes after his departure the canton authorities dropped in and carried out a search, intending to catch the unknown man. They did not find either the letter or the man.

It was obvious that the peasants had not expected anything of the kind, and they did not give me any answer at the first meeting. They must have thought that when I presented their petition to the tsar, the immediate result would be an order to release them to their homes without "signing up" and, if not a visit from the tsar himself, at least the formation of a commission which would decide the matter in their favor and satisfy all their desires.

The next day I managed to win over three (including Lazar' Tenenik), but the skepticism of the rest disturbed them and they began to waver. Some peasants flatly said that this was some kind of cunning scheme of the nobles to trick them onto the side of the minister (that is, make them tractholders) and one (subsequently very active) wondered, "Could this be some Polish prank?" I myself prompted this mistrust with a mistake of my own: the trouble was that I had spoken of the necessity, after taking the oath of fidelity to the secret society, of "signing up," in order to be able to set out for home and there serve as the founders and organizers of the Secret Druzhina. But "signing up," the peasants thought, always entailed making a cross, and this they regarded as a kind of oath, which would enslave them to the nobles. (When illiterates have to sign their names, they are usually made to inscribe a cross with their own hands, or else the so-called "taking of hands" is employed, whereby the literate who is signing for the illiterate takes him by the hand and then signs.) When I finally understood what the trouble was, I hastened to declare that if the signature is to be given by making a cross, then it should not under any circumstances be given.

This compromise seemed to reassure the peasants. The next day three of them expressed their consent to taking the oath at once, but I advised them to win over the rest, so that secret matters would not be entrusted to those who were not willing to take the oath. After a few days all of them gave their consent except for one old man, who still hestitated. They insisted that I take the oath first. I explained the words of the oath and fulfilled their request. Then, after asking the peasants to first explain what they understood the words of the oath to mean, I began the ritual; but the indecisive old man was still hesitating, and only the suasions of the rest, some of them even of a threatening kind, made him cross himself and kneel. *[The reluctant old man, whose name was Efrem Tenenik, later overcame his misgivings to the point of serving as an elder and an active recruiter for the Druzhina.*[23]*]*

Once the oath had been taken, I devoted several meetings to explaining the obligations imposed by the Code. They understood the general system at once, but some details (for example, the significance of a password) were hard to assimilate. On the other hand, they made many practical suggestions which I took into account later, in compiling the supplementary code. The peasants thought that some functions which entailed drawing a peasant away from his own work would be performed laxly, while drunkenness would certainly lead to the disclosure of the secret of the society's existence. In view of the latter circumstances, they planned, if the Druzhina had many members, to limit by a decree of the village community the number of taverns in a village.

From the Code, the peasants learned that recruiting new members was an essential obligation of a *druzhinnik,* and thus they realized the necessity of going home. I explained to them that once they had taken the oath, a simple signature, "without a cross," could not have any compulsory force. Furthermore, there was no literate among the eight of them, which would certainly limit the success of their activity as the first recruiters for the Secret Druzhina. Therefore I proposed that at least one of them should give the police chief his assent (fictitious) to "signing up," and if he was not then required to make a cross, then he would "sign up" in order to go home, initiate a trusted, literate peasant into the affair, and bring him to me. Lazar' Tenenik volunteered to do this. The next day he triumphantly informed me that not only had they not required a cross, but they had not so much as touched his hand before they inscribed his name.

I did not yet have a printed Code, and decided not to provide Lazar' with a handwritten copy, since that would not be impressive in the eyes of the peasants. Therefore Lazar' left without any documents; I simply told him that the literate whom he singled out should swear to keep secret everything that he would hear from Lazar', and then I would give him the formal oath myself.

Two weeks thereafter, in February 1877, Lazar' returned, but alone. He had found a suitable literate in the person of a retired noncommissioned officer named Efim Oleinik, but he could not come to me because of some kind of family affairs; he expressed complete willingness to serve the cause if I would come to Shabel'-niki myself and display "a real document." Furthermore, Lazar' also asked me to come since he himself, because he had signed the act and arrived without any proof that he had signed for the sake of the Secret Druzhina, was not really trusted.

It was not immediately possible for me to go with Lazar'. I provided him with a printed Code and also with printed copies of the oath and instructed him to show these documents to Oleinik and give him the oath; I promised to come in two weeks to Cherkassy *[a district town on the Dnepr, thirty miles from Shabel'niki]* ; Lazar' should wait for me there and prepare a place for a meeting.

Lazar' predicted enormous success for our cause and generally was remarkable for the optimism of his views. A gentle and trusting person, he loved to express himself allegorically; his figurative speech usually suffered from vagueness of thought, but it seems that it was just these qualities that made him appealing. A peasant, excited by the mysterious air with which Lazar' promised an escape from his life of suffering, readily deferred to him. In Lazar' I did not detect any trace of a selfish outlook on his participation in the cause; his behavior with me was simple and not marked with any element of obeisance before an important dignitary like myself, which one could not help seeing in the others. In a word, Lazar' could be a marvelous propagandist or recruiter for the secret society, but scarcely a good organizer.

Once again I could not go to Cherkassy at the time agreed upon *[because, according to Stefanovich's deposition, the railroad line was out of service]*. In the meantime, Lazar' had not been idle. A rumor spread among the *dusheviki,* and very quickly, because they were such a cohesive group, that Lazar' had brought back some reassuring news. The peasants came to him themselves and asked him to "tell all." They would say, "Wherever you go, old man, take us, too; we have suffered together and are willing to die together."

Here Lazar' showed that he was by no means a conspirator. One dark night he gathered as many as 300 people in the steppe, on an excavated burial-mound called "The Cossack Grave"; a literate read the Code by lantern light, and then and there all 300 or so took the oath.

The authorities were not slow to learn of this event. It happened in this way: a certain Leukhin, a former clerk of the canton, had been present with the others at the meeting at the Cossack Grave and was so overwhelmed by all that he heard and saw that he went out of his mind. He went to the priest and began to curse him because he had always put pressure on the peasants to agree to the tract system, while the tsar's true will was quite different; and *[he said]* that Lazar' had brought the tsar's real *ukaz* and, covered with medals and "sword in hand," had read it to the people. However disconnected Leukhin's babblings were, in any event the priest could not help noticing that something was not right in the village. The matter was officially investigated, but since searches disclosed nothing and no one would confirm the madman's words, they were simply taken for the ravings of a half-wit. When I learned about this through relatives of the *druzhinniki* who remained at Kiev, I hastened to set out for Shabel'niki, especially since breaking my promise to come at the appointed time had cooled the peasants' enthusiasm, and matters had come to a halt after the assembly at the Cossack Grave. I sent ahead two *druzhinniki* (after Lazar's example they were no longer fearful about "the cross") with an epistle to the Druzhina in general and to Lazar' in particular; I asked him to prepare a secure place for a meeting and come to get me in Kiev.

Lazar' came during Saint Thomas Week; by his report, my epistle had caused such a stir that in a few days the number of *druzhinniki* reached 500. It goes without saying that this rapid success was merely quantitative. As I was obliged to discover subsequently from conversations with some *[of the* druzhinniki*]*, a majority did not understand the meaning of the Code; there were those who did not even figure out the purpose of the secret society. These latter had simply yielded to the allure of the words "Land and Liberty," which means so much to the peasant, while the name of the tsar, which is mentioned in the Code, meant that they understood matters in this sense: anyone who takes the oath as offered will receive land and liberty from the tsar. *[This is a striking admission on Stefanovich's part, and out of line with the rest of his account. When the Druzhina was discovered by the police, many peasants testified that they had always "understood matters" in just the sense Stefanovich indicates here. If this was a general tendency, what was the practical significance of the Charter, the Code, and the Druzhina itself?]*

At the end of April, my comrade *[Ivan Bokhanovskii]* and I, accompanied by Lazar', set out for the village of Rossoshintsy, where the meeting was scheduled. *[Rossoshintsy is ten miles south of Shabel'niki, on the way to Chigirin.]* It was market day, and wagons headed for the fair at Khudiaki came towards us in a steady stream. This circumstance was very handy for Lazar', for he had departed for Kiev secretly, without official permission. "That one's one of us and

so is that one, but here's one that isn't," Lazar' would say and quickly flick the hood of his jacket up over his head so as not to be recognized by someone who was not "one of us." But over a distance
of eighteen to twenty versts *[about twelve miles]*, Lazar' had to
resort to this precaution very rarely, for a majority of those we encountered were "one of us." It was obvious that there had been a
vigorous campaign of agitation.

About six versts short of Rossoshintsy we paid off the driver and,
turning from the high road, went into the village on foot. It was
already evening when we entered the *druzhinnik's* house. About
nine or ten o'clock a group assembled in the shed where the meeting
was to take place. A ring of sentinels, both around the shed and
along the road, protected us from danger. In the village of
Rossoshintsy the *druzhinniki* as yet numbered only a few dozen, so
these precautions were not wasted.

At the meeting there were 28 elders from four villages, and their
ataman E. Oleinik. I tried first of all to learn how the peasants understood the purpose of the "Secret Druzhina," what their attitude
was to the impending task of insurrection and how they had organized themselves. It was obvious that the Druzhina elders present were,
so to speak, the most intellectual element *[of the peasantry]*; some
of them were literate. The ataman was a retired sergeant in the
guards and his deputy had been a sergeant major. They all knew the
Code of the society and understood it well, although so far there
had only been one printed copy in their hands; however, a multitude of manuscript copies had circulated from hand to hand. *[Ac-
cording to the results of the subsequent official inquiry, this
multitude amounted to two or three copies at this time.]* The slogan
used in the Code, "Land and Liberty," was wholly intelligible to
them, and passwords, which the first recruits had found incompre-
hensible, were now a widespread practice. As the elders themselves
admitted, however, there were also many who entered the Druzhina
thinking that thereby they would somehow escape the hated "minister" and his officials. The extent to which the elders and the entire
Druzhina at large clearly understood the inevitability of insurrection
was clear from the fact that the most important question bothering
the peasants before my arrival was the preparation of pikes and
other weapons. For quite obvious reasons I am not going to relate
how the *druzhinniki* coped with this question; I will only say that
they were concerned about it to an extent that I did not expect.

[In his deposition, Stefanovich stated, "By no means all" of the elders he met at Rossoshintsy had pikes, "since it was difficult to obtain them because the tractholders kept tireless watch on their doings";[24] also, see page 192.]

One Eldership was usually organized in each section of a village. Every member tried at once to induce his kinfolk into the Society; it was easier to approach a relative and, in the event of misfortune, he would be more likely to spare his brother or father-in-law. It was hard to establish how many members the Druzhina had. Only in the villages of Shabel'niki and Pogorel'tsy was there proper division into elderships. The ataman Oleinik handed over to me a list of the members of his *Atamanstvo*. The peasants attached enormous importance to the making of these lists, and although this device was very impractical from a conspiratorial point of view, it was necessary to put up with it. Usually a peasant who joined the Druzhina immediately insisted that his name be entered in the list, after which he felt, as it were, secure from any official tricks. In one village of Adamovka Canton there were only two or three dozen members, and they had not yet managed to organize elderships. Some maintained that when they spent the holidays with their relatives on the other side of the Tiasmin River, they had won them over to the Druzhina, but no one knew how matters stood there now. On the other hand, Shabel'niki Canton was almost entirely in the hands of the Druzhina. There were frequent meetings—either to discuss some question or other or to administer the oath to new members—and they could not but attract the attention of the tractholders. To discourage them from spying, the Druzhina had given an order to set up nighttime patrols. These patrols made their way around the village by night and caught spies; frequently both sides put up a fight as a result. Because they were used to hostility between the two parties, the officials of the canton had so far paid no attention to this. *[They paid so little attention that there is nothing in the official record to indicate that these patrols were ever mounted. The ataman later testified that he was planning to organize such patrols when he was arrested. But see page 157.]* The Druzhina had its own agents in the cantonal offices, and they were ordered to inform their elders about any plans or ideas the cantonal authorities might have. Yet despite the incident of the madman Leukhin, danger did not yet threaten from this quarter.

In its expansion, the Secret Society was so far limited to *dusheviki.*

They were not willing to admit *aktoviki* into the Druzhina. Many of
those they rejected, however, had been compelled by the punitive
force to accept the acts, or else had yielded to the cunning of
officials, and were now extremely dissatisfied with their unwilling
reconciliation with the authorities, but all the same they did not
enjoy the affection of the stubborn *dusheviki*. A majority of the
elders were against opening a way into the Druzhina for them. I had
to argue with the assembly for a long time about the impracticality
and injustice of this measure. The spread of the Secret Society
amidst the *aktoviki* would give the Druzhina the entire populations
not only of villages but of cantons and consequently make it possible to have its own cantonal officials. The Council of Elders yielded
to this last argument, although they ruled that any *aktovik* must
have twice as many guarantors as a *dushevik*. *[There is no evidence
that* aktoviki *were accepted into the Druzhina, and Stefanovich's
associate Deich stated many years later that they were not.*[25]*]*

There was not a kopeck in the treasury of the Druzhina *[yet there
were several hundred* druzhinniki, *each of them obliged to pay five
kopecks a month in dues]*; the ataman appealed to me to submit a
request to the tsar for a grant of money to aid the utterly ruined
Shabel'niki peasants. I tried to convince them that they should expect no aid from the tsar, that he had done all he could by indicating
the way to escape from the captivity of the squires and the officials;
they should put no more hopes on the tsar. To ease their displeasure
and disappointment, I went on to say that through me they could
appeal for aid to another *druzhina,* made up of *muzhiki* like theirs,
but a "Russian" one; for *druzhiny* were obliged to help one another
with money and other necessities. I gave them to hope that in this
way they would probably receive the sum they wanted (1,000
rubles). By so doing I wanted, on the one hand, to destroy the
hopes they placed in the tsar and, on the other, to stimulate mutual
aid among elderships and *atamanstva* by this vivid example. *[Ac-
cording to his deposition, Stefanovich also released the* druzhinniki
from the obligation to pay dues.[26]*]*

Since I intended to create the organization on founds that
would educate its members in a spirit of hostility to the existing
political order, I saw the development of so-called "illegality"
*[i.e., the status of fugitives living on false identity papers or with
none, as many radicals did]* as a major element serving this purpose.
Therefore I devoted a good deal of time to persuading the peasants

not to surrender to the authorities, but rather, if there was the slightest danger of being arrested, to hide, to go to another village. The *[fugitive] druzhinnik*'s fellow members should support his family, help them with their work, and so on. By the way, that very night one member had to become "an illegal." This was Lazar' Tenenik, whom I have already mentioned. Although he was confined to his place of residence and under the surveillance of the district police, he had twice gone to Kiev to see me without the permission of the sheriff. The tractholders somehow sniffed out the fact that Lazar' was not in the village and denounced him. Towards morning a *druzhinnik* ran from Shabel'niki (fifteen versts from the place where we were meeting) and informed us that a warning had come from the cantonal office that the sheriff had sent a constable to get Lazar'. It was decided then and there that Lazar' should appear no more in Shabel'niki, but live under another name on the other side of the Tiasmin River, enlarging the secret society there. It was decided to give three rubles to his family at once from the treasury (in which I had deposited 50 rubles) and to do the same every month. I proposed to provide Lazar' with a passport.

It was already sunrise and a wagon stood ready for us in the courtyard. After giving the ataman several printed copies of the Code, we were starting to say goodbye when the ataman called me to one side and said that, to strengthen the Druzhina's trust in us, it would be appropriate for us to take the oath of loyalty to it in the presence of all the elders. This was the sense of his irresolute remarks. My comrade and I eagerly agreed. They brought a table into the shed, spread a cloth upon it, set out the icon and lit the wax candle, not forgetting to arrange two knives in the shape of a cross. We read the text of the oath, which the ataman checked against the printed sheet. Everyone was obviously satisfied. "Now we see with our own eyes that you are *druzhinniki* just like us," they said to us. So concluded the meeting of the Council of Elders at Rossoshintsy. *[The elders present later testified that they did make Stefanovich take a solemn oath at Rossoshintsy—not the oath of loyalty to the Druzhina, which he had already taken at Kiev, but an oath that the Charter and Code were genuine.* [27] *]*

To trace the subsequent history of the Secret Society step by step is very difficult. With the decision to allow the *aktoviki* to become members, the Druzhina grew rapidly. At first the life of the Society was principally concentrated in the canton of Shabel'niki. But soon new centers formed, pursuing a more or less independent existence and not checking the opinion at Shabel'niki on every matter that arose. In my "epistles" to the Druzhina, I repeatedly but vainly urged that the massive admission of members be halted so the Druzhina could take up its internal affairs. By May there was already a rumor circulating throughout the area that those who wanted to be freed from bondage to the squires and officials should sign up in some kind of society and that the people of Shabel'niki were in charge of it. Hence the Canton of Adamovka decided to send delegates to Shabel'niki to find out for certain just what they were up to. An explanation was given, the delegates were accepted into the Druzhina, provided with the Code, and sent back. In two weeks the *druzhinniki* of Adamovka already amounted to 250. The first question that arose in this new center was the establishment of direct relations with me, by-passing Shabel'niki. Arrangements were made to send three spokesmen to Krylov *[a town on the border of Kiev and Kherson Provinces, about twenty-five miles from Shabel'- niki]*, where I was due to arrive in the middle of June. But they were not destined to see me. The trouble was that two elders from the village of Mordva set out along with the Adamovka spokesmen. These elders had already managed to lose their legal status, and the authorities were looking hard for them. They were arrested at the fair in Krylov, and the Adamovka spokesmen along with them.[28] By this time the rumor that something important was going on in Chigirin District had penetrated to every corner of the region, and the very word *"druzhinnik"* was well known as a synonym for breaking away from ordinary, peaceable folk. The *druzhinniki* from Mordva had attracted the attention of the police because people at the fair pointed to them and said they were *druzhinniki*. A list of 250 members was found on the Adamovka peasants, and on Ivan Piskavyi a list of persons in the village of Mordva who had weapons. It was only thanks to the assurances of the arrested men that these lists denoted peasants who wanted to sign some kind of petition to the governor that the authorities did not discover their real significance. However, those arrested were not released. The district officials were becoming more convinced that something was afoot among the peasants. To be sure, they imagined this "something" was related to the old business of land and the acts of lustration. All the same, surveillance was heightened, especially in the canton of Shabel'niki. Egged on by the constable, the *aktoviki*

doubled their vigilant watch on the *dusheviki.* Lazar' Tenenik, who
sneaked into his native village to see his family, was detected by the
aktoviki, seized, and taken to the district police. Although this arrest deprived the Druzhina of its most active member, the secret of
its existence remained absolutely intact. Lazar' Tenenik kept a stubborn silence, and the infuriated authorities exiled this old man of
65 years to the city of Kovno.

Constantly distracted from its own affairs by the danger of discovery, the Druzhina began to think up ways of lulling the intense
vigilance of its enemies. The *dusheviki* who, as I have already said,
comprised a majority of the canton of Shabel'niki, had so far refused to take land *[allotments].* It was largely this circumstance
that gave the authorities reason to look on them as a disloyal element, not pacified even after the punitive expedition. The Council
of Elders decided to inform the sheriff that the *dusheviki* had finally
agreed to take land according to the terms of the lustration. At first
this measure caused some to suspect the Secret Society of treachery,
but the Council persuaded the *druzhinniki* to agree, relying on this
reasoning: tenure of land on the conditions demanded by the government would not be of long duration, since soon the uprising would
change the system in accord with the goals of the Secret Society; in
the meantime the authorities, no longer regarding them as rebels,
would cease keeping watch on them, while the stirrings that had been
noticed among the people could easily be represented as caused by
the peasants' discussion of the question whether or not to take the
land. With the attention of the authorities diverted, it would be
possible for the Society calmly to take up its internal affairs, to
ascertain the number of its members, prepare weapons, and so on.
The ataman and two elders from Shabel'niki appeared at Krylov to
learn my attitude to this directive by the Council. The plan was
wisely conceived, but its effects were paralyzed by an unexpected
circumstance. The head of the canton of Shabel'niki managed to get
a recently recruited *druzhinnik* drunk and worm something out of
him. *[This was presumably Avton Omel'chenko; see page 181.]* The
head of the canton discovered that the peasants were taking an oath
to some kind of Druzhina, and while he could not elicit more def-
inite information from the drunk, all the same this incident confirmed finally the conviction that dangerous, antigovernment propaganda
was being conducted among the *narod.* The matter reached the
governor and went thence to the Gendarmerie; a special commission

headed by General Pavlov hurried to Chigirin. For two weeks the investigators rode from village to village; a great many searches were carried out, but without success. For these two weeks the *druzhinniki* halted their propaganda and, each time the enemy made an incursion, they would immediately let other villages know of the approaching danger. When one *druzhinnik* was sent to warn the people of Shabel'niki of a new descent on Mordva, his horse collapsed, but he ran all the way to the ataman's house and, utterly exhausted, brought news of the danger. Even children were infected by the universal feeling and, seeing a crowd of pilgrims at a distance on the road, ran through the village crying, "Muscovites, Muscovites!" *[i.e., Russians, not Ukrainians, and therefore officials or soldiers.]*

Thanks to this kind of precaution, the gendarme commission's two weeks of effort succeeded only in convincing the governor that the district police, in an excess of zeal, had made a mountain out of a molehill. The gendarmes returned to Kiev with nothing; no papers had been found anywhere and none of the arrested had said anything concerning the Society. The Druzhina breathed more freely than ever before.

I advised the Society, both orally and in writing, to stop recruiting new members and to start putting its affairs in order. This advice, coupled with its own experience, compelled the Druzhina to moderate its propaganda and show a concern for the inner life of the organization. This was not easy to manage. Ordinary, everyday needs were intertwined with a mass of new questions, which had never before penetrated into the life of the poor *muzhik,* whose concerns are at least few in number. I must say that I and the two comrades associated with me had a very insignificant role to play in the inner workings of the organizational machine we ourselves had created. It was necessary to live among the peasants themselves, to penetrate into every detail of the *muzhik's* life, in order to understand the real reason why this or that problem had arisen within the Society and to be able to direct the Society in accord with revolutionary goals. Our own encounters with the Druzhina were more nearly, so to speak, official, and we always stood in a relationship of authority. For this reason alone, much was hidden from our eyes; the directives I gave sometimes did not correspond to circumstances of the situation and consequently were not carried out. There seemed to be only one means of directing the inner life of the Society, and that was to take a few revolutionaries from the intelligentsia and settle them, in the capacity of simple *druzhinniki*, in the places where the Druzhina existed. We understood perfectly how necessary this measure was and searched for appropriate people. Unfortunately, we did not manage to find them, and this delayed the fulfillment of our plans. In the meantime the Druzhina coped as best it could with its internal chaos.

In the forefront of the life of the Society, and especially of the atamanstvo at Shabel'niki, was hunger. I paid out 1,000 rubles, supposedly borrowed from the Russian Druzhina, in sums of 150 or 200 rubles. *[In his deposition, Stefanovich itemized the money he paid out, totaling somewhat more than 500 rubles; according to other evidence, he paid out 800 rubles to Oleinik alone. Where did he get the money? We would like to know.* [27] *]* All this money went to feed the hungriest families. At first, the Council turned the money over to the elders, each of whom would divide it among the needy of his eldership. But this method proved extremely impractical. The trouble was that the people of Shabel'niki were famous far and wide for their poverty. Previously they had fed themselves by begging, making their way from village to village and collecting scraps of bread. All at once their destitution ended and their womenfolk began to buy bread at the fairs in Chigirin, Khudiaki, and Medvedovka, paying cash. Naturally this caused curious talk about where they got the money, and so on. All this attracted the attention of the authorities, who had reason enough anyway to take a suspicious view of the people of Shabel'niki. On the other hand, the very appearance of rubles, which had not been seen for so long, was enough to arouse passions in a major way, especially among women. Once a rumor circulated among them that the Council of Elders was hiding the Society's funds and had issued less than it should have. A mob of women surrounded the ataman's house and threateningly demanded the return of the money. It was difficult to calm them and persuade them to go home. In order to avoid talk among the people and envy among the peasant women, the Council of Elders decided henceforward to relieve the needy in kind, rather than in cash. A load or two of grain was purchased at the markets on the left bank and distributed to families according to the number of souls.

The role of women in the history of the Secret Society was rather significant. Although formally they were not part of the Druzhina, in fact they knew almost everything that happened in it; it was not possible to quarantine the *druzhinniki* from their wives. Although the Code did not mention admitting women to the Secret Druzhina, usually the wife of an entering member was also requested to swear to keep the Society's secret. However, it regularly fell to me to listen to complaints about the loose tongues of the womenfolk. Many seriously took the view that the womenfolk would ruin everything. The priests in particular elicited a good deal from them. To this end the rector of Shabel'niki made use of vodka and even flirted with the younger women in a way inappropriate to his priestly dignity. Once the elders earnestly requested me to rid them of this philandering spy, who presented a danger both to the Secret Society's cause and to the family happiness of young couples. But at the same time there were women who enjoyed universal respect and were very useful to the Druzhina. Such a one was Lazar's wife, who was entrusted with many secrets otherwise confided only to the elders. Another, the wife of a rich peasant (Adamovka Canton), was put in jail with her two small children because she would not say where her husband, who was living illegally, was. She sat in jail for half a year, her household was utterly ruined, her house boarded over and her grain carried off, but still they could get nothing from her. Yet she knew very much, and even the Code and the lists were in her keeping.

A serious circumstance, which was to cause the affair to become known, was drunkenness. In a supplement to the Code, it was necessary to include an obligatory limitation on vodka consumption; naturally, there was a good deal of talk about this. Newly entering members, after taking the oath, thought it was their duty to seal it with a drink, and the elders, to whom, by decision of the Council, fell the duty of eliminating this custom, did not always find within themselves enough firmness to resist temptation.

After the invasion of the Kiev gendarmerie in July, which was precipitated by the cantonal elder's getting a *druzhinnik* drunk, the Council began to think seriously about abolishing taverns; they intended to leave only one in the canton. Preparations were already under way for the formalities this would require [*Taverns operated in villages by permission of the peasants' elected officials.*], and only the exposure of the Secret Society forestalled them.

Apart from the reasons so far given, a further measure of chaos was brought upon the Secret Society by the hostility of individuals for one another and especially by the vanity and avarice of the ataman. Efim Oleinik exploited both his own and neighboring *druzhiny.* Taking advantage of the Council's ignorance of the mechanics of paperwork, he would include in his reports very large sums for expenses under this heading. For example, six rubles per month went to him for paper and candles. He tried to dispel my doubts about the accuracy of his accounts with assurances that for enhanced security he had to write in daytime by candlelight in a dark cellar, and since paper was a forbidden substance in their area, he had to go specially to Chigirin, thirteen miles away, to buy it. Unconvinced by these excuses, I wrote to the Council advising more careful control over the expenditure of the Society's money. And when the Council began to keep more careful track of money, the ataman found another source of income. From each new entrant into the Druzhina he exacted a tribute for entering his name on the list. Furthermore, although he received fifteen rubles monthly by virtue of a ruling of the Council of Elders, he also asked compensation from the other *druzhiny* when they turned to him for advice. Being a soldier, used to submitting blindly to authority and accurately carrying out orders, he often acted in despite of the Council of Elders. *[In this instance, of course, the "orders" were Stefanovich's.]* Seeing that nighttime patrols, especially those of the young, caused disorders in the village and only increased the vigilance of the authorities, without achieving any purpose, I advised him not to let the young *druzhinniki* engage in pointless violence. Subsequently, for whatever reason, he held to a system of tranquility and order. When the *druzhina* at Adamovka, angered by the arrest of its three spokesmen at Krylov, decided to go to Chigirin and rescue them from jail, the ataman stopped them, arousing general discontent against himself. Spies sent in by the sheriff were roaming everywhere, and the *druzhinniki* wanted to settle accounts with some of them, but here, too, the ataman prevented them in the name of order and peace which, he maintained, were necessary until the time of open insurrection. But when I wrote to the Council that spies should not on any account be spared and instructed the ataman that he should not understand "order" to mean complicity with police agents, his tactics subsequently veered in completely the opposite direction. Once he insisted on burning down the cantonal administration building, to which the Council would not agree on the grounds that the venture would be dangerous to the houses of the *druzhinniki* themselves. Another time, when a rumor was circulating that some kind of official commission was due in the canton, he ordered the road into the village blocked and the squires kept out. The commission did not come, but the wandering crowds of lads with cudgels attracted the attention of passersby. All of this taken together—avarice and administrative incapacity—set many elders up in arms against the ataman. Voices were often raised for his replacement. But he stayed on, solely thanks to his literacy.

He had an especially dangerous enemy in Kuz'ma Prudkii, one of the most remarkable individuals that I have ever encountered among the peasantry. Kuz'ma was not literate; intelligent, capable, he was unusually assiduous and wholly devoted to the cause, without any selfish consideration. He passionately believed that an insurrection was possible, but at the same time did not suffer from excessive optimism. Kuz'ma was not living on hopes of some kind of outside aid, as many others were, and his attitude to me was absolutely straightforward, without the slightest servility. In his opinion, the ataman was doing more harm to the Secret Society than anyone else. He insisted that he be replaced, at the same time he adamantly refused in advance to succeed to his place.

Finally, I myself proposed that the Council elect another ataman. On August 15, Efim Oleinik came to me at Kiev and stated that he was no longer ataman. *[In his deposition, Stefanovich put it more accurately, saying that Oleinik reported that the Council of Elders intended to replace him.*[30]*]* With him came Andrei Prikhod'ko from the Adamovka *druzhina.* The people of Adamovka and Mordva declared themselves to be separate *atamanstva,* although neither village had 500 members (there were almost 500 in the former and no more than 150 in the latter). But they had decided to manage without the ataman at Shabel'niki. He did not like this separatism at all, solely, as wicked tongues had it, because the possibility of disposing of the funds of these two *druzhiny* had slipped from his grasp. The ataman had consistently found the inclinations of the separatists groundless and illegal; therefore the people of Adamovka had sent to learn my opinion of the matter. They also had another request for me. In September the new chief of the canton would be elected.* The Druzhina was counting on putting in its own man. Since they wanted to have the whole cantonal administration in the hands of "their own," the people of Adamovka asked me to provide them with a man to be clerk, for they had no one appropriate for the post.

*[Stefanovich's note:] Adamovka was not one of the disgraced cantons, and there the elder was still elected by the community, rather than appointed by the arbiter of the peace.

There could not have been a more opportune occasion for installing a man from the intelligentsia.

Kuz'ma was supposed to come to Kiev along with the ataman, but Efim Oleinik had tried to prevent him from meeting me. He came a day earlier than the one appointed, and when Kuz'ma arrived in Kiev alone, he could not find me at the place agreed upon, and therefore returned home. The reason for this deception was that the ataman had stolen a large amount, and Kuz'ma could expose him in a meeting with me.

The trial for the old Chigirin affair, which had dragged on since 1875, had begun in Kiev in June. The trial ended rather favorably for the peasants, at least compared to what they expected. Of the several dozen found guilty, only Foma Priadko was deprived of all rights and sent to Siberia; the rest were sentenced to jail for no more than two years.* Those on trial had practically expected hard labor and firing squads. Attributing the light sentences to the lawyers for the defense, the grateful peasants decided to present them with a hundred rubles. The ataman was entrusted with this money to give it to me for transmittal. I urged them not to deprive themselves of such a sum, saying that if the lawyers are good men, they will be quite satisfied by the peasants' feelings of gratitude; I turned the money over to the ataman for return to the Council of Elders. But the Council never saw this money again. Although I only learned about this theft when I was in jail, still there were already enough other reasons for taking an extremely suspicious attitude to the ataman. Therefore, since I wanted to acquaint myself with the state of affairs in the Secret Society in more detail and from more reliable sources, I instructed Oleinik and Andrei Prikhod'ko to assemble representatives from all the villages where there were even a few *druzhinniki* for personal conversations with me. The meeting was appointed for "The Oak," a spot on the left bank of the Dnepr. After providing both *druzhinniki* with letters to their *druzhiny* and printed copies of the Code, I took my leave from them.

This meeting with the *druzhinniki* was my last as a free man. On the road to Adamovka, after parting from the ataman, Prikhod'ko turned in to an inn to rest. There he met an acquaintance, a retired soldier named Konograi. They drank a glass apiece and chatted; Konograi brought more and more. Prikhod'ko, who had a weakness

*[*Stefanovich's note:*] Seventy-four were found guilty and 262 were acquitted.

for drink, relaxed *[and wondered]* why not attract this nice man into the Druzhina? Prikhod'ko let loose his eloquence. He even forgot to take the usual preliminary oath from his listener. Konograi eagerly agreed to become a *druzhinnik*, but evaded the oath and tried to learn where the Code was kept. Although Prikhod'ko was drunk, he remembered that it is not permitted to show the Code before the oath-taking. "All right," said Konograi, "we'll finish up tomorrow at your house." They parted, Prikhod'ko going home while Konograi hurried to Chigirin to the sheriff. "So you see, Y'r Ex'ency, they insist on an oath, otherwise they won't let the paper into my hands. What is your order?" The delighted sheriff, of course, ordered him to take the oath, awarded him a ten-ruble note for his zeal, and promised more as soon as the paper was turned over to him. The next day, Konograi was at Prikhod'ko's, the oath was taken and the Code was in his hands. "Listen, cousin," he said, "let's go now together to the sheriff with this piece of paper, you tell him the whole truth; then at least you won't be punished, and maybe you'll even get a reward." Seeing the distraught Prikhod'ko was hesitating, Konograi remarked, "You know, after all, the paper isn't so important, I can testify without you." Prikhod'ko had fallen into an ambush. His own interest spoke clearly in favor of Konograi's proposal, and they set out for the sheriff together. *[This story is essentially false, as we will see on page 185.]*

Of course, once the Code had been seized in this way, it became clear enough to the authorities what was going on. The Secret Society was discovered. There were arrests. The terrified authorities, expecting armed resistance from the peasants, made raids on villages accompanied by military units. They swooped down on Shabel'niki first. Here the initial victims were the ataman and several of the elders who did not manage to flee in time.

When I was in jail I was told that when the gendarmes burst into the ataman's house, the people stood nearby in an enormous crowd, opposite the drawn-up row of soldiers. As the *druzhinniki* told it, many expressed the intention of charging forward to rescue the ataman. When I asked why they had not done it, they answered there was no one there who would make the first move.

Oleinik held firm for about two weeks and even withstood beating, but when he was brought to Kiev, the ex-soldier could not hold out against the magical effect of Pavlov's general's epaulettes and reported everything that he so much as knew about and even more than had actually happened. He and Andrei Prikhod'ko indicated the place where we had last met, and on the 4th of September my comrades and I were arrested.

Almost all the district jails of Kiev Province were overflowing with *druzhinniki.* However, by no means was everyone in low spirits after this disaster. Many fled their villages and in other places managed to begin propaganda of a kind there had been only at the very beginning of the affair. They did not yet know that I had been arrested with my comrades, and this circumstance sustained the enthusiasm of some. Kuz'ma acted with amazing energy. Many villages which had previously held apart from direct participation now, seeing the savagery with which the authorities fell upon the *druzhinniki,* were finally convinced that the Druzhina's cause was a just one. Whatever the squires and officials oppose, must on that sole account be for the common people's benefit—such is the peasants' logic. *[The Druzhina did continue to spread somewhat even after it had been crushed; in the spring of 1878, Debagorii-Mokrievich encountered a young peasant at Shabel'niki who wanted to take the oath.[31]]*

A certain Gudz', a former head of the canton and an extremely influential man, had kept the canton aloof from the enthusiasm that prevailed among the people of Shabel'niki. Now this canton *[Borovitsa]* entered the Druzhina. A rumor was circulating that anyone who had not enrolled in the Druzhina by October 1 would be left under the squires. Under the influence of this rumor, the village of Mudrovka insistently demanded that Gudz' include it at once. Gudz' declined, thinking that it would be ruinous to the cause to include a whole village in the Druzhina. So the people of Mudrovka put him in a wagon by force, brought him to their village and compelled him to read the Code to an assembly of several hundred peasants and administer the oath to them. This incident quickly became known to the gendarmes, and Gudz' was arrested. Talking to me in jail, he complained of Kuz'ma Prudkii, who had supposedly circulated the rumor that the time for insurrection was near. *[Yet Stefanovich himself, according to later testimony, had instructed the druzhinniki to be ready for insurrection by October 1.[32]]* It was this, in his opinion, that had caused the general excitement, which had been so harmful to the cause. There were instances where agitators had resorted to threats and violence when comparatively prosperous peasants had not been particularly inclined to the Druzhina.

The government understood the role that "bosses" [vatazhki]

play among the peasantry, and it was principally they who were seized. It was enough to deprive a village of one or two influential agitators for the aroused peasants to settle down. For a period of eight months the hunt was on for the bosses, who moved constantly from place to place and by this means slipped through the hands of the authorities. Without them the masses lost heart and little by little quieted down. At the end of May in 1878 the last three *druzhinniki* who had been living illegally were brought in to the Kiev jail. Among them was Kuz'ma. He seemed still to be of good courage and regretted only the upsetting of his plans to begin again in a different place and on a different basis. He was very sharp under interrogation; when he was asked how he had dared rise up against the law, he replied, "What do I care for your laws, I could write them too, if I was literate." When they learned in jail that many of the "educated" children of squires are for the common people, and when they heard of the shooting of Trepov and Kotliarevskii and the killing of Geiking [*political assassinations attempted in 1878*], the imprisoned *druzhinniki* would say, "If not today, then on Thursday there will be a celebration on our street." When I asked Kuz'ma about the mood of the masses at the present time, he replied that everything had become quiet and peaceful, but, he added, it's easy to get pitch to flare up even when it's set.

Now that I have finished this exposition of the Chigirin affair, I must say that my account has been compressed and incomplete. Some extremely characteristic episodes, the peasants' reaction to our propaganda and to the insurrection, their political and economic ideas; finally, our mutual relations in jail and the character of their conduct under interrogation by the authorities—many of these things I have mentioned only in passing or omitted altogether. The limited scale of an article, on the one hand, and "reasons which everyone will understand completely," on the other, have made my account very far from complete.

Stefanovich's apologies for the shortcomings of his narrative were wasted; at least, they were not heeded by his contemporaries. Stefanovich's article provided almost all the material that Russian radicals used in their debate over the Chigirin affair. It was only when this debate was over that sources not produced by Stefanovich became available, and only very recently that historians have begun to use these sources.[33] Thus, Stefanovich was in the advantageous position of providing the information and the frame of reference for a debate on his own activities.

A Question of Revolutionary Ethics

A mixture of ethical and practical considerations figured in this debate, which continued until the revolution of 1905 and even beyond. Stefanovich's detractors emphasized the ethical aspect. The terrorist Pribylev recalled that most revolutionaries in the 1870s took a negative view and did not "consider it moral to make use of the tsar's name, and so to deceive the population."[34] Sergei Sinegub recalled that he was in jail when he first learned of the Chigirin affair. He and the other radicals confined with him discussed it at great length, and most did not approve of Stefanovich's tactics, for "this kind of lie before the people seemed to us not only immoral from an ethical point of view but also a great political mistake, since it only confirmed the peasants in their fatal delusion concerning the tsar, which in Russia is one of the greatest obstacles to the people's liberation."[35]

Stefanovich himself, in an article published even before the account we have just read, was quick to answer the latter argument by insisting that he had actually undermined the peasants' faith in the real tsar.

> It is well known that the rebellious peasants of Chigirin imagined that the tsar himself shared all their desires, that the officials were the tsar's most vicious enemies, and that all forms of oppression, including taxes and other exactions, are not imposed by the tsar's will. When a rumor was circulating that the tsar was coming to their village, many expressed the fear that the officials would dress up an ordinary officer in the tsar's robes and represent him as the tsar. Doubtless the peasants would have held firmly to this supposition if the tsar really had appeared before them and showed how much his desires coincide with the desires of the common people. It is in such a tsar that the common people everywhere believes. This tsar's place is not in the Winter Palace, but only in the popular imagination. ... What, then, does the popular faith in the tsar express? It is a mirage, which will disperse with

the first general popular movement, as it was with Louis XVI in the Great French Revolution.[36]

From this chain of reasoning, Stefanovich could maintain that the Secret Druzhina "was oriented so that the significance of the tsar and the hopes placed on him would ultimately collapse." Plekhanov, who published Stefanovich's narrative, accepted this reasoning. He insisted that "destroying faith in the tsar is one of the necessary conditions of popular liberation," but "the dispassionate reader" of Stefanovich's narrative "will agree that the participants from the intelligentsia in this affair directed all their efforts towards weakening the authority principle and developing the people's independent revolutionary activity. All the same," he added, "we do understand just how strained is the position of a socialist who makes declarations like these to the people in the name of the tsar."[37]

Both Stefanovich and Plekhanov were trying to rise above the disillusionment which they and others had experienced in "going to the people." Russian radicals had fondly imagined that the Russian peasant was a natural socialist, but, Stefanovich recalled, "we saw that the Russian *muzhik* is full of all kinds of prejudices. He believes in God and it is only to religion that he turns for an explanation of everything around him; he is ready to consider the tsar his benefactor and put all his hopes on him; finally, he is a despot in his family and beats his wife." Instead of warring against these lamentable tendencies, the revolutionary must take the peasant as he is and exploit whatever insurrectionary potential he presents. By way of example, Stefanovich cited the grievances that religious sectarians had against the regime; he himself would subsequently try to exploit these grievances. Once again, he would be "a radical insofar as a peasant could be a radical."[38]

Implicit in Stefanovich's argument was the assumption that the experience of insurrection would destroy the myth of the tsar. Yet the Chigirin peasants, before their encounter with Stefanovich, had experienced various kinds of conflict with civil and military officials, and their faith in the distant tsar was apparently as strong as ever. It was difficult, then, to admit that the peasant was not a natural atheist or a natural socialist but still maintain he was a natural insurrectionist, and so a potential collaborator for atheist, socialist revolutionaries. Soon, indeed, Stefanovich and Plekhanov both renounced their faith in peasant revolution. By 1883, when he was finally brought to trial, Stefanovich could say:

> Only the young, who are ignorant of the entire reality of peasant life, imagine that the Russian *muzhik* is easily inflamed material, like the Parisian proletariat. ... No, Russia is not threatened by a peasant revolution, and would not be even if the entire intelligentsia was allowed to move freely among the common people and propagandize without hindrance. [39]

So the premise on which the Druzhina was founded turned out to be as vulnerable as the ardent illusions it had displaced.

While Stefanovich and his colleagues moved away from the premises of the Secret Druzhina, they never repudiated the idea. Nor did they publicly raise the ethical question that bothered their detractors. It was only in his deposition for the police that Stefanovich conceded that he had kept his activities secret from his revolutionary comrades because "only someone who had studied the peasant movement in general and the Chigirin movement in particular could understand and approve my form of action, and I did not know any such person."[40] Stefanovich's tactics were justified on pragmatic grounds. Yet seven months after Stefanovich initiated the first peasant into the Druzhina, he, his comrades, and hundreds of peasants were under arrest and the organization was destroyed. Only against the background of failure and disillusionment which Russian populists had experienced since 1874 could the Druzhina seem a success.

The Druzhina was taken for a striking practical success even by many radicals, such as S.M. Kravchinskii, who questioned its basis in fraud. Kravchinskii maintained that he and other radical propagandists had failed because they had used terms and concepts that were unintelligible to the common people. He promised success "if we really become men of the people [if] we cast away the foreign form of our ideas, which is alien to our people." For him the Chigirin affair

> signified this shift by socialists onto a purely popular ground. In the Chigirin backwater Stefanovich and his friends created the first popular organization in our revolutionary history, an organization that was unequivocally revolutionary and popular-socialist, and in a few months embraced as many as 1,500 peasants. Here for the first time revolutionary socialists became the

real, acknowledged chiefs of the popular masses. It would be
extremely shortsighted and even a violation of the basic principle of the populist program to recommend Stefanovich's
mode of action for all areas and peoples of the Russian land.
... It is possible not to agree with the principles and methods
to which socialists, under the pressure of local circumstances
and the peasant outlook, resorted in the Chigirin affair [but]
they were the first to show us that it is possible to call to life a
powerful, purely *muzhik* revolutionary organization, proceeding from local peasant interests.[41]

A.D. Mikhailov, one of the founders of the revolutionary organization *Narodnaia volia,* was similarly impressed by the fact that
Stefanovich

under unfavorable circumstances, managed all the same to
create a full-scale popular conspiracy; while it quickly collapsed, that was only due to a lack of collaborators and material resources. ... Most populists would not use Stefanovich's
method and avail themselves of the tsar's name. But none of
them would deny that Stefanovich was extremely clever in
choosing a fulcrum for action, and that to succeed one must,
as he did, take the attitudes of the common people as the
point of departure.[42]

Even Sinegub conceded that

the great success achieved by Stefanovich and Deich, their cunning and their energy favorably impressed us all and significantly softened our attitude towards their mode of action; in any
event, in our imagination their images had the aureole of
heroes and great fighters for the people's cause.[43]

Yet Sinegub, as we have already seen, rejected Stefanovich's fraud
as immoral.

Any ethical controversy presented special difficulties for Russian
populists. They were unusually high-minded and selfless men and
women. Even the practical necessity of "fibbing" about one's name
and background was so "repulsive," according to one veteran, as to
disqualify many young intellectuals from becoming propagandists.
And Vladimir Debagorii-Mokrievich, a zealous revolutionary and
eventually a terrorist, joined Stefanovich in making initial contact
with the Chigirin peasants but dropped out because he could not
bear the dishonesty involved.[44] To be sure, the populists were in
rebellion against the society that had formed them and would not

be guided by its norms. They were not yet ready, however, for the view that the revolutionary end justifies any means; indeed, most of them explicitly rejected this view because it had been advocated by their most discreditable predecessors.[45] But they lacked the common standards which usually underlie disputes about ethics. Some tried to elicit standards from the cause they served. The result was arguments that were ultimately about ethics even when they seemed to be about something else. Thus, a major part of the debate consisted of disputing whether other revolutionaries had approved of Stefanovich's tactics. Stefanovich himself withdrew from the debate and from the revolutionary movement when he was exiled to Siberia in 1883, but his comrade and bosom friend Lev Deich kept up the defense for the rest of his long life. Again and again he insisted, sometimes speciously, that all the leading revolutionaries of the 1870s admired Stefanovich and approved of his tactics in the Chigirin affair.[46] Underlying Deich's campaign was the assumption that, in a corrupt society, the consensus of the radical subculture is the only valid ethical touchstone. Others turned to the common people whom they wished to serve. E.D. Breshkovskaia, for example, held that the Chigirin peasants indignantly repudiated Stefanovich once the fraud was exposed. O.V. Aptekman, on the other hand, maintained that these peasants had not repudiated Stefanovich. He recalled that he had encountered some of them in jail, and they said, "We do not accuse Stefanovich; he wished us well. As for the oath he took, let God be his judge."[47]

More commonly, however, Stefanovich's defenders argued in broader terms, emphasizing that spontaneous popular upheavals in Russia had usually been propelled by fraud and imposture. Surely, they argued, radical intellectuals were justified in using the techniques employed by leaders who were of the people. Hence they dwelt upon the torn sheet of paper which, they said, Foma Priadko claimed to have received from the tsar's hands. And there was no lack of examples from history; Pugachev, leader of the greatest insurrection in modern Russian history, had claimed to be tsar Peter III. For P.A. Kropotkin, who insisted that he himself would not resort to fraud, these examples were enough to justify Stefanovich.

Throughout Russian history one sees the common people themselves resorting to false *ukazy*, to rumors about manifestoes from the tsar, and even to pretenders, in order to arouse the inert peasant masses. For leaders who emerged

from the common people to take an initiative, rumors that
some Garibaldi was coming to free the serfs or Stenka Razin
had appeared on the Volga were always a favorite technique.

Kropotkin went on to make an acute observation.

They did not, however, make use of rumors about *ukazy* and
charters from the tsar, etc., for the sake of deception, but
rather as a means of defense or justification in the event of
failure. Not only people who stood close to Pugachev but even
also peasants in the interior of Russia are known to have said
of him, "It doesn't matter if he's the son of the devil himself,
if he can help get rid of the landowners and officials."[48]

Neither Kropotkin nor anyone else applied this insight to the Chigirin affair. Stefanovich's detractors and defenders alike, drawing their
information from his own account, took it for granted that he was
the perfect manipulator and the peasants his guileless subjects. Thus
Kravchinskii described Stefanovich as "the absolute arbiter of so
many thousands of those obstinate peasants."[49] The possibility that
the Chigirin peasants had also manipulated Stefanovich or had even
embraced his Secret Charter "as a means of defense or justification
in the event of failure," was not considered. For if the relationship
had been one of tacit collusion, rather than pure deception, the reproaches against Stefanovich on ethical grounds would have lost
most of their force.

In fact, Stefanovich's defenders were deeply embarrassed by his
resort to fraud; this embarrassment can be inferred from their striking reluctance to describe what went on between Stefanovich and
the peasantry. We have seen that Kravchinskii held up Stefanovich as
a model for other revolutionaries and represented the Chigirin affair
as a turning point in the revolutionary movement. But, apart from
an opaque reference to "the pressure of local circumstances and the
peasant outlook," he did not say what Stefanovich had done. Instead, he promised to provide a fuller discussion in a subsequent
article, but this article never appeared. Somewhat later, in a book
intended to generate sympathy in western Europe for the Russian
revolutionary movement, he celebrated Stefanovich as one of the
movement's heroes. He conceded that Stefanovich had played upon
"the prejudices as well as the aspirations" of the peasants and that
his plan was "only partly approved" by his comrades. What that
plan was, Kravchinskii did not say.[50]

The same pattern can be seen in the memoirs of Stefanovich's associates. Debagorii-Mokrievich described the prelude and aftermath of the Chigirin affair and promised to deal with it directly, but did not.[51] Lev Deich published interminable memoirs over a period of more than twenty years and devoted pages of bilious polemic to the rehabilitation of Stefanovich. But he never got around to a narrative of his own dealings with Stefanovich and the Chigirin peasantry.[52]

If valid inferences can be made from silence and evasiveness, we can conclude that even Stefanovich's defenders were uneasy about his resort to fraud. If it was discreditable to exploit the peasants' devotion to the tsar, how did Russian radicals find themselves doing so? To understand the genesis of the fraud, we must look at the development of the revolutionary movement and at the peculiarities of Stefanovich's character.

In the middle 1870s frustration and repression had combined to demoralize Russian radicals. Peasants had not proved receptive to socialist propaganda, and most propagandists were in jail. The survivors of the "movement to the people" were fugitives and, to avoid arrest, found it necessary to isolate themselves both from educated society and from the common people. They were, in the jargon of the day, "illegals," keeping company only with themselves and a few sympathizers. By 1876, when Stefanovich launched his conspiracy, they were reflecting upon their experience and drawing lessons from it. Under these circumstances of strain and frustration, the so-called "authority principle"—the use of the tsar's name to their own ends—seemed to suggest itself. At least three of Stefanovich's comrades arrived independently at the idea of issuing false *ukazy*.[53] The use of fraud was a product of both failure and demoralization.

The particular fraud practiced by Stefanovich was the product of a particular failure. Stefanovich belonged to a radical group based in Kiev and known as "the rebels" (*buntary*).[54] The rebels were enthusiastic followers of Bakunin and believed with him that the revolutionary's task was not to spread propaganda but to precipitate an immediate peasant rebellion. Even if the rebellion was crushed, the experience would be an invaluable lesson and would provoke other rebellions, culminating in a massive insurrection that would destroy the regime and the social order. Bakunin maintained that the peasants were natural insurrectionists, so that radical intellectuals had only to ignite their rebelliousness and coordinate locally based uprisings.

The rebels had not found the peasants as volatile as Bakunin assumed, and hit upon the idea—against Bakunin's explicit advice[55]— of summoning the peasants to insurrection in the tsar's name; they believed that, however an insurrection began, the ensuing combat with the tsar's troops would convince the peasants that the tsar, no less than the squire and the sheriff, was their enemy. To this end, the rebels set up a fairly sizable organization and allocated tasks among their members. One was to get hold of a printing press on which the false *ukazy* would be printed. Others undertook to provide money and weapons. The rest settled on the fringes of the Chigirin area—since the peasants there had already demonstrated their discontent—to prepare for the rebellion. These preparations were, so to speak, purely military. The rebels did not engage in propaganda, which was dangerous and, according to their doctrine, unnecessary. Instead, they studied the geography of the area and practiced shooting and horseback riding so that, on the day when the peasantry took to arms in response to the false *ukaz,* they could ride into the villages and assume leadership.

This scheme was stillborn. The rebels could not get a significant stock of weapons or the money to buy them with. It took an interminable time to smuggle in the printing press on which the *ukazy* would be printed. In the meantime, most of the rebels simply languished in their village settlements and found the life very dull. Then, two of them tried to kill a suspected spy, botched the job, and were identified by their victim, which set an intense manhunt in motion. The combination of alarm and boredom was too much for the rebels. The organization dissolved without attempting anything.

The rebels' legacy to Stefanovich, along with a new experience of frustration, was a printing press and an idea. Stefanovich transformed the idea, trimming off some Bakuninist assumptions and injecting a new concern for organization and discipline, a concern which was taking hold of the revolutionary movement elsewhere in Russia. Stefanovich's Secret Imperial Charter was distinct from the rebels' projected *ukaz* because it did not seek to precipitate an immediate insurrection but rather to create an organization of peasant insurrectionists.

More important, Stefanovich put the idea into practice. The "authority principle" was in the air in the mid-seventies, because the demoralized radical movement was reaching for desperate expedients. But only Stefanovich was willing and able to pursue this expedient in a consistent, thoroughgoing fashion. The implementation of the principle required Stefanovich's peculiar capacities. From first to last, Stefanovich was not a typical populist of the 1870s. The son of a village priest, he had grown up in a Ukrainian village and could, in more ways than one, speak the peasants' language. He was able to pose as a peasant among peasants, and this was a valuable skill; there were other populists from similar backgrounds, but many more like Stefanovich's friend Lev Deich, who had not been outside the city of Kiev until he was nineteen. Deich was also a bookish and disputatious youngster, and here, too, he was typical of the movement. While many populists were avowedly anti-intellectual, this was the anti-intellectuality of intellectuals. They devoted most of their time to intense discussions of doctrine and tactics. Stefanovich had no interest in these discussions and did not participate. He was, by all accounts, a solitary and secretive man.[56] Most of his fellows were sustained through all their difficulties by the comradeship of the group, emotionally bound to it as to a substitute family. Apart from a durable emotional attachment to Deich, Stefanovich kept aloof from other revolutionaries.

This aloofness may have been an aspect of Stefanovich's love of mystification. Arrested in September of 1877, he managed to escape from prison in May 1878 and resume his revolutionary career for four more years. Again and again he was involved in schemes involving imposture, deception, and manipulation.[57] While most of his comrades cherished sincerity and candor, he loved to play a role. In corresponding with his friend Deich, he always used the names they had assumed for conspiratorial purposes in the Chigirin affair. In the hands of the police, Stefanovich carried duplicity further than revolutionary ethics would permit, for while he proudly withheld some kinds of information, he revealed a great deal, and some of his revelations led to the arrest of revolutionaries. Stefanovich managed to conceal from his comrades the extent of his cooperation with the authorities, and it came to light only after the October Revolution and his own death. Many of his surviving comrades then repudiated him as an informer. But perhaps Stefanovich himself supposed that in his negotiations with his prosecutors he was just playing out another role.

The Charter, the Code, and the Oath

Stefanovich, then, was a man given to duplicity. In the Chigirin affair, the instruments of duplicity were the Secret Imperial Charter and the Code of the Secret Druzhina. The Charter, which purported to be an appeal from the tsar to the common people, was the main vehicle of fraud, while the Code provided instructions and an organizational form. We have seen how Stefanovich represented them to his comrades; let us now look at the texts.

The Imperial Secret Charter[58]

Our faithful peasants!

From all parts of Our state We hear complaints from Our dear peasantry about their grievous oppression by their inveterate enemies, the nobles.

Yet even from Our accession to the throne of the Russian Empire We have tried to improve your situation. Against the wishes of the whole nobility, by Our imperial manifesto of February 19, 1861, We freed you from servile dependency and granted to you all the land without any payment for it, as well as the forests and hayfields, which theretofore had unjustly belonged only to the nobles.

This Our Freedom [Volia] We extended both to the former proprietary peasants and also to the state peasants; all the treasury lands and forests should have gone to the latter; We also ordered that all craftsmen, retired soldiers, and all landless folk without regard to religious affiliation should be alotted with land, for the Lord endowed every man with the right to enjoy this gift in equal measure.

At the same time We alleviated the obligation to military service, and granted to everyone the right to engage freely and without imposts in every kind of craft and trade—fishing, saltmaking, and all the others.

We order[ed] that the *pomeshchiki* be left only with their house lots and the same quantity of land and forest as would go to any former serf according to equal division by souls.

Such was Our will, promulgated in the manifesto of February 19,

1861. But, to Our enormous distress, the nobles prevented the fulfillment of Our orders. By cunning and deception they kept for themselves the better and greater portion of the land, all the forests and
hayfields, and assigned only the lesser and poorer portion to you,
and even so they burdened this land with excessive redemption and
quitrent payments; to many of you they did not give any allotment;
they imposed taxes on all trades and devised local taxes and other
dues. Furthermore, Our unworthy heir, despite Our opposition,
burdened you with a heavy military service obligation to benefit
the nobles, so that together they would have a force against you,
to keep you in darkness and destitution, like cattle. That is what
We wanted to do for you, but, unfortunately, Our will was
not implemented.

Our tireless 20-year struggle with the nobility has at last convinced
Us that alone We are not powerful enough to help you in your
misery and that only you yourselves can throw off the nobles' yoke
and free yourselves from grievous oppression and excessive exactions, if you rise as one man with weapons in your hands against
your hated enemies and take possession of all the land.

Guided by this conviction, to all you peasants and also the common folk of the towns, to all who are faithful to Us and not to Our
unworthy heir, Aleksandr Aleksandrovich, and his confederate
nobles and grand princes, We issue this order: unite into secret
societies called "Secret Druzhiny," in order to prepare a rebellion
against the nobles, officials, and all the higher estates of the realm.
Anyone who is ready to lay down his life for the great and holy
cause of the peasantry is obliged to give an oath of loyalty to the
"Secret Druzhina" society. These societies must be kept strictly
secret from the nobles and their officials and from the priests—for
they, in most instances, are the squires' spies, rather than worthy
shepherds of God's flock.

The treacherous should not be spared, and anyone who kills a
traitor does a good and pious work. We order Our Secret Druzhiny
to carry out the charters We have confirmed, to adhere firmly and
unanimously to their cause and not to believe the priests or the
nobles, who will try by false promises and all other means to sow
discord among you and so to weaken your forces.

In the event of Our death (or any other misfortune that may occur), this is Our testament to the Secret Druzhiny; do not abandon
your great cause, and struggle constantly, sword in hand, with the

eternal enemy of freedom and your welfare, until this plague has been extirpated from the Russian land.

When your sacred struggle with the nobles—those cunning, but weak enemies of yours—is with God's help crowned with your victory, then all the land with the forests and hayfields will be yours without payment, like water, sunlight, and the other gifts of God, which were made for man; there will be no taxes or imposts, which have been introduced by the insatiable nobility; the hated nobles and officials, who know no fellow-feeling for you, will be no more . . . and then freedom and welfare will reign in the Russian land.

And so, drape yourselves in the banner of the cross, orthodox people, and invoke God's blessing on your holy cause!

Remember, like Holy writ, these words the tsar, your benefactor, has said to you!

St. P[etersburg], the 19th day of February in the year 1875.
On the original is H[is]. I[mperial]. H[ighness].'s own seal and
signature, "Aleksandr II."

The Charter embodies the central device of Stefanovich's scheme, appealing as it does in equal measure to the peasants' discontent and to their devotion to the tsar. In the expert opinion of Stefanovich's prosecutor, it was a masterful piece of work on both counts, displaying "a deep knowledge of the popular character" and a mastery of the style peculiar to government documents.[59]

Two points are worth comment. The Charter's point of departure is the manifesto of February 19, 1861, which emancipated the serfs. The Chigirin peasants, however, had never been serfs, and the legislation of February 19 had not affected them. It may be, as one historian insists, that Stefanovich intended to extend the Druzhina to other parts of the empire and enroll ex-serfs as well as former state peasants.[60] On the other hand, perhaps the emphasis on the abolition of serfdom is a product of dilettantism. The reform of the state peasantry, promulgated in 1866, was not so well known to the general public as the abolition of serfdom; Stefanovich may simply not have known very much about it.

In the Charter, the tsar calls upon the peasants to form a *druzhina.* (In both the Charter and the Code it is not clear whether *druzhina* denotes the entire secret society or its subdivisions. This confusion is understandable since, after all, there was only one *druzhina* and one

commissar.) The word *druzhina* has two connotations. It has been
used to denote various voluntary organizations, such as the Bulgarian
units which fought with the Russians in the Russo-Turkish War of
1877–1878 or the revolutionary militia that P. A. Kropotkin proposed to form, and it is applied today to such humdrum groups as
volunteer fire departments. However, the knightly retinue of the
Great Prince of Kiev in the tenth and eleventh centuries was also
called a *druzhina,* and it is likely that Stefanovich was trying to appeal to this fabulous tradition. Yet in this sense the word was literary
and antiquarian in the nineteenth century; for an educated man,
who had been exposed to the old chronicles in school, *druzhina*
was associated with a heroic past, but it is not likely that it struck a
responsive chord among the Chigirin peasants.

In the Code (which in the original was called an "Institution," in
an archaic sense of the word), Stefanovich sought to evoke a more
recent tradition. While some of the terms used, such as *commissar*
and *treasurer (kaznachei),* were vaguely associated with the imperial
government, the key words—*elder, ataman*—denoting offices the
peasants themselves would occupy, were drawn from cossack usage.
Clearly, Stefanovich believed, as government officials did, that
Ukrainian peasants were still moved by the cossack myth and memories of "cossack liberties."

The Institution of "The Secret Druzhina"

I

The secret peasant societies, called "Druzhiny," have as their mission preparations for a rebellion against the nobles and the other
higher estates of the realm, in order to reclaim by force the land
which they have seized, to abolish the taxes and imposts which the
nobles and their officials have introduced, and to restore complete
Volia, as granted by H.I.M. the Sovereign Emperor Aleksandr
Nikolaevich.

The Druzhina is under the protection of the Sovereign Emperor
Alexsandr Nikolaevich himself and enjoys his patronage.

II

The entire Druzhina of the Russian land is directed by a Council
of Commissars, which consists of persons vested with the dignity of

Commissar by a special charter issued from H.I.M.'s own chancellery under the seal of the Sovereign Emperor Aleksandr Nikolaevich himself.

III

1. A Commissar chooses, from among the peasants known to him, those who are most honest, firm, sober, devoted to the Sovereign Emperor Aleksandr Nikolaevich, and hostile to the nobility; to them he proclaims the will of the Sovereign Emperor and, if they declare their willingness to serve the holy cause of the people, even though they may die for it, then he gives them an oath of fidelity to the cause, after which the first *druzhinniki* proceed at once to recruit new members.

2. A Commissar reports to His Majesty about the course of the Druzhina's affairs.

3. Being empowered by the Sovereign Aleksandr Nikolaevich himself, a Commissar issues supplementary charters, and these, once confirmed by the Council of Commissars under its seal, are obligatory for the Druzhina under his supervision.

4. A Commissar introduces the motion for the execution of unfaithful *druzhinniki* and, in the event of immediate danger from a member's treachery or carelessness, himself pronounces the death sentence on that member.

IV

Twenty-five *druzhinniki* comprise an Eldership. The Eldership elects its elder by a majority of at least 15 *druzhinniki*. The elders together comprise the Council of Elders; they have a password among themselves, which they change at every session of the Council of Elders; the Council of Elders elects from its members an Ataman.

Obligations of Every Member of the Druzhina

1. A peasant is only considered a real *druzhinnik* when he has taken an oath of fidelity to the cause of the whole Druzhina; he is admitted to the oath only when at least two *druzhinniki* who know him vouch for his reliability and loyalty.

2. Each *druzhinnik* is unfailingly obliged to recruit new members to the Druzhina, acting cautiously and conferring with other *druzhinniki*.

3. *Druzhinniki* should live in peace and concord and always help one another in need.

4. Each *druzhinnik* is obliged to make for himself a pike or halberd and keep it secretly until the time of rebellion.

5. Each *druzhinnik* contributes at least five kopecks every month into the treasury of the Druzhina.

6. Every two weeks a *druzhinnik* makes a report to his elder about what he has done in behalf of the Druzhina.

7. A *druzhinnik* who detects infidelity in another reports this at once to the elder.

8. A *druzhinnik* is obliged to carry out the orders of his elder.

Obligations of an Elder

1. The elder sees to it that the *druzhinniki* of his Eldership have an accurate knowledge of the Charter and punctiliously meet their obligations.

2. Every week he ascertains the number of new members and himself, before two witnesses, gives to each of them the oath, which the new member will have learned in advance from his sponsors.

3. If the number of new *druzhinniki* has reached 25 and if they reside near to one another, the elder unites them into a new Eldership and the elder they elect is brought into the council of elders.

4. Every month the elder collects the cash contributions from his Eldership and deposits them with the council of elders.

5. In the event of treachery or any other danger, the elder immediately informs the Ataman.

6. In these instances he may dispose of the matter himself, if time will not wait, but then he is accountable for unjust dispositions.

7. An elder is elected for three months; he can be replaced earlier, if a majority of 20 *druzhinniki* so desire; an elder appointed by a Commissar cannot be replaced by the *druzhinniki*.

8. An elder who leaves the office turns his Eldership over to another elected in his place.

V

The Council of Elders discusses how the directives of the commissar can be executed so as to be undetected by the nobles and their officials or by other peasants, and also discusses measures to avert danger; it issues money to the elders for the needs of their

Elderships; every three months it designates two of the elders to audit the treasury; and it elects a treasurer and an Ataman.

Obligations of an Ataman

1. The Ataman is elected from the elders for three months, but an Ataman appointed by the Commissar himself cannot be replaced by the Council of Elders. If he is not literate, he appoints a clerk for himself.

2. The Druzhina communicates with the Commissar through the Ataman, and through the latter it communicates with H.I.M. himself; hence the Ataman is chosen from the very best *druzhinniki.*

3. The Ataman personally receives the orders of the Commissar.

4. To the Commissar he reports about the affairs of the Druzhina, the names of unreliable members, and also those who are especially assiduous for the cause.

5. Since he is simultaneously the elder of his Eldership, the Ataman designates an assistant; when he leaves office, he turns matters over to the man elected in his place.

Obligations of the Treasurer

1. The treasurer is elected by the Council of Elders from among the elders, but a treasurer appointed by the Commissar cannot be replaced by the council.

2. He keeps the treasury of the Druzhina and is under strict accountability not to expend it himself; he dispenses money only to the elders and the Ataman, according to a resolution of the Council of Elders.

VI

The Elderships are named "first," "second," and so on according to the time of their origin; every order from a Commissar under the seal of the Council of Commissars should be carried out by the Druzhina like an order from the sovereign himself. The Commissar provides monetary assistance to the Druzhina.

Apart from evoking the cossack myth, the Code simply provides for a conventional conspiratorial organization. To be sure, it is a highly centralized organization. Stefanovich empowered the "commissar," to install an elder or ataman who could not be removed, to pass death sentences, to modify the Charter, and otherwise to act with the full authority of the autocratic tsar. In describing the Code to his fellow radicals, Stefanovich emphasized the democratic elements and did not mention the powers he reserved to himself. Given the role he deliberately assumed, it is little wonder that, as he admitted, his relations with the *druzhinniki* had an "official" character.

Stefanovich drew up a supplement to this Code, but it has not survived. We do have one other document by which the Druzhina was organized.

The Ceremony of the Holy Oath

The person who wishes to be a member of the Druzhina is admitted to the oath after two *druzhinniki* who know him have vouched for him; only a Commissar has the right to be admitted to the holy oath without this guarantee. The ceremony of the holy oath proceeds as follows: before an ikon of the savior and the holy cross and the holy gospel, before two crossed pikes or knives burns a waxen candle. The person admitted to the oath kneels, raising the second and third fingers of his right hand and putting his left hand on his breast, and repeats the words of the holy oath, read by the elder or a literate witness, thus:

"I (full name) before the face of the savior, the holy gospel, and the holy cross swear to sacrifice my whole life for the holy people's cause of the Druzhina. By the order of the Sovereign Aleksandr Nikolaevich I swear to fight arms in hand against the *pomeshchiki,* the officials, and all the enemies of my fellows and my Sovereign Aleksandr Nikolaevich, for they have subverted our *volia* and taken from us the land which God and the Sovereign Aleksandr Nikolaevich provided to us to hold forever and for free.

"I swear to try with all my strength continually to recruit new members into the Secret Druzhina. I swear to live in peace and concord with all *druzhinniki,* helping them in need like brothers. I swear to keep our common cause in strict secrecy, and even at confession not to betray any of my comrade *druzhinniki* to the enemy; and if I detect such an intention in another, to report it to my elder.

"I swear to carry out unfailingly the codes of the Druzhina, which proceed, through the Commissars and under the seal of the Council of Commissars, from the Sovereign Emperor Aleksandr Nikolaevich himself.

"If I should violate this my oath, I invoke the wrath of the Lord

God and all his saints on me and all my posterity, and may I then
be afflicted with every misery and misfortune, and may not the
hand of my brother *druzhinnik* spare me. Amen."
   After pronouncing these words, the oath-taker kisses the ikon, the
cross, and the gospel.
   On the original is written in H.I.M.'s own hand, "So be it. Aleksandr II."

St.P., 1875. (Beside the date is a gold seal representing a crossed
pike and axe and inscribed, "Seal of the Council of Commissars.")

   In the Oath, the Charter and the Code are distilled to their essence:
solidarity and secrecy, loyalty to the tsar and struggle against the
immediate oppressor. It strikes us today as a piece of mumbo-jumbo.
We may, if the presence of a historical document does not reduce
us to somber stupidity, recall the initiation rituals of boys' clubs.
This thought should not be rejected as frivolous, for the oath does
involve the kind of fooling around with sacred things that boys of
a certain age and education often enjoy. And Stefanovich was
twenty-one when he composed it. It is worth remembering that most
Russian radicals of the 1870s were very young; for all their dedica-
tion and courage, their activities sometimes have an element of
horseplay.
   Yet the oath also shows real intuition. We know that in other
countries, when uneducated people began to form conspiratorial
organizations of their own, they often resorted to the kind of ritual
that Stefanovich devised, and for the same reasons.[61] And Russian
peasants attached the gravest importance to oaths. In a secular and
literate society, breaking an oath is not much different from breaking a promise, but nineteenth-century peasants still did believe that
God would punish those who swore falsely in His name. We have
seen how the peasants Stefanovich recruited in Kiev were willing to
lie to the authorities but not willing to seal the lie by making an *X*,
fearing that the *X* was equivalent to a cross and a sign of the cross
would involve them in an oath. When they made Stefanovich swear
his documents were genuine, his oath was taken for adequate proof.
   The oath was a security device, intended to bind the peasants to
Stefanovich and keep the conspiracy secret. It was an effective device. During the spring and summer of 1877, only two peasants
violated their oaths of secrecy, and one of them was not an enrolled

druzhinnik. The other thousand or more kept their oaths in the face of great official pressure; in June, membership rolls fell into police hands and the 281 men listed were interrogated, but they revealed nothing.[62] It was not until September of 1877, when the police had the Charter and Code in hand and there was no longer anything to be gained by secrecy, that the peasants began to confess their involvement in the Druzhina. No conspiratorial organization drawn from the intelligentsia could match the stubborn fidelity of the Chigirin peasantry, although educated radicals would not have been so abject or so forthcoming in their confessions once the conspiracy was exposed.

The Druzhinniki

The Charter, the Code, and the Oath, taken together, reveal the basis of Stefanovich's plan. We cannot be sure that he ever worked out the further reaches of the plan even in his own mind, but the basis does seem to have corresponded to the Chigirin peasants' inclinations and outlook. One means of appraising Stefanovich's efforts is comparing what he wrote for the peasants to what they wrote for their own use. We do have some documents the *druzhinniki* produced independent of Stefanovich, but these are mostly lists— membership rolls, and so on. The only document the *druzhinniki* compiled on their own that gives any view on their attitudes is this.

Register of Traitors, Enemies, Informers, and Persecutors[63]

Name and Title	*Explanation*
1. *Traitor:* Avton Konstantinov Omel'chenko	In the cantonal administration building at Shabel'niki he testified to the tax collector Mikhail Kulinich, who made a report to the head of the canton and the clerk, and persecution ensued.
His sponsors: Fiodosii Onisov Chupurnyi and Stipan Trofimov Panchenko	

2-3. *Persecutors and informers:*
The head of the canton
Nikita Rudenko and the
clerk Mina Zabolotnyi

They have been making reports
to the authorities and are forever persecuting us.

4. *Persecutor:* Evsignei Trygu-
bov, priest of the village of
Mordva

At one o'clock at night he
leads the officials round the
village and points out our houses
for search by the warden; he
offers the *pomeshchiki* one
hundred rubles for whoever
catches us.

5. *Persecutor:* The warden of
the first ward of Chigirin
District

He carries out searches day and
night; two times at one o'clock
at night he terrified the children
with fire and also pushed our
wives around, ripping their
clothes and twisting their arms.

6. *Informer:* Iov Uzlovatyi,
of the village of Mordva

He has made reports to the
warden and the priest and
persecutes us.

7. *Informer:* Amvrosii Pan-
chenko
Informer: Efrosiniia Omel-
chenkova, wife of the
druzhinnik Akakii Kondra-
tov Omel'chenko

He reported to the priest.
She reports to the priest, the
elder, and the head of the canton.
As soon as she hears where we
might have a refuge, she reports
right away.

8. *Enemy:* The subdeacon of
the village of Mordva,
Iakov Grigor'ev Kompan

He said in our presence that
there is no need to pray to God
for the Emperor, we should only
pray for the heir, and as for
those in hiding, he said a stake
should be set up and they should
be hanged from it.

9. *Enemy:* Mariia Trygubova,
the priest's mother, who
bakes communion wafers

She also uses unseemly words
about God and the sovereign
and reports that we have found
some kind of hideous document
and are taking oaths by it.

10. *Enemy and informer:*
Samson Karpov Shutenko

He says I will catch you and put you in prison forever so your wife can't bring you food and he reports to the nobles where we are hiding.

11. *Enemy:* Matrona Snizh-chenkova, a trader's wife in Chigirin and mother of the *druzhinniki* Tit and Iakov Piskovenkov

When she is drunk she goes around to taverns and says foolish things: that she happened to be in the villages of Pogorel'tsy and Rossoshintsy during the inquiry, and she tells who set out a piece of bread, who brought a glass of vodka *[to the officials]*, and she reproaches them, saying they took bribes to become persecutors.

This register embodies the attitudes that Stefanovich was trying to play upon—piety, devotion to the tsar, hostility to officials and (even though the peasants involved had never been serfs) to the nobility. It also demonstrates vigilance, a quality which Stefanovich tried to inculcate. To be sure, the compilers did not take revenge on any of the "persecutors" and "informers" listed. Even the "traitor" Omel'-chenko escaped the death penalty prescribed by the Code and the Oath. Not, however, because he was innocent of treachery. Official sources show that he had indeed provided the tax collector Kulinich with solid information about Stefanovich's visit to Rossoshintsy.[64] The authorities made little of it, however, perhaps because the accompanying detail sounded too fanciful and because Omel'chenko denied his own involvement. The register and the other documents seized with it in early June of 1877 put more information in official hands, but the conspiracy and its design remained a secret. The investigators gave the most cautious interpretation to their evidence, disregarding everything spectacular and outlandish and reducing the new phase of the movement to the outlines familiar from past years.[65] Even the compilers of this register managed to convince the police that it and the lists found with it were simply part of a campaign to submit a petition to the governor.

How, then, was the conspiracy exposed? In his account of events,

Stefanovich identified three factors that led to the Druzhina's destruction: illiteracy, drunkenness, and overexpansion. If we examine these factors in turn, working from the official sources, we can see that Stefanovich was misled—or misled us—on each count.

When Stefanovich complained of the problem of illiteracy, he was in effect apologizing for the selection of Oleinik as ataman: he was an unworthy leader, but the choice was very limited because so few peasants had the necessary capacity to read and write. Yet there was not such an utter dearth of literate peasants in the Chigirin area.[66] The problem was that few literates would join the Druzhina. They were less likely to be taken in by Stefanovich's fraud, for they could scrutinize the documents on which it was based. Several peasants testified that they were deceived until they had an opportunity to read the Code for themselves, when they realized it was spurious. (Then, or so they maintained, it was only fear of revenge that prevented them from going to the police.[67]) Conversely, mental attitudes characteristic of illiterates helped the Druzhina to expand. In a traditional society, an illiterate is not necessarily stupid or gullible, as his literate neighbors may assume, but he is likely to have a distinctive mental set. A printed document is a great mystery for him. Not only is he unable to scrutinize it, he is likely, simply because it is printed, to regard it as authoritative. Stefanovich was aware of this attitude when he refused to let the peasants have the Charter or the Code until printed copies were available. It does seem that the illiterate's reverence for documents, like the awe of oaths, was an essential element in Stefanovich's scheme.

It can be argued, moreover, that it was not illiteracy but literacy that was fatal to the Druzhina, since only documentary evidence gave the police the leverage to destroy the conspiracy. As early as March of 1877, the police learned a good deal from the ravings of Alexander Leukhin (see page 147); they stepped up their surveillance and carried out repeated searches and interrogations. They could not find or elicit anything incriminating. So long as matters hung on the human fiber of the *druzhinniki,* the Druzhina was a remarkably resilient, impenetrable organization. The discovery of lists of members and other working documents put more cards in the hands of the authorities and led to the arrest of several leaders. But the peasants had the tenacity and cunning to explain these documents away; the police knew that something was afoot, but the Druzhina itself was intact. It was only when the police got hold of the Code and the Charter that they learned the structure, purpose, and sponsorship of the organization; only then did they give serious attention to rumors of a mysterious commissar who came from the tsar, bringing news of his favor for the Chigirin peasantry. Armed with this new intelligence, the police could extract confessions from the leaders, destroy the organization, and arrest Stefanovich, Deich, and Bokhanovskii. Any large organization requires written communication, the keeping of lists and records, and so on. Still and all, we cannot help wondering how long the Druzhina would have survived if its members had committed nothing to paper.

As for drunkenness, official records indicate that the tale about Konograi's entrapment of Andrei Prikhod'ko (see pages 159–160) is not true. Konograi was not recruited by the homeward-bound Prikhod'ko; he was a *druzhinnik* of long standing, who had enrolled others—including Andrei Prikhod'ko—as early as May. Four days after one Erofei Prudkii, a marginal member of the Druzhina arrested by chance, provided the police with new information, Konograi delivered up the Code and induced Prikhod'ko to surrender the copy of the Charter he had just received from Stefanovich.[68] We may assume that Konograi feared that Prudkii's testimony put the Druzhina in new jeopardy and thought (correctly, as it turned out) that he could win a pardon for his own involvement if he provided decisive evidence. At any rate, the tale of Konograi's manipulation of the drunken Prikhod'ko is a legend. Furthermore, while most Ukrainian peasants were not abstemious on principle, the *dusheviki* of Shabel'niki and neighboring villages were on the very edge of starvation and not likely to spend much time in taverns. Stefanovich's emphasis on the drinking problem and his accusation against Andrei Prikhod'ko represent an attempt, perhaps unwitting and certainly unfair, to shift as much blame as possible from himself to the peasants.

There remains the problem of overexpansion. We can see from the texts of the Code and even the Oath that the Druzhina was designed to grow rapidly, since the recruitment of new members was an obligation of every *druzhinnik*. This obligation was taken more seriously than the others, for it coincided with the strategy peasants tended to follow in their own conflicts with authority. What could peasants with no rights or influence, meager resources, and primitive weapons, bring to bear in such a conflict? Massive numbers and solidarity— ideally, the unanimous accord of the whole village. It did not matter much if many of the peasant participants in a disturbance were reluctant; their neighbors could keep an eye on them, and had ample means of coercion within the community. Well-armed soldiers could be stalemated by an enormous passive crowd, unless their officers were willing (like General Apraksin) to shed a lot of blood to break the community's resistance. And in the almost certain event of failure, each individual could mitigate his guilt by claiming to have acted under community pressure. So the *druzhinniki* recruited members zealously and quite openly. Some peasants later claimed to the authorities that they had been enrolled against their will. Yet even the lukewarm *druzhinniki* did not become informers until the police obtained the documents that cracked the case. It does not seem that rapid expansion was directly responsible for the ruin of the Druzhina, or that Stefanovich could have slowed this expansion even if he tried. But he did not try. His assertion that he did (see page 152) is disproved by the text of his final epistle to the *druzhinniki,* which happens (in a rather mangled state) to have been preserved.

Stefanovich's Final Epistle, August 1877[69]

To the Druzhina of Adamovka Canton, Greetings:

I rejoice from the depths of my heart that your people are maintaining the Secret Druzhina like a sacred trust. I pray to God that matters will go better for you as they are for your neighbors; try to enlighten other villages and bring them into the Druzhina, but try most of all to take over your cantonal administration. Read the Code frequently and make sure that what it says sinks in; the literates can read it to the illiterates and instruct them. Organize your treasury so it will be like *[words missing]* the Code. Make your pikes *[more words missing]* and besides the Code requires it. I will be very glad when you form an *Atamanstvo;* only do not spare traitors, but do them to death, as sovereign himself orders in his Secret Charter. Farewell. May the Lord keep you and protect you until the hour which has been foretold.

Dmitrii Naida, Commissar

Write to me in detail what the Commission has elicited from you and whose houses have been searched; report this through the ata-

man. I will make a solicitation to the appropriate place about a
grant to you for the organization's treasury, but for the moment by
your own efforts *[the last part is missing]*. ...

It is clear enough from this that to the very end, Stefanovich was
trying to keep the Druzhina growing. To be sure, he also exhorted
the Druzhina to "take up its internal affairs," as he put it in his narrative. The references to the Code and the treasury seem to be instructions of this kind. The "internal affair" which he emphasized
most forcefully, however, is the execution of traitors. Two peasants,
Leukhin and Omel'chenko, had made partial confessions to the
authorities, but neither had been killed, as the Code required. In insisting that this particular provision of the Code be fulfilled,
Stefanovich realized that the shedding of blood would constitute an
irrevocable commitment to himself and his cause. This kind of
realization lies behind his insistence (see pages 150–151) that any
druzhinnik in jeopardy should break his links to his village and the
legal order and become an "illegal." Stefanovich wanted as many of
his peasant followers as possible to "burn their boats," as the radicals called it, and become dedicated revolutionary outlaws. Involvement in murder could never be explained away, as mere membership
in the Druzhina might and would be. Stefanovich may have been inspired by the example of S.G. Nechaev, a revolutionary who, to
secure the perfect loyalty of his followers, compelled them to join
in killing one of their number. Nechaev was still so notorious among
Russian radicals that Stefanovich would scarcely admit having tried
to follow his example, and we can see that in his narrative Stefanovich minimized his emphasis on blood revenge. The *druzhinniki,*
for their part, were less malleable than Nechaev's followers and did
not make good on their pledge to kill traitors. Perhaps they were
wise. By August of 1877, Leukhin and Omel'chenko had made their
revelations and what damage they could do had been done. Their
murder could only have vastly enhanced the vigilance of the authorities, who were otherwise pretty much baffled and prone to discount most of what they had managed to learn.

From police and judicial records, we can see how the Secret
Druzhina came to grief, but we cannot learn as much as we would
like about how and why the peasants responded to Stefanovich's
fraud. Part of the problem was that the peasants were such liars;
several admitted to their interrogators that they had taken the oath,

but couldn't remember why. More important, the interrogators asked narrow, humdrum questions. Instead of exploiting this occasion for probing the peasant mind, they tried to learn who had recruited whom, who had been an elder, and so on. They were particularly anxious to track down every last copy of the Charter, the Code, and the Oath, fearing that the Druzhina would keep on growing of itself, even with Stefanovich and his confederates under arrest, so long as these inflammatory documents were in circulation.

The results of their inquiries oblige us to take a new view of these documents. Their logical priority is clear: the Charter provides the generative myth, the Code provides instructions following from the myth, and the Oath is a device to secure the secrecy demanded by the Code. In terms of circulation, however, the significance of the documents was just the reverse. No text of the Charter reached the Chigirin area until late August of 1877, when Andrei Prikhod'ko brought one and almost immediately turned it over to the police. The number of peasants who ever heard the Charter read aloud or heard Stefanovich's explanation of it was about thirty-five (that is, the peasants initially recruited at Kiev and the elders who met with Stefanovich at Rossoshintsy). For Stefanovich dealt with the peasants through intermediaries. These intermediaries were supplied first with one, ultimately with four printed texts of the Code and the Oath; from these, two or three handwritten (and possibly corrupt) copies were made.[70] Further copies were made of the Oath alone, and these were the main instruments for recruiting members. The documents Stefanovich composed and printed so laboriously were essential for providing the initial impetus for the Druzhina; beyond that his influence was diffuse, for the peasants transmitted and retransmitted his message, injecting more or less of their own interpretation and their own influence on others. To understand how the Druzhina worked, it is not enough to analyze the documents that set it in motion or the narrative of Stefanovich, who met only a few *druzhinniki;* we must discover what peasants said to other peasants.

To discover this we must turn to the depositions the *druzhinniki* made when the conspiracy was exposed. Most of these, as summarized in the Act of Indictment, are not very rewarding. Lazar' Tenenik was questioned mostly about the time and circumstances of his meetings with Stefanovich; he answered readily enough, and his answers are consistent with Stefanovich's narrative and with other testimony. Kuz'ma Prudkii, whom Stefanovich regarded as the model *druzhinnik* and was one of the last to be captured,[71] devoted most of his energies to denying particulars. Of the leading *druzhinniki*, it was the ataman Oleinik who offered the most suggestive testimony.[72] When he was arrested on August 29, 1877, he denied everything, but was soon persuaded to declare that

> he repented of the crime he had perpetrated and desired to admit everything . . . . He was sorry for the peasants who had been firm in their faith in the cause, largely as a result of the grants of money distributed by Naida [i.e., Stefanovich] and who, furthermore, respected him, Oleinik, so much that if an attempt had been made to arrest him by day, he was convinced that it would not have passed without vigorous resistance on their part.

His involvement began, he testified, when Lazar' Tenenik brought a copy of the Code and asked him to explain it for the peasants.

> After reading it, he, Oleinik, told the assembled peasants that it would be very much to their advantage to organize such a society, that according to the Code they should revere God and obey the sovereign, and that if they would swear to do that and enter the society, they would be relieved from paying taxes and would receive an adequate quantity of land. The peasants assented to this, since they do revere God and the sovereign, the authorities were against them anyway, and they did not know what kind of family the sovereign has [that is, whether he was at odds with his son and heir].

By March 1, Oleinik stated, he had recruited 250 *druzhinniki*, whereupon he convened the nighttime meeting at the "Cossack Grave" to elect the first ten elders. Thereafter he left recruiting to the elders. Furthermore, he testified that he

> read the "Code of the Secret Druzhina" only to the elders, and when he gave the oath to *druzhinniki* he would simply read them the oath, but he would say that the sovereign emperor had ordered the formation of secret societies and that peasants should prepare for an uprising against the *pomeshchiki* and the officials, to which end they should prepare pikes and keep the matter secret.

In a later deposition, Oleinik offered a still milder version. When he and Andrei Prikhod'ko met Stefanovich for the last time on August 15:

> the accused, together with Andrei Prikhod'ko, heard for the first time Dmitrii Naida's [i.e., Stefanovich's] order to have

pikes ready by the first of October; when questioned about
the purpose of these preparations, Naida replied, "What
is a *druzhinnik* without a pike?" Although the accused had indeed known earlier that the Code required the preparation of
a pike, he himself had not understood that article and usually
passed over it when he read the Code to the peasants. On returning to Shabel'niki, he, Oleinik, undertook to read aloud
the Code he had received from Dmitrii Naida at their last
meeting; appended to it he found the "Secret Charter," from
which he understood the necessity of an insurrection against
the officials and the nobles, and that the Secret Druzhiny
were formed just to meet this necessity. No such Charter had
been attached to the other [copies of the] Code, and
Dmitrii Naida had always said that the *druzhiny* were organized to submit a petition to the Sovereign and for defense against
enemies–Turks, Poles, and so on.

Or, as he put it elsewhere in this deposition, "to fight against the
tsar's enemies, but not against officials." As soon as he realized the
real purpose of the Druzhina, he became disillusioned. Oleinik was
inconsistent, however, about the timing of his disillusionment, as
about other matters. At one point he claimed that at the time of his
arrest he was coming to realize Stefanovich was an impostor and was
about to surrender, at another, that he suspected Stefanovich as
early as June, and only Kuz'ma Prudkii's threats prevented him
from tying Stefanovich up and delivering him to the police. He also
claimed that on the night of his arrest, after reading the Charter
aloud to an assembly of peasants, he had announced that he would
read no more such documents. Other witnesses denied Oleinik had
made that announcement, and challenged his testimony on
other particulars.[73]

Oleinik's strategy seems pathetically obvious. He tried to make the
Druzhina seem as innocuous as possible and to impress the authorities
with his penitent and cooperative spirit. Perhaps the authorities were
easily fooled, for the regional chief of the Third Section reported
that Oleinik was "a most intelligent and energetic person who enjoyed the boundless confidence of the members of the Secret Druzhina;
at the present time he can be considered a most useful collaborator
in the ongoing investigation. ... It would be impossible to find a
more skillful and useful collaborator." And the tsar himself was
moved by this report to promise mercy for Oleinik.[74] But perhaps
the authorities were not so foolish. Oleinik was trying to save his

skin, but his testimony can still be essentially true. His innocuous interpretation of the Druzhina's purpose has some support in other evidence. We have Stefanovich's vague remark that Oleinik was giving the peasants a misleading interpretation of the Druzhina's goal.[75] Most of the rank-and-file *druzhinniki* from Oleinik's village of Shabel'niki testified that the organization was formed to present a petition to the tsar, which corresponds to Oleinik's testimony. And while the procurator maintained that Oleinik must have known that the Druzhina was an insurrectionary conspiracy, since he had talked with Stefanovich and read the Code, he could not prove that Oleinik had represented it as such in his recruiting drive. Oleinik and all his followers might have agreed in advance on the story they would tell the police, but this agreement would have made a farce of the oath of secrecy, and we know that the Shabel'niki peasants upheld their oaths until the Code fell into police hands and the oath became pointless. We must consider the possibility that most of the *druzhinniki* of Shabel'niki, where the society developed first and fastest, were doubly deceived—deceived about the insurrectionary goals of the Druzhina as well as its august patronage.

Shabel'niki was only one community, however. The *druzhinniki* from Adamovka, seven miles away, confessed readily enough that they knew the Druzhina was organized to fight their enemies, although some of them maintained they were not to take to arms until they were attacked. The pattern of testimony from Borovitsa is still different. Here the *druzhinniki* maintained they took the oath in order to get more land, with no indication about ways and means. The Druzhina in Borovitsa was run in an independent and authoritarian manner by Mikhail Gudz'. He made very free with dire threats and was not above dragooning his fellow villagers into the conspiracy; apparently he did not burden his recruits with detailed explanations, and they did not insist upon them.[76] In general, each community tended to produce consistent testimony which might differ markedly from the testimony from a community a few miles away. There appear to have been at least four distinct centers, each with its own leadership and a more or less tenuous link to Stefanovich and the "authentic" Druzhina. Stefanovich's account indicates that he was aware of centrifugal tendencies within the Druzhina (see page 158), but it does not suggest that the *druzhinniki* reshaped the myth and the instructions he circulated.

To be sure, all these witnesses, no less than Oleinik, were charged with a grave crime and had an interest in reducing or avoiding punishment. It would not be surprising if they all lied, or astonishing if all the peasants from a village told the same lie. But it is difficult to get behind their testimony and establish their attitude to the Druzhina and its central myth.

The most reliable approach is to look for some action, apart from joining the Druzhina and recruiting others, by which the *druzhinniki* showed their devotion to the cause. Pikes, for example, were tangible evidence of commitment. According to the Code, every *druzhinnik* was bound to get a pike, and Stefanovich stated, with an air of mystery, that his followers showed "concern" for this obligation. When the conspiracy was exposed, official investigators labored to trace every last pike. They discovered that Efim Oleinik and three or four others had obtained pikes; one of them claimed to have found his around the house. More pikes had been ordered, but the blacksmith had refused to make them. A surveyor reported stumbling upon a cache of pikes in September, but he fled the district in terror and no one else could find them.[77] Even if all these pikes had materialized, they would not have been very many for a thousand or more men, with the insurrection scheduled to begin October 1. All things considered, the *druzhinniki* took this obligation rather lightly.

The same can be said of the obligation to pay dues of five kopecks per month. This is not a matter in which the investigators were much interested, but there is very little evidence to suggest that dues were systematically paid or collected, even before the elders persuaded Stefanovich to relieve the poor peasants of this burden. Certainly the *druzhinniki* received far more in subsidies from Stefanovich than they paid in dues.

For most *druzhinniki,* then, membership was a matter of forms and ceremonies. They were eager to go through the ritual of the oath, and more eager still to have their names entered on the membership rolls. These rolls were carefully kept, even though their very existence was a clear danger to the security of the Druzhina. This enthusiasm for enrollment was the obverse of the peasants' dread of "signing up" in 1874 and after. Then they feared that by participating in some formality they might inadvertently cut themselves off from the tsar's bounty. The oath was a formality of just the opposite kind, for it promised a royal reward; it would be risky to be left out.[78] To go beyond the formality, however, to pay dues or lay hold of weapons, to say nothing of rising in arms on October 1, was quite another matter.

Yet surely, if the myth of the tsar had such a hold on the peasants, they must have feared that his wrath would descend on the lukewarm *druzhinnik* who would not even bother to get a pike. Two lines of explanation suggest themselves. We can emphasize the passivity that underlay the myth of the benevolent tsar—for which, we might say, the myth provided an excuse. The bounty of the benevolent tsar, like the grace of the Lord, descended mysteriously to the faithful, and they could not bring it down by effort. The faithful should not grossly flout the canons, but there was no certain advantage in scrupulously adhering to them. Accordingly, the obligations of a *druzhinnik*—indeed, all the elements Stefanovich had added to the myth of the tsar—could be treated as extraneous.

An alternate explanation would use concepts and attitudes, such as skepticism, that are more familiar from our own experience. Peasants may have believed in the benevolence of the distant tsar as we believe in impersonal abstractions. Most of us, for example, believe in popular sovereignty as an ideal and as a functioning part of our world. We adjust our actions to the concept as the occasion may require. But the occasion very rarely moves us to activity, to say nothing of exaltation. We do not invest all our hopes in a payoff in the near term, but try to make our way in the world. We may indulge in a little cynicism even as we play out the ceremonies that this myth, in which we do still believe, requires. Of course, we are the sophisticated citizens of a modern republic. Yet we might entertain the possibility that illiterate and superstitious peasants a century ago were capable in their own way of skepticism and detachment, and half aware of the elements of fable and fantasy in the myth of the benevolent tsar. From this point of view, the Druzhina was not a matter to be taken too seriously. It was worth joining, however, since there was nothing to lose.

Responsibility and Punishment

There was, it would seem, a great deal to be lost. Ordinarily, participants in an insurrectionary conspiracy are severely punished, unless they win. The Secret Druzhina, however, was no ordinary conspiracy, and there was controversy within the government about the punishment of the *druzhinniki.* The governor of Kiev Province argued the case for severity.

Excerpt from a Report by N. P. Gesse, Governor of Kiev Province, to the Governor General at Kiev, January 12, 1878[79]

The results of investigation have shown that the peasants are inclined to believe any absurdity concerning their rights to the land, and any kind of criminal propaganda in this sense can easily take hold among them. This follows from the fact that more than 1,000 men are implicated as defendants in the case. ... It is indisputable that not all the peasant participants in the disorders entirely realize how criminal their activities were; hence some of them confessed at the very beginning of the inquiry, and in the course of time others acknowledged their guilt as a result of explanations and began to "sign out," as they call it, from the secret society. But, ever since the outbreak of disorder, amongst the dissatisfied peasants there have been and doubtless still remain leaders who consciously pursued their goals and whose influence has been shown to have won over an enormous number of collaborators in a brief time. Some of these acknowledged leaders have fled and have not yet been caught, and one can almost say with confidence that without radical measures, the peasants' present calm can easily be disrupted once more and new disorders can break out on the first convenient pretext.

Among these measures, the following is essential, in my opinion: all the peasants who took part in the formation of secret societies must, when their trial is concluded, be expelled from Chigirin District and settled with their families in one of the remote provinces, where there is land free for settlement. The necessity of this measure derives from the consideration that the main cause of the peasant disorders must be sought first of all in their social position. Antigovernment propaganda, which began to appear after the implementation of the peasant reform *[of 1861]* , has introduced communist principles into the peasant milieu, and wherever these principles have penetrated there persists among the peasants a conviction that all the land should be divided among all the estates of the realm, equally, without distinction. These communist principles found fertile soil among the former state peasants of Chigirin Dis-

trict, and therefore they began to strive with amazing stubbornness for the division of the land by souls, first under the pretext
that the acts of lustration were unjust and later under various other
pretexts. The expulsion of the discontented will achieve two purposes: the lands they leave behind can be divided among the peasants remaining in the community, and this increase of allotments
(which, indeed, are not entirely adequate in some places) will eliminate the main cause of discontent. On the other hand, the element
which has sustained the disorders among the peasants will, insofar as
possible, be uprooted, and the peasants will realize that this action
cannot simply be laid to the arbitrary authority of local officials,
as they now believe, but derives from the will of the Sovereign Emperor. Whereas if any roots of renewed disorders remain among the
peasants, one cannot guarantee that these disorders will not be repeated, especially since at the present time rumors are already circulating that at the conclusion of the *[Russo-Turkish]* War there
will be an Imperial manifesto on the division of land by souls. ...

However, if for some reason it is judged impossible to implement
the measure I have requested, then in any event it is unequivocally
necessary, both to prevent disorders in the future and to sober the
remaining mass of the discontent, to exile those who were most
active in forming the secret societies (this would amount to as many
as 80). It is absolutely impossible to be limited to the punishments
which the court will impose on those guilty of organizing and participating in the secret societies, since only a very few individuals
can be sentenced to exile in Siberia with deprivation of all rights. ...

I find it no less essential that the former student Stefanovich, who
represented himself as the Commissar of the "secret society," and
also his collaborators in organizing these societies and in disseminat-
ing the "Secret Charters" and the "Codes of the Society," in the
Emperor's name, be subjected to court-martial according to the
wartime criminal code; the sentence must be carried out in the village
of Shabel'niki, the place where they were most active. These persons,
by virtue of the character of their crime, can be punished on the
basis of articles 243 and 244 of the Penal Code of 1866, and there is
no doubt but that their exemplary punishment before the eyes of
the discontented peasants will have a very important effect: it will
provide the peasants with visible and convincing proof that the
crime in which they were implicated is a grave one in the eyes of
the law. It will further convince them that the guilty are being

punished pursuant to the Emperor's will, since there prevails among them the absurd conviction that only unusual punishments, beyond the limits of the ordinary, involve the tsar's will, whereas they attribute confinement to jail and beating with rods to the arbitrary authority of local officials who, they believe, conceal important aspects of the case; and if only the Sovereign Emperor knew of their claims, then these would be fully satisfied.

Apparently the governor of Kiev Province, no less than the commissar of the Secret Druzhina, had to contrive ways to convince the peasantry that he and his subordinates were the authentic agents of the distant tsar; the "authority principle" was not just a resort of the radicals.

Apart from this consideration, the governor took a hard line. He was, of course, responsible for the maintenance of order in Chigirin District and correspondingly anxious to strike at the roots of disorder. It is clear, however, that his severity was also inspired by a particular conception of the peasantry. Some peasants had been manipulated, others "consciously pursued their goals," but all of them were responsible adults. Though they might be "inclined to believe any absurdity," they must be held to account for the crimes into which these inclinations led them.

The governor's reasoning is clear, but it entailed difficulties. It would have been simple enough to execute Stefanovich, Deich, and Bokhanovskii, if they had not escaped; this is what the governor was suggesting by proposing a court-martial. But to resettle a thousand men and their families—four or five thousand people in all—would be an enormous and expensive operation, which might well create more problems than it could solve.

Furthermore, implicit in the governor's recommendations were judgments on the regime and social order which other officials might not find congenial. If the troubles could not be blamed on the schemes of outside agitators, but derived from the very circumstances of the peasants' life—from their "social position," as the governor called it—how could security be assured? If discontent was rational, if protest, however illegitimate, was still the intelligible product of social and political circumstances, could the regime and its officials call themselves just? It was more convenient to believe that the system was fundamentally sound, that the common people were naively devoted to their tsar, and that the "roots of disorder" were in the keeping of a handful of young intellectuals. Even the governor lapsed into this point of view when he spoke of the propagation of "communist principles"; the radical propagandists knew well enough that they had not had much success in the peasant milieu.

If protest was the product of accidental circumstances, if the regime was solid and just, then the *druzhinniki* were deluded simpletons. The procurator implicitly followed this interpretation, for he put only twenty-two *druzhinniki* on trial. The court went even further, for it sentenced six[80] and acquitted the rest. But no one insisted that the peasants were naive innocents more emphatically than the peasants themselves, as we can see from the petition in which the ringleaders ask to be let off scot-free.

A Petition to the Tsar, September 19, 1880[81]

Most Radiant Sovereign!
Most August Monarch!

In 1875[82] there began to be discontent in our village concerning the payment of money for land. The trouble was that we were unjustly allocated with an extremely small quantity of land, and much of it was not arable, but we paid for it and do pay for it as if for arable, but in 1875, apart from this, they demanded an additional 500 rubles, which our community did not desire to remit; on this account troops were sent to our village, both infantry and cavalry, with orders to make free with vodka, beef, and bread. Torturing with rods became a daily event. We will not describe, Great Sovereign, the outrages and ruination that were visited on us; it is impossible to describe such lawlessness. We sent our emissaries to You in St. Petersburg, Sovereign Emperor, seven men, but they were sent back in fetters. After this they took eight of our fellow villagers and sent them to Kiev under police custody, to say nothing of those who were confined in the fortress. One of those in police custody, Lazar' Tenenik, was working at the university when some gentlemen asked him why he was living there; he told them of all our misfortunes. Then one of the gentlemen said that there was a way of relieving our woes, but we must choose from our midst a reliable man, to whom documents from the tsar could be shown and secrets entrusted. Lazar' Tenenik went to the village and imparted all this to Efim

Oleinik, a deserving sergeant who had been awarded medals for feats of bravery in the Caucasus. Two weeks after this, that is April 23, these two gentlemen, who called themselves the Emperor's commissars and turned out to be Stefanovich and Bokhanovskii, did come to us and displayed Your appeal, August Monarch, over Your signature and seal, and the rules for the people to organize *druzhiny*. At first we could not trust them, and so we brought an ikon of the Savior, a cross, and a gospel and compelled them to take a solemn oath. Thereafter, since we had no more doubts and were deeply convinced that we were acting by Your Imperial Order, we were tirelessly active.

The persons who imparted all aforementioned to us spoke only of Your goodness, Great Monarch, and Your confidence in us, in the common people, which was flattering to us and made us inexpressibly proud of Your confidence; therefore we all unanimously swore to pledge our lives and the last drop of our blood for our Sovereign.

We did not know then that these persons were impostors, acting in despite of Your wise dispositions, Most Radiant Sovereign.

The appeal that was made to us was so righteous and so alluring that in a very short time almost the whole of Chigirin District joined us. Unanimity and faith were principally the result of the fact that the self-styled commissars gave rather large sums to aid the poorest peasants in Your name, Most Gracious Sovereign, but most important was the promise of additional land, for we were endowed with extremely little of it, to say nothing of the fact that ten of us live on one *desiatina,* and that one not arable. How could we, simple, backward people, not believe in the kindness of our beloved monarch, when the whole world attests to it, when we know of His love and trust for His people, and His concern for them?

In the meantime, the authorities conducted an investigation and on June 6, 1877,[83] we were deprived of our liberty and on June 8, 1879 we were indicted for belonging to an illegal secret society formed among the peasants of Chigirin District and sentenced to deprivation of all rights and advantages, acquired by status or as individuals and to confinement in the punishment battalions of civil jurisdiction.

For what are we so cruelly punished? For a manifestation of fidelity and self-abnegation in Your behalf, Great Sovereign! And if this be so, if we, as we did in fact, acted only at the direction of persons who represented themselves to be the Emperor's commissars, appointed by You, August Sovereign, as all the depositions taken together attest, then why are we sentenced to so severe and shameful a punishment? Is it then because through our backwardness and lack of discernment, we let ourselves be deceived and led astray, proving by this same how blindly we are ready, Most Radiant Sovereign, to respond to Your first summons? Many of us were soldiers, who have been in battles and served twenty years or more. Is it for this we are punished? And is it not enough to pay for an inadvertent error with three years of confinement?

All of this has given us the courage, Mighty Sovereign, to fall before You and most loyally request: graciously order an end to our undeserved confinement and the restoration of our rights. Restore fathers to orphaned children and husbands to wives widowed for three years! End the shame of our sundered families, which subsist by begging! Many of us are no longer among the living, having ended their lives in jail, where an epidemic disease has been raging since last year.

Casting ourselves at the foot of the royal throne, Most Radiant Sovereign, we most loyally ask: do not, August Monarch, spurn the prayer of Your unfortunate loyal subjects.

Efim Oleinik, retired sergeant of the village of Shabel'niki, Shabel'-niki Canton, Chigirin District, Kiev Province

Ivan Piskavy, retired sergeant major, of the village of Mordva in the same district

Lazar' Tenenik and Kuz'ma Prudkii, peasants, of the village of Shabel'niki; Vladimir Vykhodtsev has signed at the personal request of the two latter, they being illiterate

Perhaps this petition was a little too fulsome; perhaps eight different honorific titles for the tsar was too many. The tsar did not grant the petitioners' prayer in full, but neither did he spurn it. He had before him a verdict of the Senate, acting on an appeal from the procurator at Kiev, which sentenced each of four petitioners to twelve years of hard labor. However, the Senate proposed that the tsar should reduce these sentences, since, "although the defendants knowingly engaged in criminal activities, they were only the tools of the socialists." The tsar acquiesced and remitted the sentences to hard labor, exiling the four to various points in Siberia.

The petition failed, and yet the outlook it represented prevailed at every level of the judicial system. About a thousand peasants had been caught in an insurrectionary conspiracy, and only four of them were convicted and punished; the communities of the Chigirin District got off very cheaply indeed. Compare the case of Iu. O. Krukovskaia. She had never heard of the Secret Druzhina; her only offense was helping to clear the printing press and other paraphernalia out of Stefanovich's apartment after he was arrested. She was sentenced to thirteen years and eight months of hard labor, for she was of the intelligentsia, and could not claim to have been manipulated because of her zealous devotion to the tsar. Clearly, naiveté, simplicity, and "backwardness" were very useful qualities in the criminal courts.

Indeed, it is the usefulness of naive monarchism that made it so pervasive in the past and now makes it so difficult for us to grasp. In hard times, peasants could draw upon folklore and tradition and console themselves with the thought that the tsar was their benefactor and intercessor. A peasant leader like Priadko could arouse his fellow peasants to resistance, if not rebellion, by playing on their hopes of the tsar's favor. When the authorities broke down a village's resistance, the villagers could evade punishment by claiming they were inspired by a superstitious loyalty to the distant tsar. And it suited police and judicial officials to believe them. The professed naiveté and simplicity of the peasants justified the power these officials held; since the peasants cast themselves in a childlike role, it was so much the easier to believe that arbitrary authority was appropriately "paternal." And while paternal severity must be visited upon a few troublemakers, the bulk of the peasants, the backward and deluded, could be favored with paternal indulgence. In ordinary human transactions, we are rightly suspicious of anyone who represents himself as simple and stupid. Imperial officials, however, preferred to take the Chigirin peasants at their word. To doubt their naive devotion to the tsar necessitated punishing them in massive numbers as state criminals, which would be difficult, expensive, and dangerous. It was equally useful for the peasants to profess a naive faith in the distant tsar and for officials to believe them.

In another sense, peasant monarchism was no use at all. The tsar was not the peasants' benefactor. Until the peasants stopped believing—or saying—that he was, they were not going to attain the practical goals they had in view. Naive monarchism was a substitute for politics. And the peasants' professed faith in the tsar was of no use to nonpeasants. It did not provide the tsar's officials with any leverage on a refractory village. They had trouble enough convincing the peasants that they were the tsar's authentic agents. The peasants' monarchism was of no more use to Stefanovich. He was able to inspire a few peasants, such as Lazar' Tenenik and Kuz'ma Prudkii, with his version of the old myth; through them, he revived the hope and determination of the *dusheviki,* and so stimulated a new upsurge of resistance. He also provided the peasants with new organizational forms, although they were pretty casual in their observance of them. That was all. He was not able to inject any new elements into the myth of the tsar, which persisted in its crudest form: the tsar cares for us and will give us land. Nor could he induce the peasants to act in ways they had not acted before. From him they took encouragement and a considerable sum of money, but most of them remained as cautious, stubborn, and unreachable as ever. Stefanovich was no better able than government officials were to harness the myth of the tsar.

Stefanovich's difficult and tenuous relationship to the peasants should come as no surprise, even though his contemporaries and later historians did not perceive it in that way. By his own admission, he dealt with peasants on a distant, official footing—necessarily so, perhaps, since he represented himself as an official. The peasants treated this official much like any other; they were obsequious and compliant in his presence, and otherwise went their own way. They might have treated him better, since, unlike other officials, he brought good news, but the news was so good as to arouse a skepticism. Like the myth of the Second Coming, the myth of the good tsar required its adherents to take a cautious attitude to those who claimed to bring it down to earth: they might make a show of compliance but not a possibly fatal commitment. So the peasants responded to Stefanovich, as to anyone from the educated classes, with reserve; he was, as the four petitioners put it, "a gentleman."

Stefanovich was more of a gentleman than he knew. Despite his long-standing and close contact with Ukrainian peasants, he still perceived them across the same social and cultural gulf, and in much the same terms, as the tsar's officials did. And he perceived them in much the same terms. His tactics and his narrative both show that he believed the peasants to be passive, although potentially explosive, and credulous. He shared the official outlook even in its details. He assumed, for example, that however desperate their plight, peasants could only be roused out of their inertia by "passers-by" or other outsiders, and that peasant resistance was always the work of a few "bosses." He drew uncritically on the fund of conventional wisdom about peasants. Indeed, he may have failed in his attempt to exploit the myth of the tsar primarily because he himself was in the grip of the myth of the peasant.

Notes

Over the years there has been a great deal of comment and speculation about the Chigirin affair. Nonetheless, the publications offering solid information about it can be very quickly listed. There is, first of all, Stefanovich's account, which is reproduced here in full on pages 131–162; the memoirs of his comrades Deich and Debagorii-Mokrievich paraphrase and, more rarely, supplement this narrative. *Materialy do istorii selians'kykh rukhiv na Chyhyrynshchyni (1875–1879)*, Khar'kov, 1934, very sloppily edited by K. Grebenkin, is a major compendium of official sources bearing on both phases of the Chigirin affair. It is cited in the notes below as *Materialy*. Some new and important sources are given in P.A. Zaionchkovskii, ed., *Krest'ianskoe dvizhenie v Rossii v 1870–1880 gg. Sbornik dokumentov*, Moscow, 1968, cited below as *Krest'ianskoe dvizhenie*. The only sustained discussion of the Chigirin affair in the secondary literature is in Poida's monograph cited below in note 11.

1. Gesse to Dondukov-Korsakov, May 9, 1875, *Materialy*, p. 80.
2. *Krest'ianskoe dvizhenie*, pp. 139–141.
3. Pankevich to Gesse, June 30, 1875, *Materialy*, p. 146.
4. Pankevich to Gesse, November 28, 1876, *Materialy*, pp. 187–188.
5. *Materialy*, p. 201.
6. "Volnenie v Starostve," *Vpered!*, no. 15 (August 15, 1875), p. 470.
7. Staal' to Gesse, December 21, 1875, *Materialy*, pp. 181–182.
8. *Materialy*, p. 18.
9. Dondukov-Korsakov to the minister of state properties, June 9, 1870, *Materialy*, pp. 22–23.
10. The minister of state properties to Dondukov-Korsakov, June 18, 1870, *Materialy*, p. 26.
11. D.P. Poida, *Krest'ianskoe dvizhenie na Pravoberezhnoi Ukraine*

v poreformennyi period (1866–1900 gg.), Dnepropetrovsk, 1960, p. 197.

12. Gesse to Dondukov-Korsakov, May 6, 1875, *Materialy,* p. 73.
13. *Materialy,* p. 168.
14. See Stefanovich's remark on page 134, which Poida (p. 212) accepts as factual; it is not confirmed by the reports in *Materialy.*
15. D.I. Danilevskii, the procurator at Kiev, to the minister of justice, May 13, 1875, *Krest'ianskoe dvizhenie,* p. 132.
16. Pankevich to Gesse, Janury 4, 1876, *Materialy,* p. 183.
17. In his deposition *(Materialy,* p. 255), Stefanovich stated that he first learned of the Chigirin affair from "the émigré press"; more probably from *Vpered!* than from N. Tsvilenev's sketchy account in *Rabotnik,* no. 8 (August 1875), pp. 5–6.
18. First published in 1880 in G.V. Plekhanov's underground journal *Chernyi peredel,* nos. 1 and 2; reprinted in *Pamiatniki agitatsionnoi literatury,* vol. I, Petrograd, 1923, pp. 141–156 and 199–214, from which this translation was made.
19. See L. Deich, *Chetyre pobega,* Berlin, 1908, p. 55, and *Materialy,* p. 353.
20. *Materialy,* p. 257.
21. Because of inconsistency in spelling and the garbling of names, it is uncertain which peasants were involved, but at least five and perhaps eight of them had signed the petition of 1876; see *Materialy,* pp. 317 and 336.
22. The Russian text has *starostva ili atamanstva* here, but surely *ili* is inserted in error. The actual charter makes no mention of *atamanstva.*
23. See *Materialy,* pp. 311, 347.
24. *Materialy,* p. 261.
25. Deich, *Chetyre pobega,* p. 48.
26. *Materialy,* p. 261.
27. *Materialy,* pp. 337 and 347.
28. Deich later recalled that, in the wake of these arrests, he proposed that he, Stefanovich, and Bokhanovskii should submit to arrest to forestall further arrests of their followers, but he was overruled by his two comrades; L. Deich, *Chyhyrynska sprava,* Khar'kov, 1929, pp. 31–32.
29. A police informer claimed that Stefanovich got his funds from liberal Ukrainian nationalists, but no other evidence supports this implausible charge. Deich wrote in 1902 that *Zemlia i volia* had financed the Chigirin affair, and in 1929 specified that Mark Natonson, a leader of *Zemlia i volia,* had provided 2,000 rubles "for famine relief," but this version does not

square with Deich's account of his attempts to raise money in
St. Petersburg; see *Materialy*, p. 309; "Svod pokazanii dannykh
nekotorymi iz gosudarstvennykh prestupnikov," *Byloe*, no. 19
(July 1907), pp. 142–143; L. Deich, "Oproverzhenie ili
otstuplenie?" *Iskra*, no. 29 (December 1, 1902), p. 3; Deich,
Chyhyrynska sprava, p. 29; L. Deich, *Za polveka*, 2 vols., Berlin,
1923, II, p. 119, and (for a hint that D.A. Lizogub provided
funds) pp. 89–90. On the "rebels," chronic lack of money, see
V. Debagorii-Mokrievich, *Ot buntarstva k terrorizmu*, 2 vols.,
Leningrad, 1930, I, p. 270.

30. *Materialy*, p. 265.
31. Debagorii-Mokrievich, *Ot buntarstva k terrorizmu*, vol. II,
pp. 24–25.
32. *Materialy*, p. 338.
33. In their surveys of the revolutionary movement, Bogucharskii,
Thun, Glinskii, Levin, and Venturi all rely on Stefanovich's account and on the texts of the Charter, Oath, and Code in dealing with the Chigirin affair; Poida, writing in 1960, was the
first historian to make significant use of other sources.
34. A. Pribylev, *Narodnaia volia pered tsarskim sudom*, Moscow,
1930, p. 130.
35. S. Sinegub, "Vospominaniia chaikovtsa," *Byloe*, no. 10 (1906),
p. 63.
36. Ia[kov] S[tefanovich], "Nashi zadachi v sele," *Obshchina*, no.
8/9 (1878), p. 36.
37. [G.V. Plekhanov], "Ot redakstii," *Pamiatniki agitatsionnoi
literatury*, vol. I, p. 213.
38. [Stefanovich], "Nashi zadachi v sele," p. 38.
39. *Rechi podsudimykh ot protsessa 17-i*, St. Petersburg, 1883,
quoted in V. Bogucharskii [Iakovlev], *Aktivnoe narodnichestvo
semidesiatykh godov*, Moscow, 1912, p. 207.
40. *Materialy*, p. 258. To be sure, in this deposition Stefanovich
minimized the involvement of his fellow radicals in order to
avoid implicating them; similarly, in his speech of 1883, it was
in his interest to emphasize the fatuity of *buntarstvo* so as to
minimize the danger it posed.
41. S.M. Kravchinskii writing in the underground newspaper *Zemlia
i volia!*, no. 1 (October 25, 1878), republished by V. Bogucharskii in *Revoliutsionnaia zhurnalistika semidesiatykh godov*,
Rostov n/Donu, n.d., p. 77.
42. A.D. Mikhailov, "Pokazaniia. . .," in A.P. Pribylev-Korba and
V.N. Figner, eds., *Narodovolets Aleksandr Dmitrievich
Mikhailov*, Leningrad, 1925, p. 147.
43. Sinegub, "Vospominaniia chaikovtsa," p. 63.

44. A.O. Lukashevich, "Nechto iz popytochnoi praktiki," *Krasnyi arkhiv,* no. 15 (1926), p. 124; Debagorii-Mokrievich, *Ot buntarstva k terrorizmu,* vol. I, p. 249.

45. Revulsion against Nechaev and his Machiavellian tactics prevailed among populists for most of the 1870s. Even when, in May of 1878, *Zemlia i volia* took the view that "the end justifies the means," the proposition was hedged about with qualifications; see the variants of the *Ustav* of 1878 in S.S. Volk, ed., *Revoliutsionnoe narodnichestvo 70-kh godov XIX veka,* vol. II, Moscow-Leningrad, 1965, p. 35.

46. See, for example, L. Deich, "Na rubezhe," *Vestnik Evropy,* July 1912, pp. 178–179. Both Deich and Plekhanov, of course, subsequently became Marxists and from this vantage point could take a patronizing attitude towards the Chigirin affair. They maintained that imposture was an appropriate technique at the populist stage of the revolutionary movement, which they had now happily transcended; see also G.V. Plekhanov, "G-zha Breshkovskaia i Chigirinskoe delo," *Sochineniia,* 24 vols., Moscow, 1923–1927, XII, p. 355.

47. E. Breshko-Breshkovskaia, "Pis'mo v redaktsiiu," *Revoliutsionnaia Rossiia,* no. 20 (March 15, 1903), pp. 5-6; O.V. Aptekman, *Obshchestvo "Zemlia i Volia" 70-kh gg.,* Petrograd, 1924, p. 282.

48. P.A. Kropotkin, "Pis'mo v redaktsiiu," *Revoliutsionnaia Rossiia,* no. 12 (October 1902), p. 26.

49. "Stepniak" [S.M. Kravchinskii], *Underground Russia,* New York, 1892, p. 55. The number of *druzhinniki* grew in the telling. In 1878, Kravchinskii credited Stefanovich with 1,500 recruits (see page 165), but here with "thousands." The government calculated that they numbered about a thousand.

50. "Stepniak," *Underground Russia,* pp. 51–52. Elsewhere, Kravchinskii opposed resorting to "the authority principle"; see his letter to Vera Zasulich, *Krasnyi arkhiv,* no. 19 (1926), pp. 196–197, and his *Nihilism as It Is,* London, n.d., pp. 46–47.

51. Debagorii-Mokrievich, *Ot buntarstva k terrotizmu,* vol. I, pp. 249, 261.

52. Among Deich's writings dealing with the 1870s are *Za polveka; Chetyre pobega;* six articles in *Vestnik Evropy* published between 1911 and 1914; various articles in *Gruppa "Osvobozhdenie truda,"* 6 vols., Moscow, 1923–1928; and *Chyhyrynska sprava,* a pamphlet for a Ukrainian series called "The Peasants' Library." One or another of these provides minute coverage of everything Deich thought or did, but on the Chigirin affair he is either silent or closely paraphrases Stefanovich's account.

53. Deich, *Za polveka,* vol. II, p. 11; Debagorii-Mokrievich, *Ot buntarstva k terrorizmu,* vol. I, p. 242; Franco Venturi, *Roots of Revolution,* Knopf, New York, 1960, p. 584.

54. These remarks about "the rebels" are largely based on the memoirs of Deich and Debagorii-Mokrievich already cited; see also Deich's autobiography in the appendix to vol. XL of the "Granat" encyclopedia, 7th ed., pp. 111–114.

55. Debagorii-Mokrievich, *Ot buntarstva k terrorizmu,* vol. I, p. 244.

56. On this point, Stefanovich's friend Kravchinskii and the police spy Kuritsyn were in remarkable accord; compare "Stepniak," *Underground Russia,* p. 56, and Volk, *Revoliutsionnoe narodnichestvo,* vol. II, p. 125.

57. For example, his plan to revive the Secret Druzhina after his escape from prison; his scheme for propaganda among religious sectarians; and the abortive antigovernmental "Christian brotherhood." His enemies later charged that his adhesion to the terrorist organization *Narodnaia volia* was fraudulent and that he meant to destroy it from within; see Aptekman, *Obshchestvo "Zemlia i Volia,"* p. 385; S.S. Volk, *Narodnaia volia,* Moscow, 1966, p. 378; "Protsess 17i narodovol'tsev v 1883 godu," *Byloe,* no. 10 (October 1906), pp. 236–237. Stefanovich may also have briefly pretended to repudiate his resort to fraud with the Chigirin peasants in order to insinuate himself into *Narodnaia volia;* see Sh. M. Levin, *Ocherki po istorii russkoi obshchestvennoi mysli. V toraia polovina XIX–nachalo XX veka,* Leningrad, 1974, p. 133.

58. The texts of the Charter, the Code, and the Oath are all taken from *Krest'ianskoe dvizhenie,* pp. 141–147, with some orthographic details taken from the otherwise inferior text in *Byloe,* 1906, no. 12, pp. 259–261.

59. Deich, *Chetyre pobega,* p. 55.

60. Poida, *Krest'ianskoe dvizhenie,* p. 222.

61. See Eric Hobsbawm, *Primitive Rebels,* New York, 1965, pp. 166ff.

62. *Materialy,* pp. 231, 300.

63. *Materialy,* pp. 234–235.

64. *Materialy,* p. 238.

65. We can observe this mental process by comparing Gesse's report to Chertkov of July 7, 1877 *(Materialy,* pp. 236–243), which is a digest of evidence, with the interpretation of this evidence he submitted to the minister of internal affairs on July 11 *(Krest'ianskoe dvizhenie,* pp. 147–149).

66. Working from the information I.M. Bogdanov provides *(Gramotnost' i obrazovanie v dorevoliutsionnoi Rossii i v SSSR,*

Moscow, 1964, pp. 24, 54, 57), one would suppose that at least one Chigirin peasant in ten was literate, and the indictment of the *druzhinniki,* which tends to single out literates, reinforces this supposition.

67. *Materialy,* pp. 328–329, 344, 346.

68. *Materialy,* pp. 301–302, 307, 309.

69. *Materialy,* p. 307.

70. See the Act of Indictment, *Materialy,* pp. 311, 313, 337.

71. See Debagorii-Mokrievich, *Ot buntarstva k terrorizmu,* vol. II, pp. 29–34.

72. Summaries of Oleinik's testimony are given in *Materialy,* pp. 311–313, 338–339, 359–361.

73. For example, Kuz'ma Prudkii denied that he had prevented Oleinik from turning Stefanovich over to the police; in a face-to-face confrontation, he angrily insisted that Oleinik was the main culprit and was trying to shift the burden of guilt; *Materialy,* pp. 341–342.

74. L. Deich, "Zagovor sredi krest'ian Chigirinskogo uezda," *Sbornik materialov i statei,* Moscow, 1921, p. 76.

75. *Materialy,* p. 353.

76. See *Materialy,* pp. 344–346 (Adamovka), and pp. 331–334, 382–385 (Borovitsa).

77. *Materialy,* pp. 301, 313, 319, 326, 348, 379 (the Act of Indictment), and pp. 248–249.

78. The fear of exclusion from the tsar's bounty appears to have been crucial; compare the unsuccessful signature campaigns conducted by some propagandists in 1874, when peasants were asked, in essence, to enroll in the army of insurrection; Volk, *Revoliutsionnoe narodnichestvo,* vol. I, p. 294, and V.N. Ginev, *Narodnicheskoe dvizhenie v Srednem Povolzh'e,* Moscow-Leningrad, 1966, p. 87.

79. *Materialy,* pp. 269–271.

80. Of these, one was convicted of dereliction of official duty for failing to report the existence of the Druzhina, but not for belonging to it; another died during the appeal process. The other four signed the petition given here; see *Krest'ianskoe dvizhenie,* p. 433, and *Materialy,* pp. 426–427.

81. *Krest'ianskoe dvizhenie,* pp. 149–151.

82. The original here and just below reads 1877, which is surely an error.

83. This is the date of Piskavyi's initial arrest; *Materialy,* p. 297.

When they are up to something,
it is cunning, not stupidity,
that prevails.

A gendarmes officer, 1861

4

The Myth of the Peasant

The Bezdna and Chigirin affairs differed from one another in significant particulars, and they were both extraordinary. Nonetheless,
they do provide a very full record of two groups of peasant monarchists. Inferences from this record confirm some long-standing
assumptions and call others into question.

First of all, faith in the tsar seems to have been universal among
the peasants in the Bezdna and Chigirin areas. Some peasants found
occasion to profess this faith, others responded to appeals based
upon it, and there were, so far as we know, no dissidents. No peasant stood aloof and maintained that the tsar was just another squire
or boyar. We know from other instances that peasant communities
in conflict with outsiders had ample means of imposing solidarity
and conformity on their members. The myth of the tsar, however,
had a compelling force of its own. Even in the divided villages of
the Chigirin area, the obdurate minority of *aktoviki* did not
challenge the myth.

Peasants professed their faith in the tsar in the simplest form.
The adage, "The tsar wants it but the boyars resist," not only
epitomized the myth; it encompassed it. It was members of educated
society, whether in sympathy or revulsion, who attempted to flesh
the myth out. Common sense seemed to require supporting detail,

for who would take desperate action on the basis of a bare adage? Krylov gave the myth, as it functioned at Bezdna, the trappings of legend; Stefanovich tried to elaborate upon the myth to make it more plausible. Peasants sloughed these accretions off, insofar as they were aware of them. The legend of the tsar-deliverer had a variety of scenarios, but the myth of the tsar as a pretext for protest had no scenario at all. The adage itself, the assertion of the tsar's favor for the peasantry, was an adequate rationale for behavior, and added elements could only impair it. In contrast to a slogan, which serves to summarize an extended program, the adage functioned as a kind of talisman.

The myth of the tsar was potentially subversive and, in these two cases, exclusively subversive. Insofar as it encouraged patience and submission, the myth contributed to the stability of the regime. We cannot, however, reproach tsarism, as Kravchinskii did, for "the foul perfidy involved in the abuse of this touching, childlike confidence" of "the simple-hearted millions."[1] For the myth did not give officials any leverage on insubordinate peasants. The myth taught hostility and at least passive resistance to these officials, who figured as the wicked boyars of the adage. Once this lesson had been drawn and put into practice, the adage's other lesson—submissive patience until the tsar's favor should descend—was of no account. It took force and intimidation to restore submission, and officials could not subdue peasant monarchists by invoking the monarch they served.

Most important, the myth of the tsar was useful to peasants in conflict with the authorities. Naive or not, the peasants professed their faith in the tsar in forms, and only in those forms, that corresponded to their interests. Peasant leaders, finding the myth ready to hand in its folkloric expressions, used it to arouse, galvanize, and unify other peasants. It was a pretext to resistance against heavy odds, and there was no other likely means to that end. We can appreciate the difficulties these leaders faced by rendering the peasants' actions in the language of conventional politics. In these hypothetical terms, the peasants at Bezdna participated in a demonstration. The Chigirin peasants were involved first in stubborn chicanery, or the manipulation of the language of the law to their own ends, and then in an insurrectionary conspiracy. Without the impetus and the rationale the myth provided, these tactics were beyond the reach of peasants. They did not have the standing at law and in the chancelleries that these tactics would otherwise require. A peasant who worked free of the myth of the tsar had no resorts at all—except to cease being a peasant.

Furthermore, the goals peasants pursued under the aegis of the myth were eminently practical: more land, tax relief, and self-rule. Their means were draped in mystery, but their ends were worldly. This discrepancy between means and ends, of course, is by no means unusual. It underlies almost every consultation of an astrologer or witch doctor. Indeed, this descrepancy may be the irreducible element of naiveté in peasant monarchism.

Yet naiveté was useful in confrontations with the authorities. The myth of the tsar provided a ready-made and acceptable excuse for insubordination. The peasants at Bezdna and Chigirin committed acts for which peasants and other citizens were ordinarily punished severely. Because they could and did plead that they were inspired to these acts by a boundless and naive devotion to the tsar, they were not punished. The execution of one peasant, short terms of confinement for a few peasants out of thousands—from the point of view of the community as a whole, this was scarcely any punishment at all. Indeed, unless it encountered an inexperienced blunderer like Apraksin, a peasant community could, under the banner of naive monarchism, commit illegal acts of protest with virtual impunity. And this impunity was part and parcel of the initial rationale of these acts, and so provided encouragement to participate in them. The chances of practical success might be remote, but the myth of the tsar provided a ready-made excuse in the event of failure. Peasants could plead their delusion and foolishness, these pleas were accepted, and the peasants were sent home. The plea did require a sacrifice of pride, which peasants readily made: better to confess to folly and let the wise suffer penal exile.

All in all, the peasants of Bezdna and Chigirin were cunning and opportunistic. The myth of the tsar provided them with a pretext, which they otherwise lacked, to probe the intentions and determination of the regime in behalf of their own material interests and with minimal risk. If we should meet people who behaved in that way in a modern urban setting, we would hesitate to call them naive, and hesitate all the more as they blandly insisted on their naiveté.

The real naiveté of these peasants, then, must lie in their failure to

attain their goals. Armed with sophistication and hindsight, we see
that success was impossible. We know that a peasant movement can
never achieve *volia* or a "black repartition." We know this from the
writings of Marx and his followers, in Russia and elsewhere, and no
serious historian or sociologist would dispute the point. If only
Marx and the wisest social scientists could have magically materialized in Bezdna or Shabel'niki, they would have given the peasants un-
answerable arguments as to the hopelessness of their cause. They
would have advised the peasants to wait for several generations until
workers and intellectuals could accomplish a revolution in which
peasants would only be ancillary forces. Only then could *volia* and a
redistribution of land descend to the village, not by favor of the
tsar but by grace of the urban revolution. This imaginary advice
from the wisest of men would mean, in its practical application,
forbearing patience. The peasants had priests and officials aplenty
to tell them to be patient. To be patient meant to forgo hope or
relief for oneself and one's children. The alternative to naiveté was
not sober wisdom but despair.

The myth of the tsar, then, was a necessary, unexamined ingredient in the peasants' substitute for politics. The monarchism was
naive, from the vantage point of transcendent wisdom, but the monarchists themselves were manipulative, practical, and cunning. Can
we say that the peasants of Bezdna and Chigirin, who did manifest
these qualities, sincerely believed that the flesh-and-blood tsar was
their frustrated benefactor?

A distinguished historian has examined some of the considerations
reviewed here and reduced them to the view that " the Russian peasants' monarchism was largely a defensive trick." This, he finds, "is
probably pushing peasant pragmatism too far, but there is a grain of
truth in such a view."[2] If the manipulation of one's own monarchism
must indicate that faith in the monarch is a cynical pose, then the
grain of truth would be very small. There is, however, no necessary
contradiction between sincere belief and manipulation, defensive or
otherwise. Down through the ages, husbands, monarchs, and employ-
ers have manipulated the injunctions of Saint Paul to justify and exalt
their authority over others. We cannot conclude from their convenient use of these texts, nor from their neglect of other scriptural
injunctions, that their Christianity was mere hypocrisy. Moreover,
peasants may be especially inclined to mingle articles of belief with

earth. Robert Redfield found that peasants half a world away from Russia manifested "a state of mind at once practical and reverent, the inseparable mixture of prudence and piety."[3] The peasants' use of their own monarchism does not make hypocrisy a psychological necessity.

More than that we cannot say. We know that these peasants professed their faith in the tsar and acted in conformity to these professions, that these professions were useful to them, and that nonpeasants accepted them. We may wonder about the sincerity of these professions, but we cannot appraise it. The sincerity of peasants is out of our reach. A hypothetical peasant hypocrite, or community of peasant hypocrites, would leave no trace in the written records on which we depend. We must rely on what educated Russians have conveyed to us. And in any encounter between peasants and members of educated society, the peasants had an overwhelming impulse to dissemble.

It is obvious that peasants under interrogation would profess devotion to the tsar. Even in situations with no element of criminal jeopardy, however, the cultural distance between peasants and educated society was so great, suspicion and distrust were so deep-seated, that peasants dissembled on innocuous matters. Consider Bazarov, the archplebeian of nineteenth-century Russian literature. Finding himself in a village, he cross-questioned the peasants about their naive cosmological views, and the peasants duly played out their roles. From their point of view, straightforward talk with the archplebeian was out of the question, for he was "a gentleman," like all the rest. Indeed, Turgenev observes, "that self-confident Bazarov, who knew how to talk to peasants (as he had boasted . . .) did not even suspect that in their eyes he was all the while something of a buffoon."[4] If the peasants of Bezdna or Chigirin had even faint doubts about the benevolence of the tsar, we can be sure they concealed these doubts from the "gentlemen" with whom they had to deal.

While we may wonder about the peasants' sincerity, these gentlemen did not. The peasants' successful dissimulation and reticence required a certain disposition among the educated classes, and this was not lacking. Standing on the other side of the cultural divide, literates supplemented whatever was oblique or obscure in peasants' utterances from their own conceptions of peasants in general. These conceptions varied in important respects, but they were uniformly patronizing. The *muzhik* was understood to be superstitious, irrational, and credulous. He was less than adult, and his childishness served to justify the authority of educated adults. Naive faith in the tsar was simply an expression of well-known traits. The peasant might be conceived as impulsive and bestial or as vulnerable and innocent. In either event, he required authoritative guidance. Thus the childlike innocent and the "uncouth half-beast"[5] were two expressions of one myth, the myth of the peasant.

Sentimental idolators of the peasantry and case-hardened bureaucrats drew upon this myth. So, in their own way, did radicals, even when they broke with educated society and identified with the peasants. Lev Deich, recalling his first encounter with Chigirin peasants, wrote, "We wished to help these blind and ignorant adherents of the tsar," but this was difficult because they were heedless, garrulous, and drunken.[6] Peasants were proper objects of compassion, but not respect. Stefanovich was wiser in the ways of peasants than Deich, but he perceived them in much the same terms as his bureaucratic antagonists did. It never occurred to him that the Chigirin peasants manipulated him.

The myth of the peasant, in one or more of its variants, was pervasive in the eighteenth and nineteenth centuries and it is not dead yet, even among historians, whose task it is to penetrate the illusions generated by past events. Many historians today are the descendants of peasants or identify with them. Yet they, too, are often under the sway of the myth because they tend to perceive events from the perspective of the educated and articulate. By professional necessity, historians are literates, and the solidarity of literates across the ages is stronger than the bonds of class or confession.

The myth of the tsar and the myth of the peasant were complementary, and have much in common. They both had a basis in reality. Peasants surely were, in many respects, superstitious, ignorant, and brutal; similarly, the tsar's true will, as expressed in the laws, was more favorable to the peasantry than the actions of most of his officials. Each myth was the product of the cultural gulf between educated society and the *narod*, and each made it easier to negotiate across the gulf. Each was an instrument of accommodation, rather than change, and, insofar as it justified inaction, each served to bolster the existing order. Each was invoked as if by reflex to meet certain practical needs. And both myths persisted because, at least in the short run, it suited everyone involved that they should persist. Finally, and most important for our purposes, the myth of the peasant made it possible for peasants to manipulate their reputation for naive monarchism. They maintained that they were naive, credulous, and deluded; officials, whether stern or indulgent, took these professions at face value, acknowledged the peasants' fulsome expressions of repentance, and let them go. Order was restored. The peasants avoided punishment, officials were spared the difficulties and dangers of judging and punishing large numbers of peasants. The complicity of officials and peasants was tacit, but it was so complete that we cannot push our inquiry any further.

We know that the peasants of Bezdna and Chigirin professed their faith in the beneficent tsar, and their actions were consistent with these professions. We know that nonpeasants maintained that peasants were gullible and irresponsible, and they, too, acted consistently. Our case studies indicate that these particular nonpeasants were deceived, or tried to deceive one another, and that the peasants were not naive, in the ordinary meaning of the word. The myth of the tsar and the myth of the peasant were both so useful and so ubiquitous, however, that we cannot establish the balance of sincerity and dissembling within the peasants themselves. Peasants were intractable to their contemporaries and, a century or more later, they are intractable to us.

Notes

1. "Stepniak" [S.M. Kravchinskii], *The Russian Peasantry: Their Agrarian Condition, Social Life and Religion,* Routledge, London, 1905, p. 114.
2. Eric Hobsbawm, "Peasants and Politics," *Journal of Peasant Studies,* I, 1 (October 1973), p. 21, commenting on D. Field, review essay on S.B. Okun' and K.V. Sivkov, eds., *Krest'ianskoe dvizhenie v Rossii v 1857–mae 1861 gg.: Sbornik dokumentov,* Moscow, 1963.
3. Robert Redfield, *Peasant Society and Culture,* University of Chicago Press, Chicago, 1956, p. 70.
4. I.S. Turgenev, *Fathers and Sons,* ch. 27.
5. Raeff aptly observes, "the educated nobles reacted [to the Pugachev rebellion] by trying to create a new image of the peasant which would emphasize those very qualities that could put

their fears to rest. Instead of the view of the serf as an uncouth half-beast, who could be kept down only by force, we observe the emergence of the notion of the peasant as a child, a child who has to be protected against himself and carefully guided into the new 'civilization' '"; Marc Raeff, "Pugachev's Rebellion," in R. Forster and J.P. Greene, eds., *Preconditions of Revolution in Early Modern Europe*, Johns Hopkins Press, Baltimore, 1970, p. 200. In situations reminiscent of the Pugachev rebellion, however, such as the confrontation at Bezdna, the earlier image of the peasant emerged once more.

6. L. Deich, *Chyhyrynska sprava,* Khar'kov, 1929, pp. 19, 25.

Index

As a rule, personal names that occur only once in the documents and text have not been included in this index.